SAP NetWeaver™/Microsoft .NET™ Interoperability

 PRESS

SAP PRESS is a joint initiative of SAP and Galileo Press. The know-how offered by SAP specialists combined with the expertise of the publishing house Galileo Press offers the reader expert books in the field. SAP PRESS features first-hand information and expert advice, and provides useful skills for professional decision-making.

SAP PRESS offers a variety of books on technical and business related topics for the SAP user. For further information, please visit our website: *www.sap-press.com*.

Johannes Meiners, Wilhelm Nüßer
SAP Interface Programming
2004, 379 pp.
ISBN 978-1-59229-034-5

Patrick Theobald
SAP Business Connector-Applications and Development
2005, 66 pp.
SAP PRESS Essentials 3
ISBN 978-1-59229-052-9

Jens Stumpe, Joachim Orb
SAP Exchange Infrastructure
2005, 270 pp.
ISBN 978-1-59229-037-6

Egger, Fiechter, Salzmann, Sawicki, Thielen
SAP BW Data Retrieval
2006, 552 pp.
ISBN 978-1-59229-044-4

Andreas Rohr, Thomas Meigen, André Fischer

SAP NetWeaver™/Microsoft .NET™ Interoperability

Galileo Press

Bonn • Boston

ISBN   978-1-59229-088-8

1st edition 2007

Editor Florian Zimniak
Translation Lemoine International, Inc., Salt Lake City, UT
Copy Editor Laurel Ruma, Boston, MA
Cover Design Silke Braun
Layout Design Vera Brauner
Production Bernadette Blümel
Typesetting Typographie & Computer, Krefeld
Printed and bound in Germany

Contents at a Glance

Contents

Contents

Acknowledgements

Even though there are only three authors mentioned on the book cover, this book could not have been finished without the support of and the discussion with colleagues, partners, and friends who participated directly or indirectly in creating and correcting the manuscript. Unfortunately, we can't mention everyone who contributed to the successful completion of this book, but would like to mention the following people.

We would like to thank the following SAP AG and SAP AG Germany employees for proofreading sections in their area of expertise and for taking time to answer our questions despite time constraints: Claudia Bossong-Iselborn, Rainer Ehre, Thomas Grassl, Martin Guther, Chris Hearn, Reiner Hille-Doering, Christopher Kästner, Jens Koster, Jürgen Kremp, Guangwei Li, Wulff-Heinrich Knapp, Razi Mateen, Rolf Müller, Marc Noe, Udo Paltzer, Susanne Rothaug, Michael Sambeth, Eric Schemer, Serge Saelens, and Christian Stadler.

We would like to thank the following Microsoft employees for checking chapters referring to their area of expertise: Jürgen Daiberl, Hermann Däubler, and Jürgen Grebe.

In particular, André Fischer would like to thank the following colleagues for their help in configuring the XI integration scenarios and for their support in creating chapter 5, *Process Integration*: Matthias Allgaier, Patrick Bollinger, Stefan Grube, Daniel Möllenbeck, and Frank Pfeil.

André Fischer and Thomas Meigen would like to thank Michael Byczkowski for supporting the writing of this manuscript during their work hours.

André Fischer would like to thank his family for their understanding. Several of their evenings and weekends were sacrificed for the sake of this book. A notebook just doesn't belong at the dinner table...

Andreas Rohr would like to thank Anna and Zora for their understanding and support. He promises to be back to his old self again in the near future. Andreas would also like to thank his friends and colleagues Sebastian Ekat and Jens Oldenburg, whose tips and comments have always been very helpful. Thank you!

Andreas Rohr
Thomas Meigen
André Fischer
Berlin and Walldorf, February 2007

This chapter will introduce you to the topic of integration between the software solutions provided by SAP and Microsoft. We will also discuss the historic development in the context of the entire software industry and how the integration of both vendors has developed until today.

1 Introduction

The integration between software solutions is an important and often problematic topic, particularly when different vendors' products are combined into a comprehensive system landscape that meets all of the enterprise's requirements. This book addresses the integration between the products of two of the most significant software vendors worldwide—SAP AG in Walldorf, Germany, and Microsoft Corporation in Redmond, USA.

SAP is the leading vendor for industry standard software and one of the largest software vendors worldwide. Microsoft is the largest software vendor and the largest provider of operating systems and productivity tools worldwide. Virtually all of SAP's more than 28,000 enterprise customers use Microsoft software at the same time, either on the PCs of the more than 12 million end users or for operating their servers.

Together, the software developed by SAP and Microsoft creates the basis of a functioning IT enterprise in a multifaceted way. The topic of this book is the integration of SAP and Microsoft products.

Integration is not usually thought of as a state. In fact, the full integration between the extensive product ranges of both software vendors is an ideal state that must be continuously strived for across coordination processes and product decisions. A large number of influences within the two enterprises—and, naturally, with the affected customers and within the entire software industry—need to be taken into account.

Integration as the ideal state

Figure 1.1 shows the current status (as of summer 2006) of the integration between the components of SAP NetWeaver and Microsoft .NET.

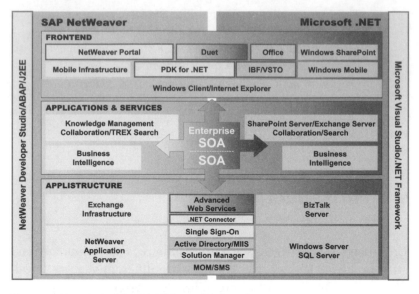

Figure 1.1 Snapshot of the SAP/Microsoft Integration

1.1   About This Book

This book was written for all SAP and Microsoft experts who deal with the integration of components developed by these companies. This includes developers and administrators, but IT decision-makers and consultants will also find valuable information for the architecture of their system landscape.

As the authors of this book, we hopefully covered all essential integration aspects of the extensive SAP and Microsoft product portfolios. We based our selection of topics on the many discussions we had with customers during our daily work in the past years. However, we are well aware that there are other aspects that we might not have dealt with at all or not sufficiently in the first edition of this book.

Structure of this Book   The structure of this book is based on the structure and levels of the SAP NetWeaver architecture.

Chapter 2 of this book is for software developers who want to use Microsoft development tools to create integration solutions with SAP applications. We will first explain legacy technologies like SAP RFC, and then the SAP Connector for Microsoft .NET, which is still widely in use today, will be introduced in detail with some sample scenarios. Since the future of integration lies in web services, how they can be used today in enterprises with different SAP releases and components is discussed at the end of this chapter.

The main topic of **Chapter 3** is user integration, specifically end-user functionality. Here, you will find topics on subjects like the SAP Portal Development Kit for Microsoft .NET, which should be of primary interest to Microsoft developers, and office integration, which naturally includes Duet.

Chapter 4 highlights the various integration aspects of the SAP NetWeaver components (Business Intelligence and Knowledge Management) with Microsoft products (Microsoft Analysis Services, SQL Server and Windows Explorer).

Chapter 5 is dedicated to the integration at the process level, e. g., the communication between SAP NetWeaver Exchange Infrastructure and Microsoft BizTalk Server, or .NET-based clients based on web service. The chapter thus addresses issues for both system administrators and developers.

The broad field of identity management, which includes user management, as well as the interesting topic of single sign-on are explained in detail in **Chapter 6**. This chapter is particularly interesting to system administrators as well.

Finally, we provide an outlook on the future of the integration between Microsoft and SAP software in **Chapter 7**.

Annotation About Listings

An underscore (_) at the end of a VB listing line indicates a line break caused by typesetting. Most of the listings included in this book can also be downloaded from the web page for this book under *http://www.sap-press.com.*

1.2   Integration History

For a profound understanding of the current state of the integration and its potential development, it is important to know its history. Even though it is more common in the short-lived computer industry to look into the future, some aspects are easier to understand and to classify by looking at their history, which also enables us to draw conclusions for potential future developments.

Now that SAP and Microsoft are large providers in the software industry, there naturally are many points of contacts between various products that require a partnership. This has not always been the case. Until the beginning of the 1990s, SAP R/2 exclusively and successfully operated on the mainframe by running IBM MVS or DOS/VSE, or Siemens BS2000. End users usually used IBM or Siemens terminals. Even as enterprises gradually replaced mainframes with PCs running terminal-emulating software there was no real integration between SAP and Microsoft.

Beginning · However, two crucial decisions changed this:

▸ **SAP running on the client**
SAP developed SAP R/3 based on a client/server architecture. R/3 was then based on a graphical user interface that could only be used on expensive X terminals. Very soon, however, PCs running *Microsoft Windows for Workgroups* were established as the standard platform for SAP frontends. In contrast to terminals, PCs provided the option of running several programs in parallel, each in its own window. This opened up new integration possibilities for SAP applications. With this step, SAP had access to the Windows client.

▸ **Microsoft on the server**
At the beginning of the 1990s and in parallel with the very successful DOS operating system using the Windows interface, Microsoft developed a new server operating system called Windows NT. In contrast to the rather primitive Windows for Workgroups, this operating system was not just an extension of DOS. Instead, Windows NT was a completely new operating system providing the essential features of then current Unix or mainframe operating systems. With this step, Microsoft moved toward servers.

1.2.1 SAP R/3 on Windows Server

Windows NT was first introduced in 1992 as Windows NT 3.1 and contained some significant innovations for the Microsoft operating system. Advanced process and memory management with 32-bit support, the NTFS file system and full network support made NT the inexpensive operating system for the LAN server market, which was booming at the time. At the same time, NT also attracted the attention of the R/3 Basis developers.

The shift from mainframes to Unix-based client/server systems led to a significant cost reduction in hardware required for running an R/3 system. However, R/3 was to be deployed in market segments where even Unix servers were still too expensive. On one hand, this deployment clearly required more servers because in addition to the production system, SAP also called for a development system and a quality assurance system. On the other hand, more users could be served and performance could be improved with R/3 by adding more application servers. Therefore, people were always looking for ways to achieve a more favorable cost/performance ratio (today called TCO, total operating costs). Windows NT was an interesting candidate for that purpose.

R/3 as a client/server system

At the beginning of 1993, SAP examined the option of porting the R/3 Application Server to Windows NT 3.51 and found the results so promising that a full porting was resolved, which then took four months.

It was the official beginning of the successful partnership between SAP and Microsoft; and Hasso Plattner and Bill Gates then signed an agreement regarding a technical collaboration (see Figure 1.2).

At the American Sapphire Conference in October 1993, an operating R/3 2.0B running on a Windows server was presented and it was a sensation. In March 1994, release 2.0D was delivered to the first customers. The target audience was medium-sized enterprises with at least 250 employees and 16 computer workplaces.

Until a few years ago, the scalability of Windows servers was limited simply by the available hardware. For example, the most powerful 2-way server featuring 66 MHz Intel 486 processors served approximately 50 to 60 users. Even though Windows NT supported Intel processors as well as MIPS, PowerPC, and Alpha, SAP focused on Intel processors this early stage. The main reason was that the leading Oracle database was available only on Intel processors.

Scalability of Windows servers

Figure 1.2 Bill Gates and Hasso Plattner, 1993

It took a while until Intel processors were a good fit for servers; in 1995, the Intel Pentium Pro, which had its own chipset, allowed for ready-made 4-way servers. However, none of these architectures provided the scalability of coexistent Unix servers which is why NT servers were rarely used in large enterprises and then only as application servers with a connection to a Unix-based database instance.

Proof of this continuous restriction was the frequently performed SD benchmarks.[1] By introducing a hardware certification for Windows-based R/3 servers, interested SAP customers had a quality controlled, reliable and powerful system.

64-bit architecture Nowadays, available hardware is no longer a limiting factor. With the introduction of the Intel Architecture 64 (IA-64) in 2002 and the Itanium CPUs based thereafter, multiway servers with up to 128 CPUs were made available that were sufficient even for most demanding SAP installations. Shortly after, the previous IA-32 standard architecture was extended with 64-bit addressability for Windows servers. EM64T (Intel) or AMD64 processor are increasingly

---

1 The SD benchmark is a load test defined by SAP that is used to detect the maximum supported number of accepted sales and distribution users for a given hardware.

equipped with several processor kernels and growing caches. The continued close collaboration of the SAP, Microsoft, and Intel development groups ensures that these technologies are enabled for SAP applications immediately after their release.

By taking all these measures, performance, scalability, and availability are no longer unachievable goals. Instead, SAP and Microsoft customers can look to the topic that led to the porting of R/3 to Windows servers in 1993: TCO. Today, Microsoft Windows Server provides the most successful server operating system for SAP solutions by far, with a market share of about 50%.

1.2.2 SAP R/3 on Microsoft SQL Server

Microsoft realized at an early stage that in addition to a server operating system, a powerful database was indispensable for their software to be successful in enterprises. Therefore, the SQL Server database software originally licensed by Sybase was gradually improved to provide a powerful database. At the same time, a consolidation took place in the highly competitive market of relational databases in the early 1990s, leaving three large providers: Oracle, IBM with DB2, and Microsoft with SQL Server.

The first porting of an R/3 Application Server by SAP took place in 1996 at Microsoft in Redmond. The SAP porting team is still based there. At the time, SQL Server 6.0 had a serious weak point, though, that was not fixed in its more frequently used successor, 6.5. Instead of the row-level locking commonly used today, where individual rows of database tables can be locked from being accessed by other users, SQL Server only supported page-level locking. This often resulted in a so-called deadlock where many SAP applications running simultaneously locked up when accessing the database tables. Therefore, an R/3 installation based on SQL Server 6.5 had to be restricted to very few users. With the release of the thoroughly revised SQL Server 7.0 in 1999, this problem was completely smoothed out and the database could then be widely distributed.

Porting of R/3 to SQL Server

Over the years, the close collaboration between SAP and Microsoft in Redmond has turned out to be very fruitful. The lessons learned from operating large SAP systems with SQL Server are immediately incorporated in the SQL Server development. Likewise, the latest developments and functions of SQL Server can immediately be integrated in the current SAP NetWeaver Application Server. Among other aspects, high integration quality is ensured by the fact that Microsoft (as a large SAP customer) uses the newest version of SQL Server (when it is still in the beta phase). So when SQL Server 2005 was introduced in November 2005, the SAP systems using Microsoft internally had already been used productively for a full year.

1.2.3 From SAP RFC via COM Connector to .NET Connector

Worldwide, hundreds of thousands of software developers trust in Microsoft tools when developing all kinds of applications. Microsoft Visual Studio, currently the central Microsoft development tool, provides a comparatively intuitive work environment, which makes programming easy—even to programmers with only basic knowledge. On the other hand, SAP R/3 provides data and processes that exist only on a limited scale in a pure Microsoft world. Therefore, the idea of having Microsoft-based programs and applications access SAP data seemed to be the next logical step.

The mainframe-based SAP R/2 already provided the possibility to exchange data with the outside world via protocols like CPI/C and LU6.2. R/3 also offers this option. However, the developer needs to determine every single step of communication, which is very complex and, therefore, error prone.

SAP Remote Function Call (SAP RFC) SAP developed the proprietary SAP Remote Function Call protocol (SAP RFC), which provides two significant advantages:

▸ The greatest part of communication control was now performed by the SAP system or by software development kits (RFC SDK), which relieved the developer from this duty and helped to avoid many sources of error.

▸ The SAP functions were encapsulated in function modules that had to be identified as RFC-enabled. To the outside, they provided typed interfaces. With this, both tools and developers knew what information needed to be delivered or was expected.

The data stream of the RFC protocol is largely based on ABAP data structures, and since it is a binary protocol, it is also compact and efficient.

SAP RFC, essentially consisting of *librfc32.dll*, was initially offered with R/3 release 2.1A. With 2.1E, an SDK was included that contained program samples and metadata. While the support for Microsoft developers was first restricted to C developers, Visual Basic was later supported as well.

In 1993, Microsoft introduced the Component Object Model (COM) and then the Distributed Component Object Model (DCOM), which followed similar objectives: Logical components were encapsulated in standalone software modules that provided clearly defined interfaces to the outside. Microsoft expected to create a booming market of business components that could be compiled as desired to form entire business applications. Although this did not exactly happen according to plan, the technology was still interesting to SAP customers because SAP already had thousands of business objects that were virtually waiting to be addressed via DCOM.

For this reason, SAP developed the DCOM Component Connector (DCOM Connector) based on SAP RFC. It essentially consisted of another DLL that translated the RFC files into COM format and vice versa. This step was not particularly difficult for scalar data but could reach any degree of complexity when structures were nested.

SAP DCOM Component Connector

In 1997, the DCOM Connector was first introduced during SAP Technology Days in Karlsruhe—by Bill Gates himself, who posted a sales order to SAP R/3 with a mouse click from a Microsoft application. Although the first version of the DCOM Connector was delivered without the desired development tools they were added later in the form of a browser-based generator for the required proxy classes.

The DCOM Connector was an attractive tool for enterprises that basically wanted to synchronously access central enterprise data in R/3 from their own applications to:

▶ Use the data in real-time within their own applications

▶ Design alternative user interfaces to SAP applications

At the end of 2004, SAP discontinued the support of the DCOM Connector when it was replaced with the SAP .NET Connector.

The SAP .NET Connector (NCO) wraps function modules and BAPIs that are released for use via RFC as .NET objects. The .NET developer

SAP Connector for Microsoft .NET

is able to extensively use SAP business objects without having to leave the familiar environment of Visual Studio and without having to deal with another programming language like ABAP or Java.

The NCO was a huge step forward in the field of SAP development tools for Microsoft. It supported the new Microsoft .NET platform, but an add-in to Microsoft Visual Studio was also delivered as a part of the Connector for the first time, which developers could use to access SAP business objects and processes with a minimum effort.

Today, the NCO works reliably and fast and is successfully implemented in many enterprises and applications. From the perspective of SAP, the development of this product is largely completed and the team is already working on replacing it with newer and open technologies. In the context of moving to Enterprise Service-Oriented Architecture (Enterprise SOA), it is possible to access SAP applications from the .NET world using web services without using a connector. How this is done is one of the core topics of this book.

1.2.4   Integration with Microsoft Office

Another integration for SAP and Microsoft developed at a very early stage during their partnership. Microsoft Office had quickly become the standard for office applications and SAP systems contained the valuable data and processes. Therefore, the request came up to be able to use and edit the SAP data within the various Office products (Word, Excel, Outlook, etc.).

Structured vs. unstructured data

As natural as this idea was, the conceptual and technical requirements were just as complex. SAP data has a clear structure and integrity, while Office is particularly suitable for working with unstructured or semistructured data. Only two Office components are excluded from this perspective:

▶ Microsoft Outlook (or Microsoft Exchange Server). The Messaging Application Programming Interface (MAPI) protocol has been a broadly accepted standard for many years, ensuring a controlled exchange of e-mail, appointments, etc.

▶ Microsoft Project, which always works with structured data.

The transfer of structured SAP data to Office is relatively easy and can be performed in many different scenarios. For example, a sales order list can simply be transferred to Microsoft Excel, sorted, changed, formatted and printed.

The other way around, however, it is much more difficult to transfer unstructured data to SAP because consistency must always be ensured. You can easily imagine that not every sales order list, especially those manually edited, can be uploaded to an SAP system. Every single data element must be checked for integrity.

Therefore, it is understandable that there cannot be a generic solution for SAP Office integration across all SAP applications. Instead, a deeper integration between SAP and Office was provided only for those scenarios in which it was required by many Office users so that the immense development effort was justified.

With the availability of SAP RFC, the technical requirements for interfaces between Microsoft Office and SAP R/3 were established. Within a few years, a number of individual solutions were created based on this protocol. However, the developers kept facing the same challenges:

▶ What if Microsoft Office is not installed on the PC but another product is or none at all?

▶ What about compatibility with different Office versions?

▶ How should communication errors or other errors be dealt with?

It did not make sense to attempt to solve these questions again and again for every single scenario. A unified interface was developed from the ABAP environment for the different Office solutions available on the market—the Desktop Office Integration (DOI).

Desktop Office Integration

DOI uses OLE documents to start applications included in the Microsoft Office suite (or others) from the ABAP stack. OLE, which stands for Object Linking and Embedding, is the Microsoft technology that enables the program-based embedding of applications or their documents in other applications. The Office application is either displayed in its own window or can even be visually integrated in the SAP GUI so that the user hardly notices the transition between the SAP and the Office application.

The DOI was very popular among the SAP application developers, and a large number of application scenarios have been implemented using this solution. Older applications that were still based on native

RFC frameworks were gradually converted. At conferences, the DOI was a popular topic because customers could now build their own extensions to their SAP systems with relatively little effort.

SAP GUI and Microsoft Office are both fat clients (or rich clients, to put it more positively), providing a high amount of interaction and flexibility at the cost of installation effort and a higher demand on resources. Because people are no longer willing to accept this cost, the DOI integration method cannot be directly transferred to the now more preferred SAP thin client—the SAP NetWeaver Portal. Therefore, two different approaches are pursued:

▶ As a part of the SAP NetWeaver Portal, SAP Knowledge Management can store Office-based documents either locally or in an integrated repository (e. g., Windows SharePoint Services) and search and edit them from the SAP NetWeaver Portal. The editing takes place in the locally installed client.

▶ With the new joint SAP and Microsoft product, Duet (previously known as Project Mendocino), a new path is struck to embed scenarios into the Office application. Figure 1.3 shows an overview of the development of the partnership between Microsoft and SAP.

Development of the Partnership

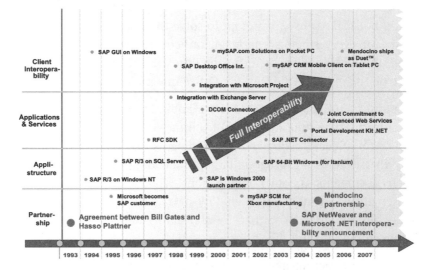

Figure 1.3 History of the Partnership Between Microsoft and SAP

1.3 Platforms for a Service-Oriented Architecture

Due to dynamic economic changes, enterprises face the challenge of creating a flexible IT infrastructure that enables a constant change and innovation of business processes. Such a flexibility can only be achieved using service-oriented architectures (SOA). SOA is an important trend that has had a lasting effect on the IT industry. Both SAP and Microsoft not only realized this trend at an early stage, but also acted as driving forces in creating this common endeavor for the IT industry and customers.

1.3.1 SAP NetWeaver

At the end of 2002, SAP introduced a new application and integration platform—SAP NetWeaver. It was the most significant technological announcement since the introduction of SAP R/3 ten years previously. Essentially, two developments led to NetWeaver:

In the second half of the 1990s, the functionality scope and the number of technical components (e. g., APO, ITS, BW, etc.) for the SAP R/3 system notably increased. While every single component had its right to exist from a technical and functional perspective, the system landscapes of the SAP customers became more complex, maintenance-intensive and, thus, unnecessarily expensive. These components would gradually be grouped together again in an application server, which is the current SAP NetWeaver Application Server.

Increasing complexity of the SAP solutions

Enterprises and analysts realized there was an immense integration need between different vendors' applications and this demand could only be met by handling the communication between the different application components on the basis of commonly defined open standards. The emerging e-business and the bad experiences with best-of-breed landscapes accelerated this perception. SAP supports all relevant open standards and is a driving force on many standards committees. The decision to centrally support J2EE in addition to ABAP in SAP NetWeaver Application Server was an immediate result of this philosophy.

The call for open standards

Meanwhile, SAP NetWeaver is so far advanced that the SAP strategists also call it a business process platform (BPP). Effectively, this is the combination of technology platform and the infrastructure for business applications. Apart from the SAP NetWeaver Application

Server, the NetWeaver components include business intelligence, exchange infrastructure, mobile infrastructure, and portals. As a whole, this combination of platform and infrastructure is referred to as *applistructure*.

SAP NetWeaver was originally introduced using the following definition:

> *The SAP NetWeaver technology platform brings people, information, and business processes together—across all organisational and technological boundaries. SAP NetWeaver integrates information and applications from different sources. The SAP platform is compatible with the widely used Microsoft .NET and IBM WebSphere technologies. It is extensible and supports the Java 2 platform, Enterprise Edition (J2EE). SAP NetWeaver is the technical basis of mySAP Business Suite and SAP xApps. The technology ensures a maximum of reliability, security, and scalability so that your business processes run smoothly. The platform based on web services delivers a comprehensive, fully integrated function portfolio. The preconfigured contents reduce the need for customer-specific integration effort.*

NetWeaver and .NET With regard to Microsoft .NET, the following statements are very significant:

▶ SAP NetWeaver is compatible with Microsoft .NET and "offers full interoperability with .NET." This is a goal still pursued by SAP and Microsoft.

▶ SAP NetWeaver is based on web services. SAP announced the full support of SOA and associated open standards such as XML, SOAP, WSDL, UDDI, and many others. Microsoft .NET implements these in a largely similar way so the technological basis for the interoperability between these two platforms is established for the years to come.

Considering its complexity and importance, NetWeaver is definitely the largest SAP technology project.

1.3.2 Microsoft .NET

In the late 1990s, Microsoft also had to create a new software platform, for two reasons:

▶ The implications of emerging open standards were realized at an early stage. Their support required a fundamental reorganization of the programming model.

▶ At the same time, different Microsoft technologies like COM, DCOM, and Win32, which formed the basis of the Windows operating system and most applications, were exhausted. The Java world provided more progressive concepts and a modern programming language.

▶ The legal dispute between Microsoft and Sun Microsystems (at the end of which Microsoft was enjoined from proprietarily extending the Java standard) confirmed the decision of Microsoft management to cut their own path with the Microsoft .NET platform.

Microsoft .NET provides a virtual runtime environment (like the Java Virtual Machine), the C# programming language (which is largely identical to Java but includes small conceptual improvements), and a very extensive class library that comprehensively supports the creation of modern applications based on web services and open standards. With Microsoft Visual Studio, the software developers have an excellent development environment that enables the use of C#, Visual Basic .NET, and C++ as well as many more programming languages.

A severe disadvantage of Microsoft .NET is that although it more or less follows the same objectives as the J2EE platform (Java 2 Platform, Enterprise Edition), it is not compatible with it. Applications developed in J2EE cannot be run in a .NET runtime environment and vice versa. Communication can only take place based on the web services and open standards mentioned above, but even this is not always guaranteed (see Figure 1.4).

J2EE or .NET?

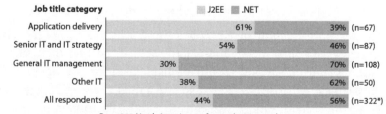

Base: 322 North American software decision-makers

* "All respondents" includes 10 respondents with business-focused titles – to few to include in this chart.
Source: Forrester's Business Technographics® April 2004 North American Benchmark Study

Figure 1.4 Acceptance of J2EE and Microsoft .NET

For software vendors, like SAP, this is annoying because it is not possible to develop applications that run on both platforms. Duplicating development of applications for both software platforms is not an option, if only for sheer cost reasons. Therefore, SAP had to make a fundamental decision for its future development strategy.

SAP employees were invited to Redmond at a very early stage to be showed the new .NET platform. So, when a beta version of the new platform and development environment became available at the end of 2000 it was not a surprise to SAP. First tests showed an amazing quality and maturity of this newly developed technology.

.NET in Web AS?   Still, the .NET runtime environment was not included in SAP's Web Application Server (Web AS), unlike J2EE. This was based on Microsoft's decision to provide .NET for the Windows operating system only—a decision that is still applicable. Fifty percent of SAP customers use servers that do not run Microsoft Windows Server. However, since the R/2 mainframe days SAP has pursued a strategy of platform independence for operating systems and databases. Wherever possible, products are developed only once and then distributed to be available on any platform requested by a SAP customer.

Even if individual parts have been accepted as standard by the European Computer Manufacturers Association (ECMA), .NET is still Microsoft's proprietary technology. And a large software provider, like SAP, cannot afford to be dependent on a single technology provider, certainly not for the benefit of their customers.

But even though the .NET runtime environment was not an integral part of Web AS, along side ABAP and J2EE, there were other ways to create a sound interoperability between the worlds.

1.3.3   A New Level of Partnership Using Web Services

After the introduction of NetWeaver and .NET as comprehensive technology platforms, SAP and Microsoft realized that their shared customers must be provided with a reliable plan for interoperability. Many large enterprises have switched to a dual-vendor strategy, particularly in recent years. This means that those customers always try to obtain all software solutions from SAP or Microsoft first.

For this reason, SAP and Microsoft, represented by Henning Kager-mann and Bill Gates, presented an agreement at the Sapphire 2004 Conference, which showed the shared planning (roadmap) for the years to come regarding both companies' technical and non-technical aspects (see Figure 1.5). The crucial points of this agreement included:

The shared roadmap

▶ SAP Enterprise Portal Development Kit for Microsoft .NET, using which iViews for the NetWeaver Portal can be developed in Visual Studio

▶ SAP Connector for Microsoft .NET version 2.0, using which data and processes of SAP applications can be made available to the .NET world

▶ SAP support for Visual Studio .NET

▶ SAP NetWeaver support for Advanced Web Services Protocols

▶ SAP NetWeaver support for the Microsoft Smart Client Technology

▶ Integration between SAP NetWeaver, Microsoft Exchange, and Microsoft Windows SharePoint Services

▶ The joint Collaboration Technology Support Center (CTSC), which exclusively takes care of interoperability aspects

▶ Shared sales and marketing activities

All of the technical initiatives as well as the CTSC are presented in this book.

Microsoft and SAP Raise the Stakes for Web Services for the Enterprise
Companies Deepen Relationship Through Broad Integration of SAP NetWeaver With Microsoft .NET

NEW ORLEANS, WALLDORF, Germany, and REDMOND, Wash. — May 12, 2004 — Microsoft Corp. and SAP AG today announced a significant expansion of their long-standing relationship based on a shared commitment to Web services as the foundation for the next generation of enterprise software. The two companies detailed a road map for deeper integration between Microsoft® .NET and SAP NetWeaver™, the companies' respective strategic platform initiatives, allowing customers to get more out of business-critical SAP® applications and technologies running in collaboration with Microsoft .NET. The jointly developed solutions will greatly enhance access to SAP NetWeaver functionality for developers using Microsoft Visual Studio® .NET and will increase the interoperability between SAP solutions and the Microsoft Office System.

Figure 1.5 The Presentation of the Shared Roadmap, 2004

With the presentation of the roadmap, the main course was set for technologies and standards to be shared in the future. Concrete function enhancements for end users were not contained in the roadmap. This co-presentation was received with great interest, particularly by enterprises who selected SAP and Microsoft for their chosen strategy.

SAP Developer Network

After the presentation there was, naturally, a significant demand for clarification regarding the details and the current progress of the roadmap implementation. One of the tasks of the CTSC is to provide this background information via publications on the SAP Developer Network (SDN, *http://sdn.sap.com*), during customer meetings and events.

Meanwhile, SAP and Microsoft have almost completely implemented the roadmap.

The Mendocino project

At the Sapphire 2005 Conference in Copenhagen, SAP and Microsoft took another step ahead and addressed the topic of Office integration with a completely new approach. Under the code name *Mendocino*, a jointly built and sold solution for a deep integration between SAP NetWeaver and Microsoft Office was announced (see Figure 1.6). The announcement of this product (now called Duet) was remarkable for several reasons:

▶ In version 1.0, Duet only contains four application scenarios, which is a relatively limited number, especially in comparison to the more than 80 business packages and 7,000 iViews of the SAP NetWeaver Portal. However, Duet is based on a comprehensive infrastructure and on the Enterprise Service-Oriented Architecture (Enterprise SOA). Thus, a basis is established for more ready-to-use SAP scenarios but also for extensibility by SAP customers and partners in future versions.

▶ Duet is the first joint product between SAP and Microsoft, that is, sales and support are provided jointly, which is a further improvement from the customer perspective.

Duet is not a renunciation of the SAP portal strategy but is rather a supplement for those users who spend 80% or more of their time with Microsoft Office, and particularly with Outlook. From this point, they can navigate to the more complex tasks in the portal.

SAP and Microsoft Announce First Joint Product Designed to Revolutionize How Information Workers Access Enterprise Applications

New product, code-named "Mendocino," will present SAP processes and data within familiar, easy-to-use Microsoft Office software.

COPENHAGEN, Denmark — April 26, 2005 -- SAP AG and Microsoft Corp. today announced they are jointly developing and planning to offer a new product, code-named "Mendocino," that will help companies gain a competitive advantage by revolutionizing the way information workers access, analyze and use enterprise data to make better business decisions. "Mendocino" will link SAP process functionality directly to Microsoft® Office applications. Users of this product, the first to be developed jointly between SAP and Microsoft, will enjoy the familiarity of Microsoft Office as they access SAP's best-practice business processes and information. The announcement was made at SAPPHIRE® '05, SAP's international customer conference being held in Copenhagen, Denmark, April 26–28.

Figure 1.6 The Mendocino Announcement

1.4 A Living Partnership

Like any other partnership, the partnership between enterprises is not static. It evolves and adapts to various circumstances and challenges. New customer requests, new technologies, market changes, expectations of shareholders and analysts—all influence companies like SAP and Microsoft to continuously reconsider new topics and how shared solutions can be found. Naturally, this requires people to deal with the integration of products and an organizational framework for a smooth cooperation must be provided.

1.4.1 Cooperation of Engineering Departments

On a daily basis, integration takes place in the many affected product groups. Both enterprises communicate in a relatively open way about future technologies to stay synchronized. This is crucial because new products that cannot be integrated with partner products would not be accepted in the market. A new SAP Web AS that cannot run on Windows Server is out of the question, just as is a new Windows Server that is incompatible with Web AS.

The following are a few examples of how integration and compatibility are aimed for and ensured:

▶ SAP employees work in Redmond on the Microsoft site. Microsoft employees work in Walldorf and in the SAP labs all over the world directly with the SAP development teams.

▶ Each company shares new technologies and products, which helps define a common direction at an early development stage.

▶ Each group is invited for ramp-up or beta programs so that experiences with new product versions can be incorporated in the development process before they become problems.

▶ Employees are enabled in developing, consulting, support, etc. to have easy access to each partner's key products.

▶ Mutual support contracts provide access to official support channels with defined processes and response times.

1.4.2 The SAP Microsoft Alliance Team

For many years, both SAP and Microsoft have had dedicated teams that primarily market their own products with the products of their partner. These teams are:

▶ the SAP Microsoft Competence Center in Walldorf, based at SAP's in the PartnerPort building

▶ the Microsoft SAP Global Alliance Team in Redmond at Microsoft's site

Both teams consult customers regarding existing technologies within the sales cycle, perform sales initiatives, and organize events.

1.4.3 Collaboration Technology Support Center (CTSC)

To ensure that the right technology decisions can be taken and implemented despite the continuously changing conditions, specialists in both enterprises must deal with possible integration scenarios. Within the SAP Microsoft alliance team, a dedicated team was created in 2003 to exclusively deal with technical interoperability: the Collaboration Technology Support Center (CTSC).

The CTSC is a team of technology experts that is operated equally by SAP and Microsoft. The CTSC employees work together on one single topic: the interoperability between the SAP and Microsoft solutions. They act globally, even though they are based in the SAP Microsoft Competence Center in Walldorf (see Figure 1.7).

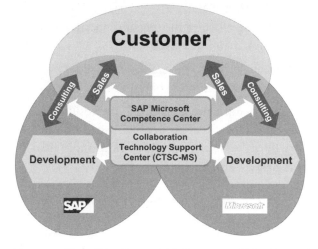

Figure 1.7 Three-Way Partnership: Customer—SAP—Microsoft

The CTSC has extraordinary abilities because it talks directly to shared customers about integration and records their requirements, which can then be directly transferred to the respective engineering departments. This happens according to a clearly defined process (see Figure 1.8).

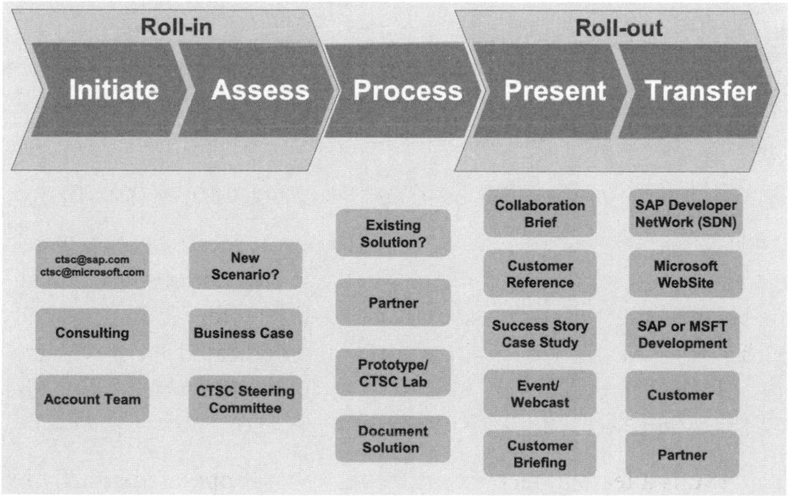

CTSC process

Figure 1.8 The CTSC Process

Simplified, the CTSC process is as follows:

▶ Customer requests and requirements or the release of new products and technologies cause the CTSC to examine if a new integration scenario already exists or is required.

▶ In coordination with the mutual product groups, possible integration concepts are developed and assessed.

▶ The best approach is transferred to development based on a business case. There, the implementation is determined.

▶ Even if no additional development is required, the result is documented in a collaboration brief that is then published on the SAP Developer Network (*http://sdn.sap.com*). Up to now, more than 20 collaboration briefs have been published.

This chapter examines SAP Basis interface technologies and SAP/Microsoft integration tools both past and present. The basics of the SAP integration technologies, the SAP Connector for Microsoft .NET, and web services are presented as possible tools for SAP/Microsoft integration.

2   Basis: Integration Tools

SAP NetWeaver distinguishes between three integration levels and the *application platform*. The application platform contains the technologies that form the basis for higher integration levels. These include the operating system, database management system, user management as well as (Web) application server and development tools. Figure 2.1 illustrates the points of contact between Microsoft and SAP products at all of these levels.

Application platform

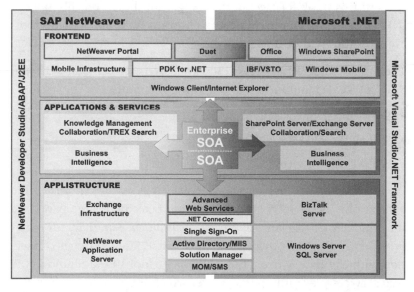

Figure 2.1 SAP NetWeaver Integration Level

To better understand the technical background of the possibilities of a NetWeaver/.NET integration, it is necessary to first take a look back at the development of SAP interface technologies. We will focus especially on SAP technologies that were usable in a Microsoft environment, particularly:

▶ Remote Function Call (RFC)

▶ Business Application Programming Interface (BAPI)

▶ Intermediate Document (IDoc)

Early tools for SAP/Microsoft integration These SAP technologies, some of which formed the basis of SAP interface technologies in the SAP NetWeaver infrastructure, are described in detail in this chapter. There were tools that made these SAP interface technologies usable in the Microsoft environment, including:

▶ Remote Function Call Software Development Kit (RFC SDK) with the function library *librfc32.dll*

▶ RFC components

▶ BAPI components

▶ DCOM Connector

Their architectures and functions are only briefly explained, though, because this book focuses on the integration based on the modern .NET and NetWeaver architectures. Moreover, some of these tools are not supported by SAP.

Current tools The current integration possibilities are based on Microsoft .NET and SAP NetWeaver and include the following variants:

▶ SAP Connector for Microsoft .NET

▶ SAP NetWeaver AS web services

▶ SAP XI web services

In this chapter, the use of SAP NetWeaver AS web services in the context of a .NET/NetWeaver integration takes up a large part since it has increasing relevance as a basic technology, especially for *Enterprise Service-Oriented Architecture* (Enterprise SOA). Also in connection with the new Microsoft development tool Visual Studio 2005, web services play an important role, which is also discussed in this chapter.

2.1   SAP Legacy Interface Technologies

Even at the time of SAP R/2, there were always other applications and IT systems in an enterprise other than an SAP system, including legacy systems or systems for a specialized work area. Because these systems might either need data from R/2 or were supposed to deliver data to R/2, there was an early demand for the corresponding functions.

To enable both the external access to SAP data and the other way around, SAP developed and provided the relevant technologies. These were the real-time integration variants RFC and BAPI, as well as the transactional variant of IDoc. Before NetWeaver (up to version SAP R/3 4.6C), these provided the technological basis for integration and interoperability scenarios. They are also referred to as *SAP legacy interface technologies*.

Because these technologies continue to play a role for newer interface technologies, although encapsulated internally, it is helpful if not necessary to know them, which is why they are discussed here.

2.1.1   Remote Function Call (RFC)

The RFC is a technology originally developed by SAP for the communication between SAP systems, such as between SAP R/2 and SAP R/3, but also for the communication with external applications. It is based on the Remote Procedure Call implementation already used in the Unix environment.

The basis for a RFC is the *Common Programming Interface for Communications* (CPI-C), which was originally standardized by IBM and is based on the TCP/IP communication protocol. SAP has implemented CPI-C for ABAP and uses it for the RFC technology.

CPI-C

The RFC technology enables bi-directional access to an ABAP function module[1] in SAP R/3 via an existing TCP/IP network connection. This triggers the execution of the function module in the SAP system. This function module can then receive external data and return it after processing. On this basis, it is possible to develop the appropri-

---

1   ABAP is the programming language for SAP systems, and ABAP function modules are implemented functions within an SAP system.

ate point-to-point interface applications where both partners can communicate and exchange data for a concrete case via a concrete function module.

Remote-enabled function modules

SAP provides a large number of ready-made, remotely-callable function modules. A list of ABAP function modules that are declared as remotely callable can be viewed in the SAP system via the Object Navigator (Transaction SE84).

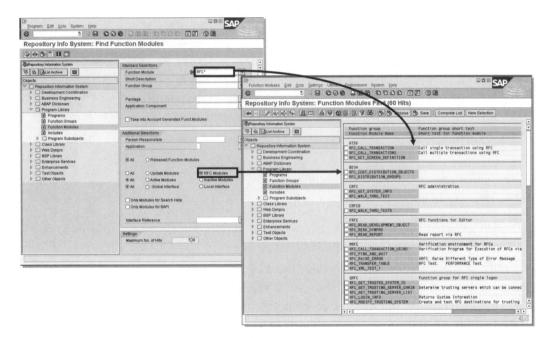

Figure 2.2 RFC Search in the Object Builder

Additionally, customers can also create remote-enabled function modules via the ABAP Workbench and the Function Builder (Transaction SE37). However, they need to make sure that the function module contains the remote-enabled attribute. Figure 2.3 illustrates the corresponding example.

Import, export and table parameters

All ABAP function modules have import, export and table parameters for data communication.[2] Changing parameters have been added in later releases. The function of import and export parameters should not need any further explanation. But what about the tables?

---

2   Note: All parameters of an RFC must have a reference to the ABAP Dictionary.

Tables enable the program to return more than one data record. They are similar to record sets in database queries.

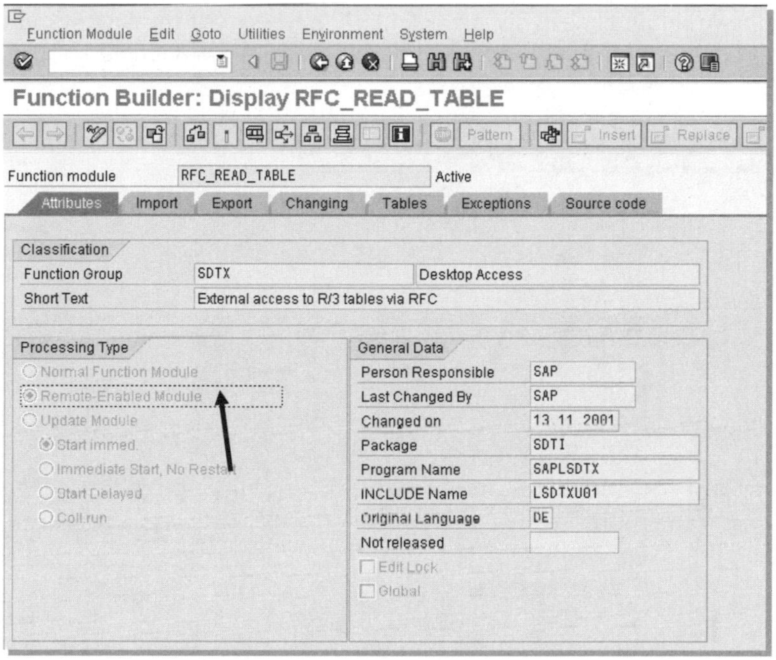

Figure 2.3 Remote Properties of an RFC in Function Builder

The following ABAP program code shows the call of a remote-enabled function module (RFC):

```
CALL FUNCTION 'FUNC1'
   DESTINATION 'ABC'
   EXPORTING ...
   IMPORTING ...
   TABLES ...
   EXCEPTIONS ...
```

While CALL FUNCTION generally calls other functions in ABAP, EXPORTING and TABLES describe the file transfer, and IMPORTING and TABLES describe the data return. The EXCEPTIONS area describes the error handling.

In this context, the keyword DESTINATION is important, because the DESTINATION parameter of the CALL FUNCTION call describes the target of the RFC communication. This can be an SAP R/2, SAP R/3, or a

Destination

39

non-SAP system. The data and parameters of such a target are stored in the RFCDES table and can be maintained there accordingly. If the desired target is entered there it can be directly addressed as shown in the program code. This is particularly necessary if the SAP system takes the initiative and addresses an external system (see Figure 2.4).

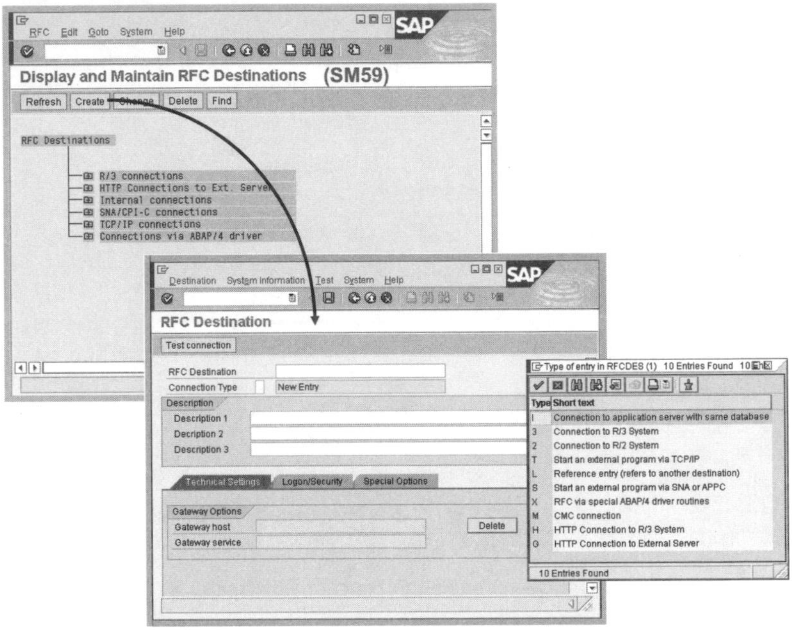

Figure 2.4 Display and Maintenance of RFC Destinations

Testing an RFC   A very helpful aspect for developing an interface is the possibility of testing or simulating parts of the interface. As far as the RFC is concerned, this possibility exists via the *Function Builder*. Figure 2.5 shows an example of testing an RFC. In such an RFC test, the import parameters of the RFC are queried by the user, the result of the function module is then displayed. The same result values should then also be received by the interface application if the import parameters are identical.

(A)synchronous RFC, tRFC, and qRFC   An essential characteristic of an RFC communication is the communication in real time, i.e., it takes place synchronously. Therefore, these RFCs are also referred to as *synchronous RFCs* (sRFC). For synchronous RFCs, the calling program waits for the processing of the called function module to be finished and continues its work only after it receives an answer.

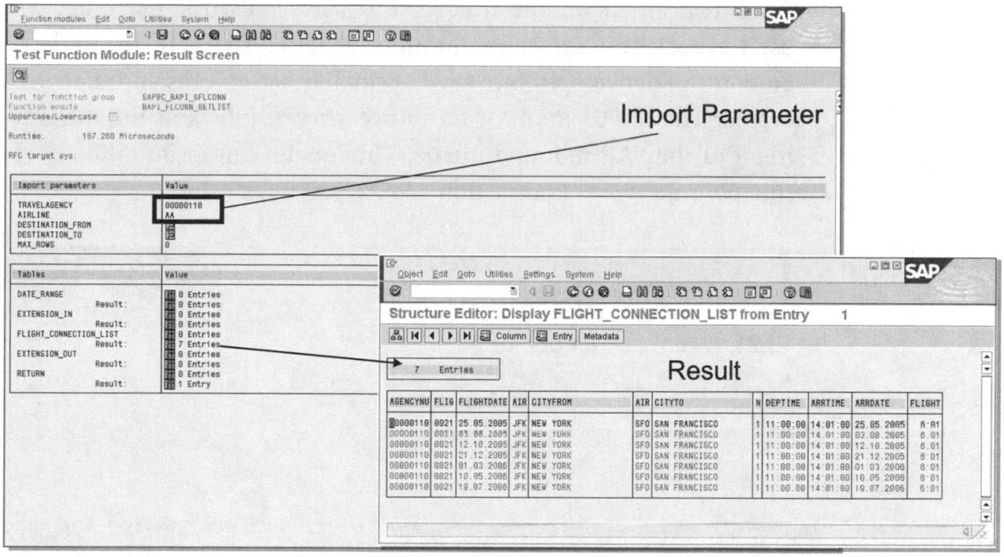

Figure 2.5 Testing an RFC Via Function Builder

It is also possible to use an asynchronous variant to perform the data exchange via RFC in a decoupled way. The calling program then continues. This can have the advantage since the possible unavailability of one of the interface systems will not block the other system in this case. However, an asynchronous interface requires specific functions that check if an RFC was started only once and if it was fully completed. These are the transaction controls. They handle the transaction management of the SAP system and the *transactional RFCs* (tRFCs). tRFCs are coupled with the transaction management of the SAP system. In the ABAP code, tRFCs are marked with the annotation IN BACKGROUND TASK, and COMMIT WORK then triggers the execution—not CALL FUNCTION, as usual:

```
CALL FUNCTION 'FUNC1'
   IN BACKGROUND TASK
   DESTINATION 'ABC'
   EXPORTING ...
     TABLES ...
COMMIT WORK
```

You also need to consider that no data return can be defined with tRFCs and that only the *exception* (i. e., error message, SYSTEM_FAILURE) can be returned.

An enhancement of the tRFCs are *queued RFCs* (qRFCs). They are used especially with large amounts of data. The transfer of large amounts of data is split into several small function calls and then processed. The qRFCs monitor the processing of jobs and the management of the SAP inbound queue. This queue can be monitored via the qRFC monitor (Transaction SMQ2, see Figure 2.6).

Figure 2.6 SAP Inbound Queue

RFC SDK   To support the use of the RFC technology in the Microsoft Windows environment, SAP created the RFC Software Development Kit (SDK). The RFC SDK is included on every SAP GUI installation CD and can also be installed during the installation of the SAP GUI. It is then stored in the directory */SAPGUI.../rfcsdk/*.

The RFC SDK contains several tools that deserve a closer look. The RFC SDK contains the DCOM Connector, a group of ActiveX controls and a function library that plays a special role which is why it should be dealt with in detail. The DCOM Connector and the ActiveX controls will be discussed later (see Figure 2.7).

Figure 2.7 Contents of the RFC SDK

The function library called *librfc32.dll* provides all required functions   librfc32.dll
of an RFC communication for a Windows environment (Win32). It
can be addressed and used in a Visual-C++ program as well as in a
Visual Basic program like any other function library, i. e., the functions must be declared accordingly.

In Visual Basic 6.0 code, an example of the syntax is:[3]

```
Declare Function RFCCLOSE Lib "librfc32.dll"(...)
```

The *librfc32.dll* function library provides approximately 100 functions. These are functions for logging on/logging off (RfcOpenEx /
RfcClose) from the SAP system as well as functions for the actual
function module call (RfcCallReceiveEx) and for reading the relevant import/export parameters (e. g., RfcGetImportParam) or the RFC
tables. A complete overview of all functions in this function library
can be found in the directory *rfcsdk/text* in the Windows help file
saprfc.hlp.

Besides, the program logic of a program using the function library
librfc32.dll is to be regarded as an example of all programs communicating with SAP. It has remained almost the same, as we will see in
examples later in this book.

The program logic is as follows:

1. Log on to the SAP host

2. Define transfer and return parameters

3. Reserve memory for the parameters, if necessary

4. Fill the transfer parameters with values

5. Call function modules (RFC call)

6. Evaluate returned values

7. Release memory

8. Log off from the SAP host

---

3   Not all RFC API functions can be called in this way from Visual Basic.

RFC components

Although encapsulated, the library *librfrc32.dll* is the basis of the *SAP RFC components*. These are ActiveX controls[4] that could be embedded as components in Visual Basic 5.0/6.0. The most important ActiveX control is the SAP function control WDTFUNCS.OCX.

If you added this control as a component to your VB 6.0 program via the **References** menu, as shown in Figure 2.8, the developer could easily address RFCs instead of using the function library *librfrc32.dll*.

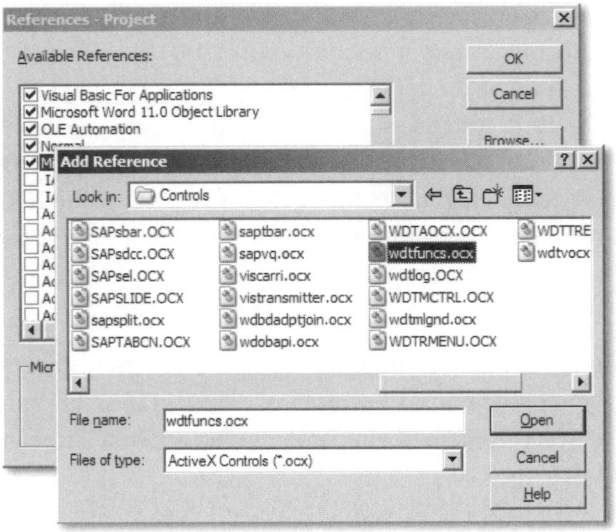

Figure 2.8 Embedding the SAP Function Control

If the ActiveX control WDTFUNCS.OCX was placed on the VB form, no coding was needed to specify the RFC to be addressed, e. g., via the object properties, and the RFC properties could be edited while the SAP host system was accessing it.

In the program code, the ActiveX control would be addressed as follows:

```
Private Button_Click()
Dim mSAP_RFC As SAPFunctionsOCX.Function
Set mSAP_RFC = SAPFunctions1.Item(1)
```

---

4 ActiveX controls are precompiled software components based on the COM software architecture developed by Microsoft. Concerning Microsoft Visual Basic, ActiveX controls are usually control elements, while COM generally defines the distribution of components and the communication between objects.

When the control was embedded, in the property window it was assigned the RFC_READ_TABLE per Drag&Drop on the VB form as Item1.

In addition to the SAP function control WDTFUNCS.OCX, the RFC components also included the SAP logon control WDTLOG.OCX, the SAP TableFactory control WDTAOCX.OCX, and the SAP table view control WDTVOC.OCX. These controls could be integrated into VB projects as well and were based on the functions of the RFC basis function library *librfc32.dll* depending on their functionalities and characteristics (see Figure 2.9).

More controls

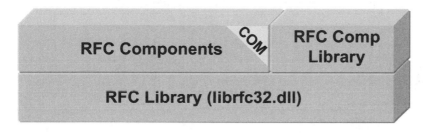

Figure 2.9 Classification of RFC Components

As an alternative to the embedding of controls in the VB project or on the VB form, it was also possible to address the corresponding control library in VB 6.0 via CreateObject.

For example, a class would be initialized as follows in VB 6.0:

```
Private Sub RFC_Function_Class_Initialize()
   Set objSAP_RFC = CreateObject("SAP.Functions")
   Set  mSAP_RFC = objSAP_RFC.Add("RFC_READ_TABLE")
End Sub
```

The call took place in the actual program code via

```
mSAP_RFC.Call
```

2.1.2   Business Application Programming Interface (BAPI)

The object-oriented version of the SAP interface technology is the use of Business Application Programming Interface (BAPI).

SAP business objects The BAPI is a standardized and fixed method of an SAP business object (BO). SAP BOs are economically defined objects. They are part of the *SAP Business Framework* concept and defined and documented in the *Business Object Repository* (BOR).

With SAP business objects, SAP moved another step toward integration at a business level because an SAP BO encapsulates parts of the SAP data model according to economic relevance. Thus, objects like *material* or *customer* are addressed, not tables or structures (see Figure 2.10).

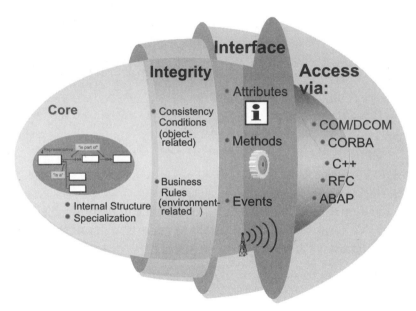

Figure 2.10 Layers of a Business Object

An SAP BO consists of the following layers:

▶ **BO kernel**
Contains the data of the object.

▶ **BO integrity layer**
This layer implements the relevant object-related dependencies and the business logics via business rules and environment-related conditions.

▶ **BO interface layer**
This layer contains the attributes, methods, events, and I/O functions. It describes the implementation and structure of the object.

► **BO access layer**
  This is where the concrete access to the business object is implemented and the access technology is defined.

The BO interface layer with attributes and methods is particularly interesting.

The data covered by a BO is described using attributes. These can be virtual attributes, field references, or object references with dependency attributes.

Attributes

The methods (BAPIs) of a BO are operations that edit the attributes of a business object. The method of a business object is defined via a name as well as parameters and exceptions. The method is technically implemented via remote-enabled SAP function modules. Thus, an RFC can access the BAPIs as described in Section 2.1.2 and illustrated in Figure 2.11.

Methods

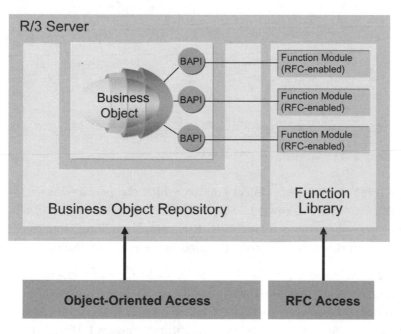

Figure 2.11 Possibilities of Accessing BAPIs

The main tool for BAPIs in SAP R/3 is the *BAPI Explorer* (Transaction BAPI), which is a part of the ABAP Workbench and the Business Framework. It serves as a documentation and information instrument as well as a development tool for editing BAPIs.

BAPI Explorer

On the one hand, the BAPI Explorer lists all BOs implemented in the respective SAP system and their methods. Their properties and parameters are documented in detail. Figure 2.12 shows an example.

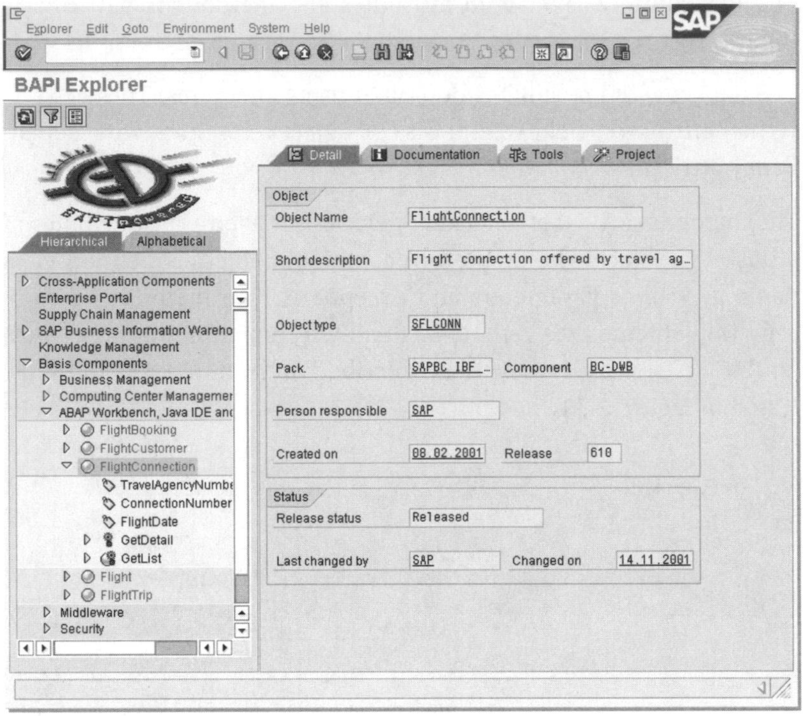

Figure 2.12 BAPI Explorer

Business Object Builder

By using the Business Object Builder, which can be called from the BAPI Explorer as shown in Figure 2.13, customers can create new business objects and their BAPIs. It is completely integrated in the ABAP Workbench and tightly coupled to the Function Builder.

Interface Repository

Primarily, however, the BAPIs provided by SAP are addressed within interfaces and may be slightly modified to meet the customers' demands. To allow a SAP interfaces developer who cannot always access an SAP system to still provide information via BAPIs, SAP put the Interface Repository (IFR) on the Internet. Via the web address *http://ifr.sap.com*, the developer could obtain a detailed description in XML of the BAPI from which he needed information (see Figure 2.14).

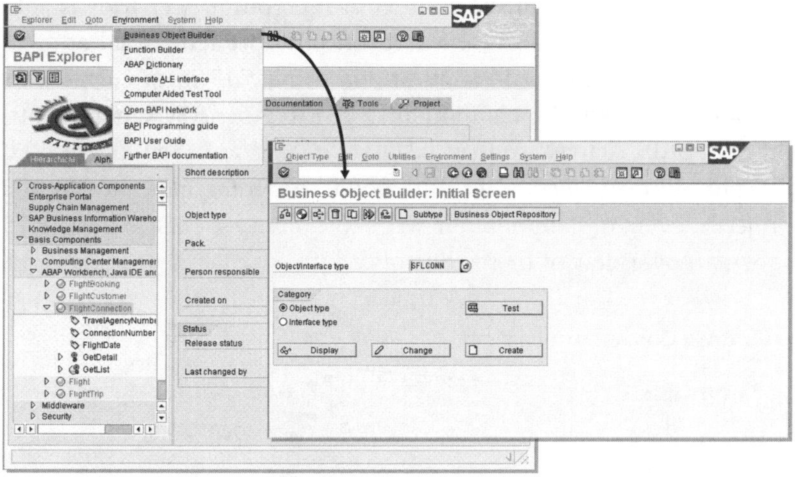

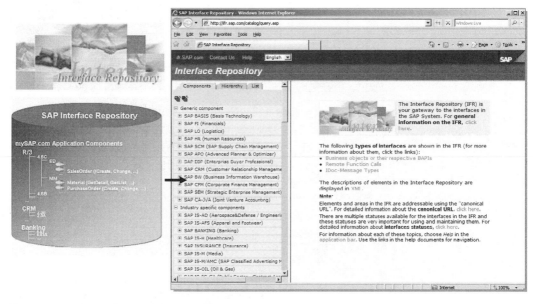

Figure 2.13 Business Object Builder

Figure 2.14 SAP Interface Repository on the Internet

The IFR was last updated in August 2005, and that was probably the last update. According to SAP, the site is no longer maintained. The development of an *Enterprise Service Repository* will replace the Interface Repository.

BAPI components As far as using BAPIs in the context of integration scenarios is concerned, developers from the Microsoft environment could address the BAPIs in Visual Basic applications using *SAP BAPI components* that are similar to RFC components. Just like the RFC components, the SAP BAPI ActiveX control (WDOBAPI.OCX) was based on the RFC function library *librfc32.dll* and could be integrated in VB 6.0 projects, even in combination with RFC components. Figure 2.15 shows an overview of these controls.

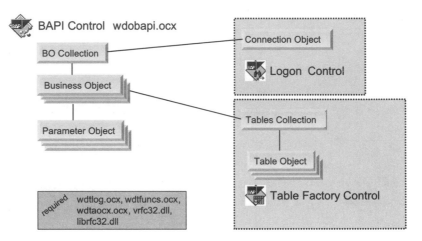

Figure 2.15 Overview of the SAP BAPI ActiveX Controls

Figure 2.15 and Figure 2.16 show the classification of the BAPI components and their relationship to the RFC function library *librfc32.dll.* They are based on each other.

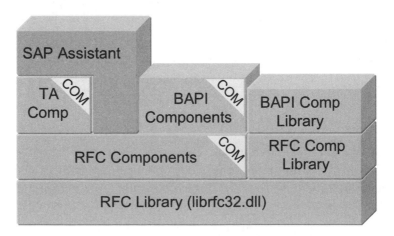

Figure 2.16 Classification of the BAPI Components

Just like the RFC components previously described, the BAPI ActiveX control could be integrated and used in VB 6.0 applications via **References • Add References**. Please note that the BAPI control needs to be addressed in an object-based way, which could read as follows:

```
Dim objSAP_Customer as Object
Set objSAP_Customer = SAPBAPIControl.GETSAPObject _
  ("Customer", strCustomerID)
```

`SAPBAPIControl` refers to the name of the SAP BAPI control object on the VB form.

2.1.3 DCOM Connector

A popular reason for creating integration applications in the Microsoft COM environment was to address BAPIs and RFCs via the SAP DCOM Connector. This real-time connector was jointly designed by SAP and Microsoft and developed by SAP. It was based on Microsoft's DCOM and COM+ technology.

While SAP provided predefined components, e.g., RFC and BAPI components, to the developers, the DCOM Connector takes one step further. It could now be used to create proprietary components for accessing BAPIs and RFCs. These encapsulated the SAP-specific interface functionalities as proxy objects. The DCOM Connector creates C++ program code for one or several selected SAP function modules. This program code can then be compiled to a reusable function library (DLL) or ActiveX component using a VC++ compiler. This component used the *Microsoft Transaction Server* (MTS) or, in newer versions, *COM+* as a runtime environment. However, it always accessed the *librfc32.dll* library mentioned above as well.

Creating your own components using the DCOM Connector

Due to integration in a software architecture based on distributed components, the implementation of the DCOM Connector made sense particularly for server-based applications or web-based applications (see Figure 2.17).

Up to SAP Web AS 6.20, the SAP DCOM Connector was delivered on the installation CD of the SAP GUI and is contained in the RFC SDK, as described above. However, the DCOM Connector is no longer being developed, and SAP support and maintenance were discontinued on December 31, 2004.[5]

Figure 2.17 Object Builder of the DCOM Connector

In the most recent version 6.20, the DCOM Connector consisted of the following components:

▶ **Destination Manager**
Manages the R/3 connections

▶ **Object Builder**
Supports the generation of reusable DCOM components as wrappers or proxy classes for BAPIs or RFCs

▶ **Catalog**
Displays all components created using the Object Builder

▶ **Monitor**
Displays the current R/3 connections and their status during productive operations

For developers, the main tool was the DCOM Object Builder. Using this wizard, a developer could address the requested SAP function modules or BAPIs after a successful logon to the SAP target server and create the C++ code mentioned above.

---

5 For more information, see SAP Note 533055.

The DCOM Connector was an important module in the evolution of SAP integration in the Windows world. However, it had its limits: for example, there was no support for Unicode or the complex structures of newer BAPIs.

The successor of the DCOM Connector in a Microsoft world is the *SAP Connector for Microsoft .NET* (see Section 2.2). However, SAP points out that no migration tool for migrating the SAP DCOM Connector to the SAP Connector for Microsoft .NET is provided. This is understandable, since the serious architectural differences between traditional Microsoft development and Microsoft .NET make a sensible automatic conversion impossible.

SAP Connector for Microsoft .NET

2.1.4 Intermediate Document (IDoc)

In addition to the real-time variants RFC/BAPI, there is another possibility for exchanging data between SAP and third-party systems. *Intermediate Documents* (IDocs) are particularly suitable for an asynchronous and structured exchange of large amounts of business data. IDocs are proprietary SAP file formats for data exchange (see Figure 2.18).

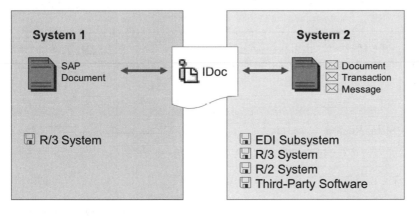

Figure 2.18 IDoc Concept

IDocs are usually used in business processes where large amounts of data is exchanged, for example, the exchange of material master data. The appropriate IDocs are provided for the electronic transfer of purchase orders, delivery notes, and invoices to or from a supplier, i.e., the exchange of business documents that used to take place on paper.

Although the IDocs format is an ASCII format, it is not compatible with formats from the area of *Electronic Data Interchange* (EDI) or *EDIFACT*. The IDoc format has a fixed data structure and consists of the following elements (see Figure 2.19):

▶ **Control record**
An envelope, consisting of management and control information for technical processing

▶ **Data record(s)**
Segments and segment fields that make up the actual data of the application

▶ **Status record(s)**
One or several status data sets containing the processing status, as well as error information

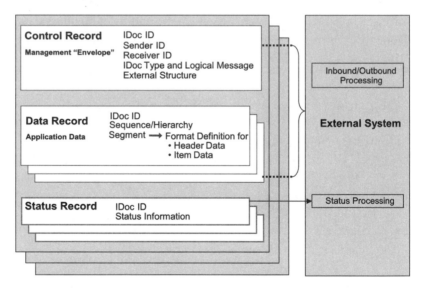

Figure 2.19 Structure of an IDoc

In contrast to the modern XML format, an IDoc is not self-descriptive—it is not readable for people without detailed skills.

ALE When exchanging data based on IDocs, the proprietary SAP integration service *Application Link Enabling* (ALE) is used. This is a message-oriented middleware architecture that uses the IDoc document for a controlled data distribution between SAP systems and external applications to map the business processes accordingly. The goal is to ensure consistent data storage and the process's transaction security. With ALE, the systems are all loosely coupled and data is exchanged asynchronously—data storage is redundant and databases are accessed locally. Figure 2.20 shows an example of an ALE process.

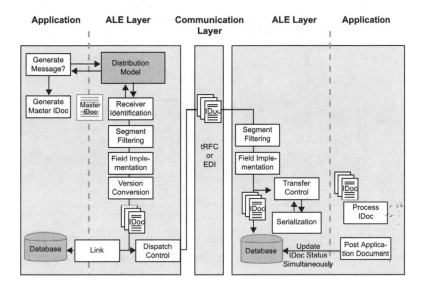

Figure 2.20 Example of an ALE Process

2.2 Development Tool SAP Connector for Microsoft .NET

With the introduction of the Microsoft .NET Framework and the associated development tool Visual Studio 2003, Microsoft has created a comfortable engineering environment for developers. This, and the fact that the tools for SAP/Microsoft integration (see Section 2.1) had reached the end of their lifecycle, caused SAP to work together with Microsoft to provide a contemporary tool for the Microsoft .NET developers.

The successor of all previous integration tools for developers in the Microsoft world is the *SAP Connector for Microsoft .NET* (NCO) in its current version 2.0. It supports the developer both at design time and at runtime by creating or operating SAP interface applications based on the Microsoft .NET Framework. The SAP NCO is integrated in Microsoft Visual Studio 2003 and enables the .NET developer to completely work in his familiar engineering environment. Figure 2.21 illustrates the functionality of SAP NCO at design time and at runtime.

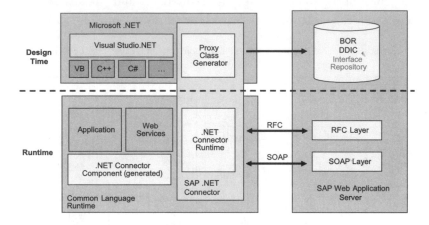

Figure 2.21 Overview of SAP Connector for .NET

Protocols and languages

The SAP NCO supports the access to RFC and BAPI as well as the access to SOAP as of SAP Web AS 6.20. The decision about the respective protocol does not immediately affect the development process, though, because it can be switched at runtime.

In contrast to the predecessor, version 2.0 permits the use of the Microsoft .NET development languages Visual Basic .NET and C# for engineering.

Access to SAP NCO

The SAP NCO is available in the SAP Service Marketplace.[6] Every customer and partner can obtain it there. Please note that developers using the SAP NCO must have an SAP developer license. Additionally, all end users must be properly licensed for the SAP functionality used via the SAP NCO.

After the successful installation on the development system, the developer will notice the SAP logo in the Visual Studio startup screen. From there he will see another new item in the Server Explorer. As an extension, the Server Explorer now shows an SAP server branch as a new type (see Figure 2.22).

---

6 See *http://service.sap.com*.

Figure 2.22 SAP Branch in the Server Explorer

Thus, it is possible to add one or more SAP servers to the development environment that is similar to other server types such as an SQL server. For example, the developer can directly access the server resources via Drag&Drop and reference them in his program code.

The developer will also notice that there is an SAP Proxy group in the Toolbox that contains the appropriate controls, as shown in Figure 2.23.

Figure 2.23 SAP Proxy Components

But how can the NCO be used to create integration applications? This will be shown in the following sections.

2.2.1   Example of a .NET Application

This example is a .NET WindowsForm application that should address the SAP BAPI `Bapi_Flconn_Getlist`. This BAPI is part of the training application of the SAP flight data model[7] of the ABAP Workbench. It returns lists of possible flight connections filtered by various search criteria.

We will now create a WindowsForms application based on Microsoft .NET that queries a fictitious travel agency, airline and their identification codes as search criteria and then displays the result as a list of flight connections in the same mask.

Creating a Visual Basic project

At first we will create a new Visual Basic project (see Figure 2.24). A new project element is added to this project in the Solution Explorer (see Figure 2.25).

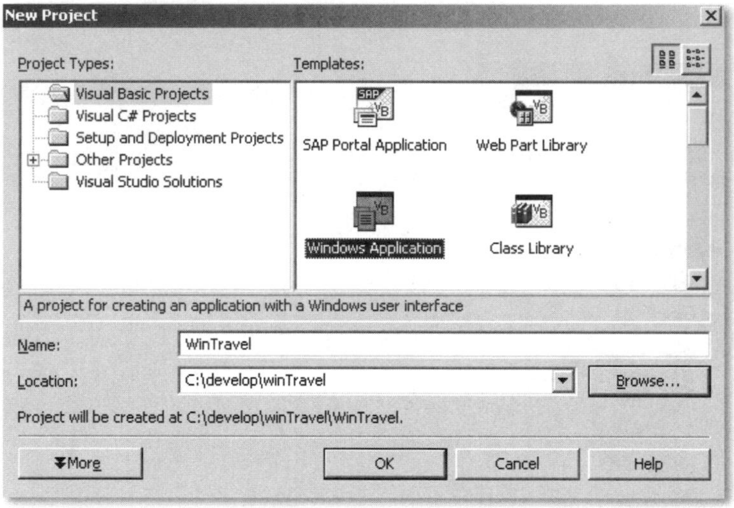

Figure 2.24 Select New Project

In the **SAP** category, the **SAP Connector Proxy** template should be selected. This SAP Connector Proxy is the core element of this application.

---

7 This flight data model is used as a training scenario during SAP ABAP training courses. It is also included in the SAP NetWeaver Preview 6.40 ABAP and can be created using the ABAP program `S_FLIGHT_MODEL_DATA_GENERATOR`.

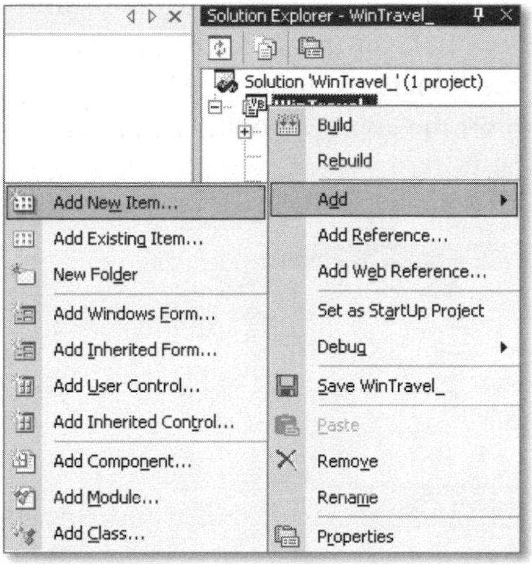

Figure 2.25 Add New Element

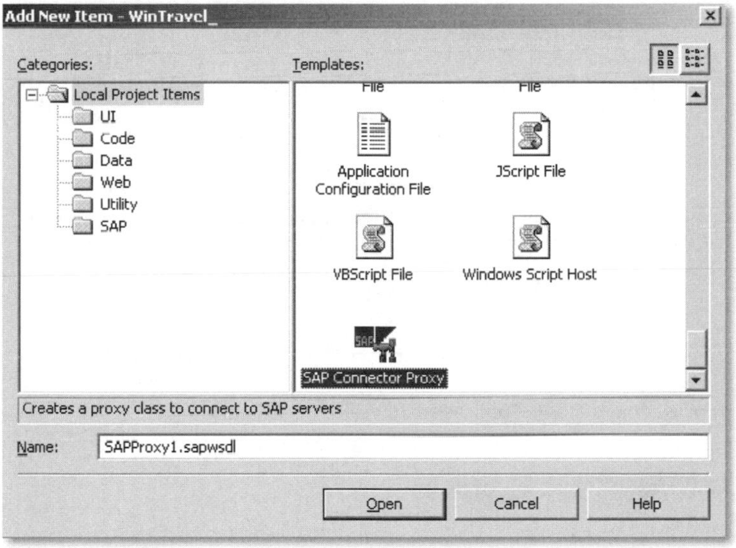

Figure 2.26 Adding the SAP Connector Proxy Element

However, this only adds an empty Web Service Definition Language (WSDL) file called *SAPProxy1.sapwsdl* to the project. At the same time, you should add the appropriate SAP Application Server in the VS Server Explorer, if it is not displayed yet (see Figure 2.27).

Selecting the BAPI or RFC

In the Server Explorer you can now select the respective BAPI from the Business Object Repository (BOR) of the selected SAP Application Server or an RFC from the **Functions** group (see Figure 2.28). For this purpose, you need to set the appropriate filter in the **Functions** group.

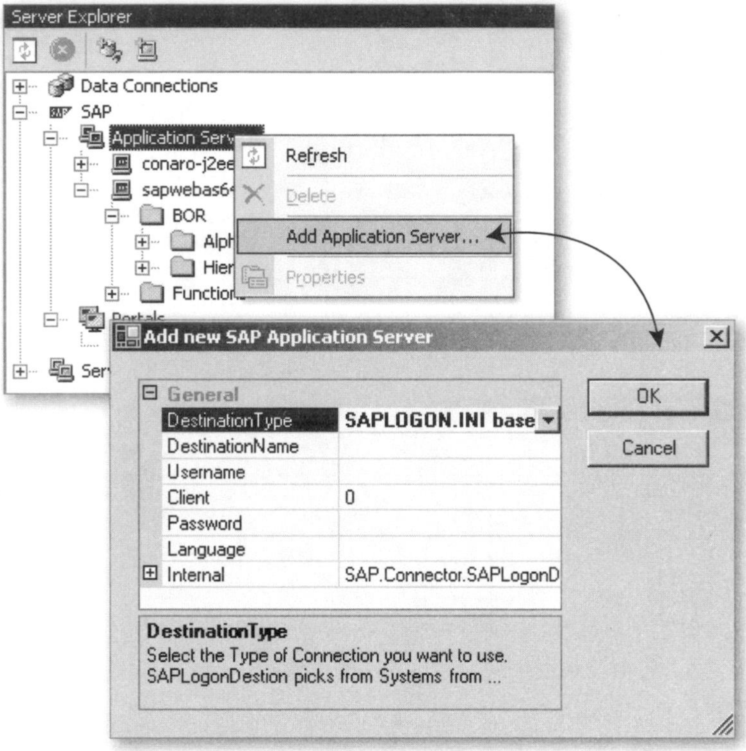

Figure 2.27 Adding the SAP Application Server

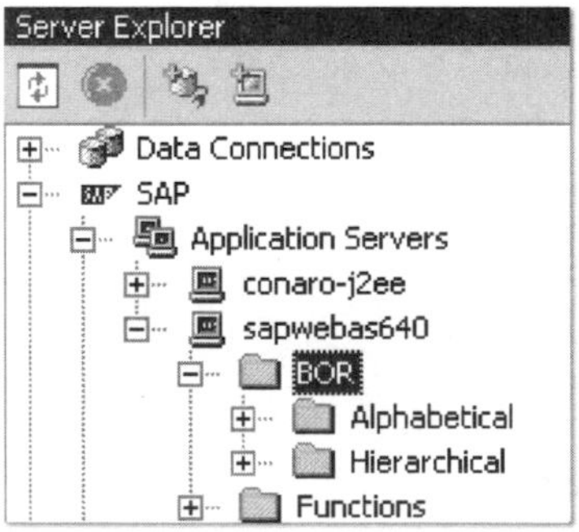

Figure 2.28 BOR in the Server Explorer

Now, we want to access a BAPI. Thus, we need to select the relevant business object and the desired method in the BOR branch. Figure 2.29 shows the relevant BAPI branch **Flight connection offered by travel agency** (Flconn) and the wanted method (BAPI) GetList.

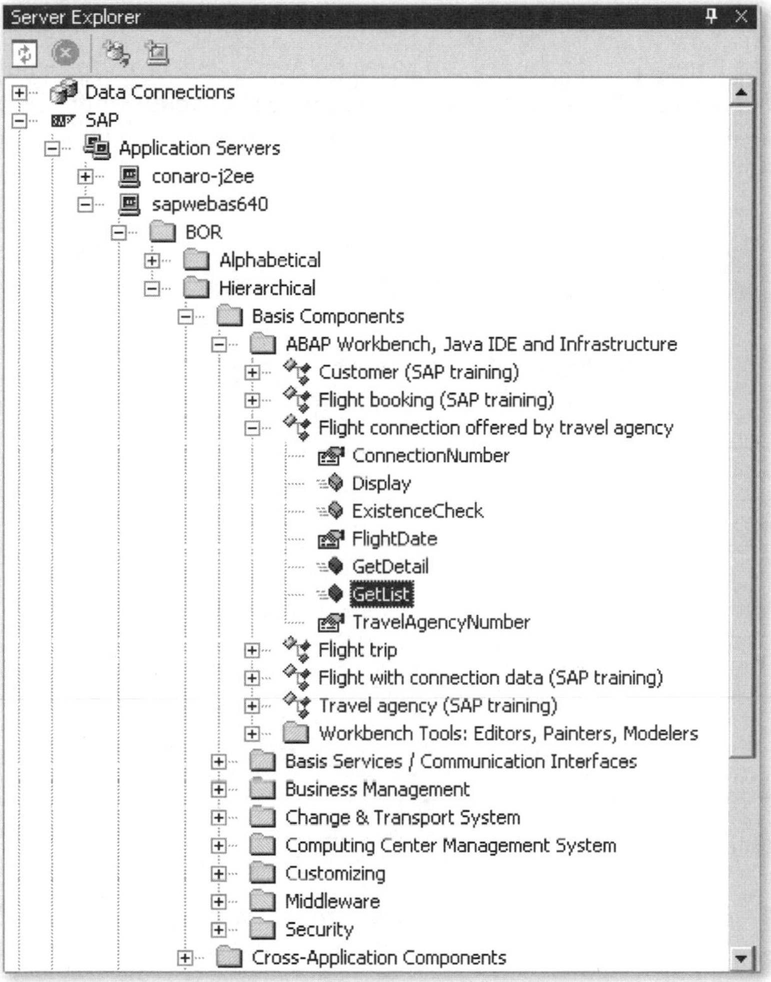

Figure 2.29 Server Explorer/Selection of the BAPI

Via Drag&Drop, this entry is drawn to the form of the WSDL file we created previously. The Connector then automatically creates the SAP Proxy code.

The SAP data structures and methods are transferred and the appropriate classes are generated. In the example, SAP tables like `BAPISCODATTABLE1` were generated as derived classes of the `SAPTable` basis class, and the BAPI was generated as the method `Bapi_Flconn_Getlist`.

Additionally, ABAP data types were converted to .NET-compliant data types. The developer can view the generated Proxy program code, and the Parameter Collection Editor even enables a more comfortable view of the BAPI parameters as shown in Figure 2.30.

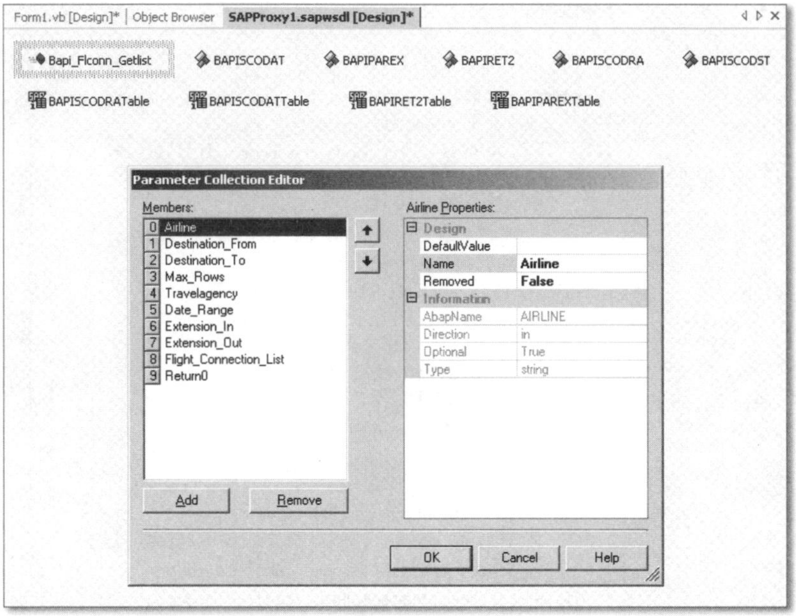

Figure 2.30 SAP Proxy Parameters

Windows form We still need to edit the Windows form (WinForm). A form is required that provides the input fields for the **Agency** and the **Airline** and contains a list view in the form of a DataGrid for the result. For the actual BAPI call, a button is provided. Figure 2.31 shows the example form.

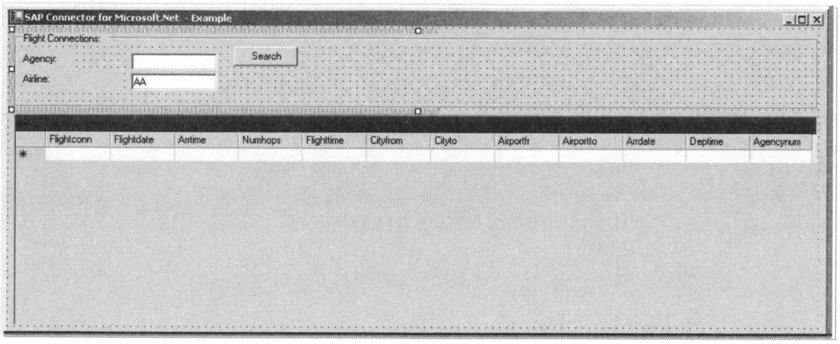

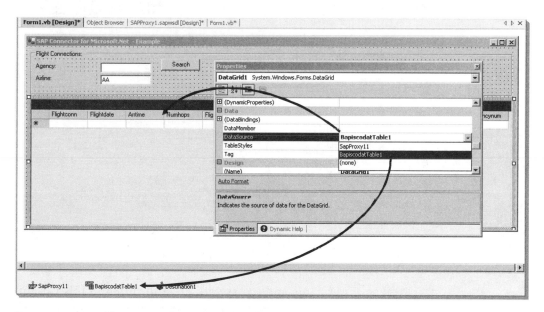

Figure 2.31 WinForm of the NCO Example

Additionally, it is recommended to specify the SAP table BAPISCODATTABLE1 as a data source for the DataGrid in the properties. This has the advantage of then applying the SAP table structure to the DataGrid (see Figure 2.32).

Figure 2.32 SAP Table as a Data Source for the DataGrid

Talk about convenience, even the logon to the SAP host can be performed via the Destination Control from the SAP Proxy Toolbox without much program code. You just have to drag the Destination Control to the form. Then you can store the logon parameters in the Control properties, as shown in Figure 2.33. These parameters are

Logon to the SAP host

added as key elements of the Microsoft .NET configuration file *App.config*. An excerpt follows:

```xml
<?xml version="1.0" encoding="utf-8"?>
<configuration>
  <appSettings>
   <add key="Destination1.AppServerHost"
       value="192.168.0.23" />
   <add key="Destination1.Client" value="000" />
   <add key="Destination1.Language" value="EN" />
   <add key="Destination1.SystemNumber" value="0" />
   <add key="Destination1.Trace" value="False" />
    ...
  </appSettings>
</configuration>
```

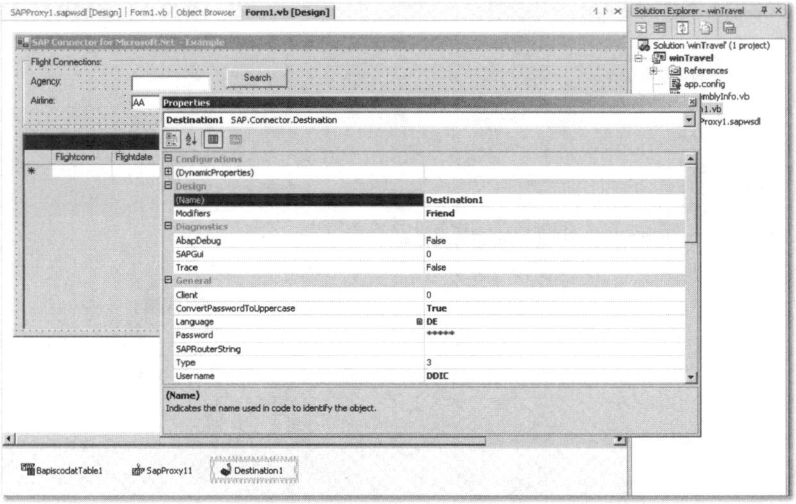

Figure 2.33 Maintenance of Logon Data Via Destination Control

Because a user name and a password are also stored in this variant, this procedure is recommended for testing environments only. It would make more sense to create a separate logon dialog for entering those parameters.

SOAP support   In this context, it should be mentioned that the SOAP support for the SAP Connector has been enhanced in version 2.0. If the SAP host is SAP Web AS 6.20 or higher it can now also be addressed via SOAP. For this purpose, you need to change the connection type in the property dialog. Set the UseSOAP property to True and specify the httpPath. These parameters are then stored accordingly in the configuration file and can thus be used as follows:

```
<add key="Destination1.UseSoap" value="True" />
<add key="Destination1.HttpPath"
     value="/sap/bc/soap/rfc" />
```

Additionally, a new feature of SAP Connector version 2.0 is *Connection Pooling*. This means that an existing connection to the SAP target host will continue to be used. Every open connection to the SAP system is a valuable resource. Thus, a connection management via Connection Pooling is recommended.

Up to this point, we almost exclusively work with Drag&Drop. Now we get to the coding. Although the SAP Connector for Microsoft .NET created the framework and generated the most important (proxy) classes, there is still something left to do for the developer. In this example, the query of the import parameters **Airline** and **Agency** need to be coded, as well as the display of the expected result.

Coding

Once the entry fields for **Airline** and **Agency** are filled accordingly, the user clicks on the search button. This should be the triggering event for this application. Here is the program code:

```
Private Sub btnSearch_Click(ByVal sender As _
   System.Object, ByVal e As System.EventArgs) Handles _
   btnSearch.Click
```

The definition of all required variables and SAP tables looks as follows:

```
Dim strTravelAgency As String
Dim strConnection As String
Dim oProxy As New SAPProxy1
Dim oList As New BAPISCODATTable

Dim oReturn As New BAPIRET2Table
Dim oExtOut As New BAPIPAREXTable
Dim oExtin As New BAPIPAREXTable
Dim oDateRange As New BAPISCODRATable
Dim oDest_To As New BAPISCODST
Dim oDest_From As New BAPISCODST
```

```
Dim iMaxRows As Integer
Dim strConn As String
iMaxRows = 20
```

Then the connection to the SAP system is established using the data from the Destination Control:

```
strConn = Me.Destination1.ConnectionString
oProxy.Connection = _
  New SAP.Connector.SAPConnection(strConn)
```

Next is the first call of the BAPI:

```
Try
  oProxy.Bapi_Flconn_Getlist(txtAirline.Text,
    oDest_From, oDest_To, iMaxRows,
    txtTravelAgency.Text, oDateRange, oExtin, _
    oExtOut, oList, oReturn)
```

The BAPI call result is then bound to the DataGrid:

```
  DataGrid1.DataSource = oList
  DataGrid1.Refresh()
```

In case of an error, an error message is returned:

```
  Catch ex As Exception
    MsgBox(ex.ToString)
    Return
End Try
```

Then the connection is closed and the routine is finished:

```
oProxy.Connection.Close()
End Sub
```

If the SAP host cannot be reached, you can perform a test. After you enter the search criteria **Agency: 110** and **Airline: AA**, the result should be displayed as presented in Figure 2.34.

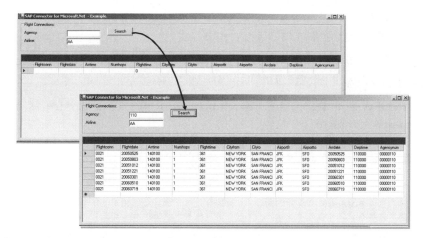

Figure 2.34 The Final SAP .NET WindowsForm Application

The enhancement of the Smart DataSet needs to be mentioned. With this enhancement it is possible to preset the parameters of the BAPI or RFC call. In the property dialog of the RFC method or the BAPI, the parameters are assigned so-called SAP Proxy fields as default values. Where do these come from? The Visual Studio 2003 toolbox contains the **SAP Proxy Field** component. Using Drag&Drop, this component is moved to the Designer and the corresponding type information is defined in the properties of the component. In this example, the BAPI call could then be shortened:

Smart DataSet

```
oProxy.Bapi_Flconn_Getlist()
```

Whether it actually makes sense to use the Smart DataSet is up to the individual developer. However, the trend is toward configuration instead of coding.

2.2.2 Example of an ASP.NET Web Service

Just as simple as the creation of a Windows application is the generation of an ASP.NET web service (ASMX) using VS 2003 and the SAP NCO. This scenario is suitable only for systems running Basis release 4.6 or lower because SAP applications that are based on the SAP Web Application Server or the SAP NetWeaver Application Server are able to publish web services themselves. Instead of using an ASP.NET service, you should first try using the SAP Exchange Infrastructure without having to modify the actual application.

In this example, the previous scenario is now implemented as ASP.NET web service. The steps are very much the same.

Initially, you select the VB template **ASP.NET Web Service** as a project template (see Figure 2.35).

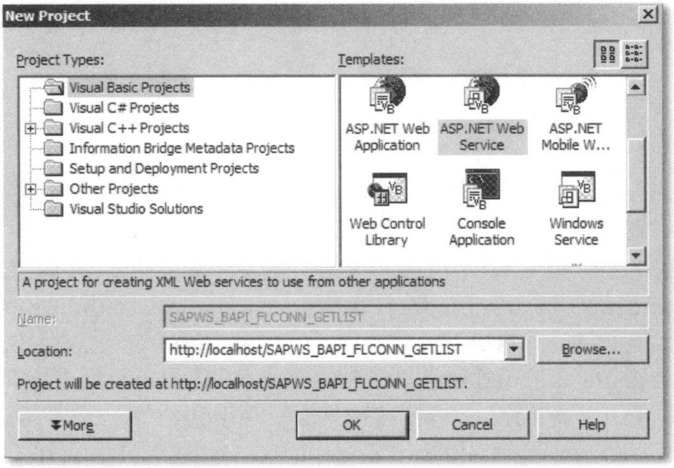

Figure 2.35 Selection of the VB Template ASP.NET Web Service

An SAP Proxy is added to this project as well (see Figure 2.36).

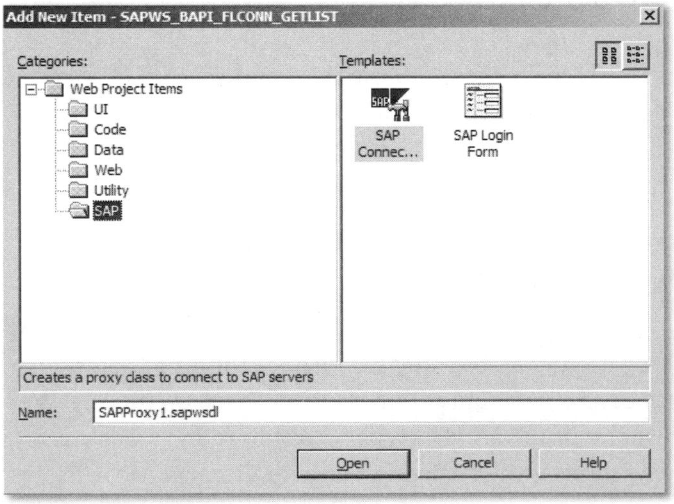

Figure 2.36 Adding the SAP Proxy

Again, we address the BAPI FLCONN_GETLIST. The procedure is the same as in the last example. The BAPI is selected from the Server Explorer and dragged to the SAP Proxy file form (see Figure 2.37).

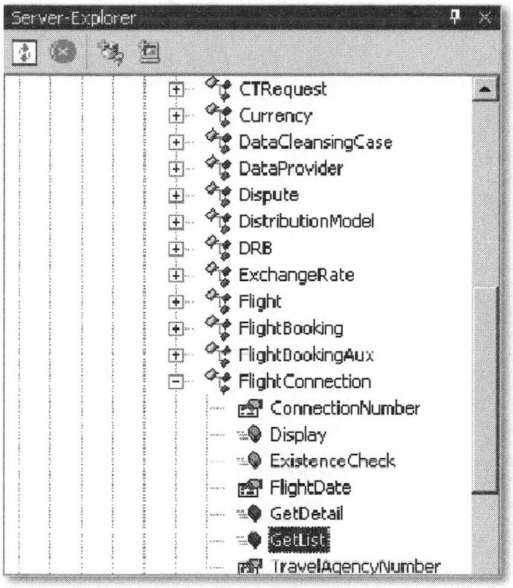

Figure 2.37 Selection of the BAPI FLCONN_GETLIST

Then, the coding for the web service functionality is created in the ASMX file of the project.

We start with the web service declaration:

```
<WebMethod()>
Public Function sapws_BAPI_FLCONN_GETLIST(ByVal _
  Airline As String, ByVal TravelAgency As String) _
  As BAPISCODATTable
```

Next follows the definition of all required variables and SAP tables:

```
Dim SAPServer As New SAP.Connector.Destination
Dim oProxy As New SAPProxy1
Dim oList As New BAPISCODATTable
Dim oReturn As New BAPIRET2Table
Dim oExtOut As New BAPIPAREXTable
Dim oExtin As New BAPIPAREXTable
Dim oDateRange As New BAPISCODRATable
Dim oDest_To As New BAPISCODST
```

```
Dim oDest_From As New BAPISCODST
Dim iMaxRows As Integer = 20
```

The logon data for the SAP host is stored in the code this time:

```
SAPServer.Client = "000"
SAPServer.AppServerHost = "192.168.0.23"
SAPServer.SystemNumber = "00"
SAPServer.Username = "BCUSER"
SAPServer.Password = "MINISAP"
SAPServer.Language = "EN"
oProxy.Connection = New SAP.Connector.SAPConnection(SAPS-
erver)
```

Then the BAPI is called:

```
oProxy.Bapi_Flconn_Getlist(Airline, oDest_From, _
  oDest_To, iMaxRows, TravelAgency, oDateRange, _
  oExtin, oExtOut, oList, oReturn)
```

The result of the BAPI call is returned:

```
Return oList
```

Finally, the connection is closed and the routine is finished:

```
oProxy.Connection.Close()
End Function
```

After compiling and starting this ASP.NET web service, it can then be addressed and consumed. Figure 2.38 shows the corresponding confirmation when calling the ASP.NET web service.

Note, if another ASP.NET web application or a Windows application based on the .NET Framework were to be the consumer of this ASP.NET web service, it would make more sense to attach this application directly to the SAP host using the SAP Connector for Microsoft .NET instead of taking the long way via ASP.NET web services and SAP Connector for Microsoft .NET Proxy classes.

Figure 2.38 Calling the SAP ASP.NET Web Service

2.3 Web Services

With the rapidly increasing popularity of e-business scenarios (e. g., web shops) and the related demand to couple these to ERP systems, such as the mySAP Business Suite, the topic of web services in the SAP environment comes up early.

Web services are an extension of the client/server concept known from the R/3 world. Instead of proprietary protocols like the SAP-proprietary RFC protocol, open Internet standards like, such as HTTP, SOAP, and WSDL are used. Particularly the use of open standards suggests the possibility of implementing interfaces that are independent of programming languages and vendors. Therefore, processes become more adaptable and can be implemented more flexibly so that innovations can be implemented in a quicker and more cost-effective way.

Open Internet standards

The SAP Business Connector plainly showed the future of web services for the SAP system. However, it was designed as an interim solution. At the same time, SAP NetWeaver was further developed to where web services or enterprise services play a central role.

Variants for creating web services

SAP NetWeaver provides two variants for creating the requested web services:

1. SAP NetWeaver Application Server (SAP NetWeaver AS)

2. SAP NetWeaver Exchange Infrastructure (SAP XI)

If both SAP NetWeaver AS and SAP XI can be used for generating web services, you might legitimately question which SAP product should be used for generating and managing web services.

Figure 2.39 shows situations or areas of application to use each variant.

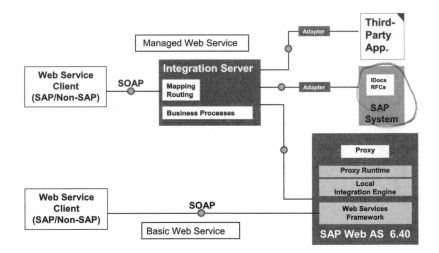

Figure 2.39 Providing Value-Added Web Services Via XI

At SAP, the first case is referred to as *Basic Web Services* or *Point2Point Web Services*, which are simple point-to-point scenarios. A web service is only used to publish the functionality of a single application, which is currently still the common practice in many cases.

Point2Point web services

For the Point2Point version of a web service, two variants can be distinguished: the inside-out method, i.e., the direct provision of an existing functionality (function module, BAPI) as a web service, and the outside-in method where at first an inbound message interface is modelled in the XI Integration Repository, then an XI server proxy is generated in the ABAP backend that is then implemented in a third step. Via the *Web Service Creation Wizard*, basic web services can be implemented quickly and easily using the SAP NetWeaver Application Server, as is shown in this chapter. The advantage of the outside-in method are that web service metadata like data types and message types, is stored in the integration repository and can be used in various implementations of the service. This approach already anticipates important aspects of the Enterprise SOA, where the ESR as an enhancement of the IR will be the central design-time repository for all service objects. Please note that XI is only used for modelling, not for executing the service. Therefore, it still is a simple Point2Point web service.

However, if a complex, cross-system business process is to be published as a web service, it is strongly recommended to use the *Integration Server* of the SAP Exchange Infrastructure. In this case, SAP refers to *managed* or *brokered web services*. By centrally storing a collaborative process's entire integration knowledge, the information is accessible to other processes as well and can be reused.

Managed web services

Web services also had a large impact on the developments in the Microsoft .NET environment. One consequence was the enhanced support of web service development in Microsoft Visual Studio 2003.

We will first discuss the SAP Business Connector and the SAP Web Application Server 6.20: real-life examples are used to illustrate the possibilities available to developers for implementing web service-based interoperability scenarios between the Microsoft .NET and the SAP NetWeaver platform.

The following integration examples are presented:

- SAP NetWeaver Application Server as a web service provider
- SAP NetWeaver Application Server as a web service client
- SAP XI as a web service provider

2.3.1 SAP Business Connector

Up to version 4.6, SAP R/3 did not support any web services or other Internet technologies. However, customers required more and more sophisticated solutions. Therefore, in addition to the SAP Internet Transaction Server (SAP ITS), SAP provided an add-on to the ERP system SAP R/3 as an (interim) solution for R/3 customers: The SAP Business Connector (BC). Originally, this was a licensing of the web-Methods Integration Server that was completely implemented in Java (see Figure 2.40).

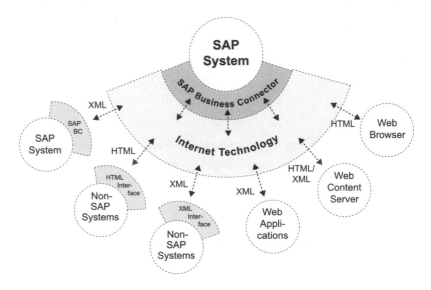

Figure 2.40 SAP Business Connector

Characteristics of the SAP BC
The SAP Business Connector was able to process HTML, XML, and web services and, as a server-based intermediate layer or EAI component, enable the appropriate communication with SAP R/3. It could be both an RFC client and an RFC server. The BC communication was based on the BC services, which were additional Java classes. The standard version was delivered with services for the integration with SAP R/3 via RFC and ALE as well as with services for FTP, HTTP(S), and JDBC.

The BC could address web services as a client, or it could publish RFCs as web services.

The invaluable advantage of the SAP Business Connector was primarily that the third-party system did not need any detailed knowledge of the SAP technology, but communication could take place based on vendor-independent standards. Figure 2.41 shows an example of the communication via web services.

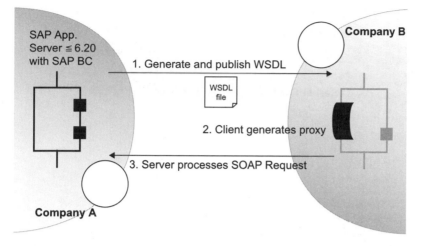

Figure 2.41 Business Connector and Web Services

The SAP Business Connector was very successful and has been implemented by SAP R/3 customers in many scenarios. However, SAP discontinued the development of the SAP Business Connector in 2003.[8]

The strategic solution for the business process integration is a part of SAP NetWeaver—the SAP NetWeaver Exchange Infrastructure (SAP XI). Because new and revised SAP solutions for process integration and messaging use the Exchange Infrastructure, customers should not consider the Business Connector during their strategic planning phase.

SAP NetWeaver Exchange Infrastructure

2.3.2 SAP Web Application Server 6.20

Starting with SAP Web Application Server (Web AS) version 6.20, it is possible to generate and consume web services (see Figure 2.42).

The components required for that purpose are Integration Engine and the Internet Communication Manager, which is an integral part of SAP Web AS 6.20 and supplements it with the necessary communication protocols like HTTP and SMTP.

---

8 Detailed information about the SAP Business Connector is available in the SAP PRESS Essentials Guide 7, *SAP Business Connector—Applications and Development* by Patrick Theobald (SAP PRESS 2005). Current information about the availability of the SAP Business Connector can be found in SAP Note 571530, Availability of SAP Business Connector.

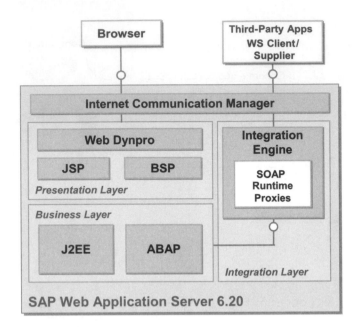

Figure 2.42 Overview of SAP Web AS 6.20

SAP NetWeaver
Developer Studio

In a development environment for creating web services in SAP Web AS 6.20, you can use SAP NetWeaver Developer Studio, which is based on the open development environment Eclipse. As an alternative to the *ABAP Workbench*, this development environment enables the creation of new applications based on Java or J2EE, and the EJB interfaces can afterwards be published as web services.

SOAP runtime

On the other hand, it is also possible to create web services in the ABAP area of SAP Web AS 6.20. This is done via the SOAP runtime of SAP Web AS 6.20. This SOAP runtime enables the calling of RFCs from SAP Web AS 6.20 using the SOAP protocol via HTTP. The business server pages application of the SAP Web AS 6.20 Web Service Browser can be used to determine the web service description (see Figure 2.43).[9] The URL of the SAP Web AS 6.20 Web Service Browser is:

http://[host]:[port]/sap/bc/bsp/sap/WebServiceBrowser/search.html? sap-client=[client]

where:

---

9 The BSP framework must be active.

- *[host]* represents the name of the SAP server.

- *[port]* refers to the channel. In a standard installation, this would be 5000.

- *[client]* stands for the number of the SAP client.

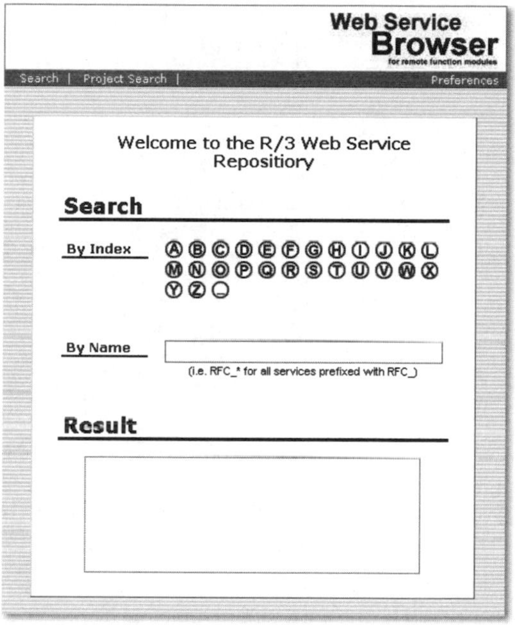

Figure 2.43 SAP Web AS 6.20 Web Service Browser

The weak point of SAP Web AS 6.20's SOAP runtime is that it isn't possible to publish a single function module as a web service but the entire SOAP functionality, for example for RFCs, is enabled or disabled for the node default_host • sap • bc • soap • rfc via Transaction SICF (Maintenance of the Internet Communication Framework services). Thus, either all or no RFCs can be reached as a web service.

2.3.3 SAP NetWeaver Application Server as a Web Service Provider

With SAP NetWeaver Application Server 6.40, the SOAP runtime of the predecessor was replaced with the Web Service Framework and extended by the Web Service Creation Wizard. The Web Service Creation Wizard supports the creation of web services out of the box. It can be launched either from the Function Builder or from the BAPI

Web Service
Creation Wizard

Explorer, as shown in Figure 2.44 and in Figure 2.45. However, it can also be started via Transaction SE80.

Figure 2.44 Launching Web Services from Function Builder

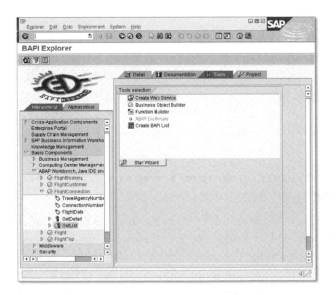

Figure 2.45 Launching Web Services from BAPI Explorer

For example, if the wizard has been started for the BAPI FlightCon-nection.GETLIST, as shown in Figure 2.45, the next steps of the Web Service Creation Wizard query the following parameters, as shown in Figure 2.46.

▶ **Virtual interface**

Steps of the Web Service Creation Wizard

This represents an interface to the outside world. If necessary, it can be used to prevent the web service from being recognized as an SAP web service.

▶ **End point of the virtual interface**
What should the VI refer to? Usually, this is the already named function or the BO. In the case of an outside-in web service, the XI server proxy must be selected as the end point.

▶ **Operation**
Choose the method (BAPI) of the selected BO.

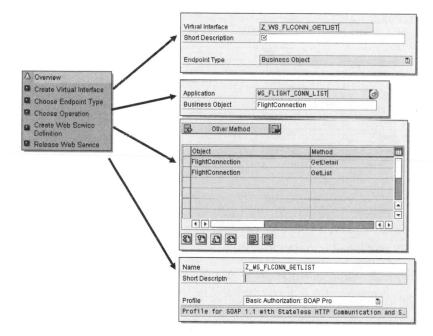

Figure 2.46 Steps of the Web Service Creation Wizard

In this example, the end point of the VI is the FlightConnection object, and the BAPI FlightConnection.GetList is used as the operation. In the next steps, the web service definition is created and the web service is released. Using Transaction WSCONFIG, the web service

79

can now be further edited and configured. Then, using Transaction WSADMIN, the web service can be managed and tested, as shown in Figure 2.47.

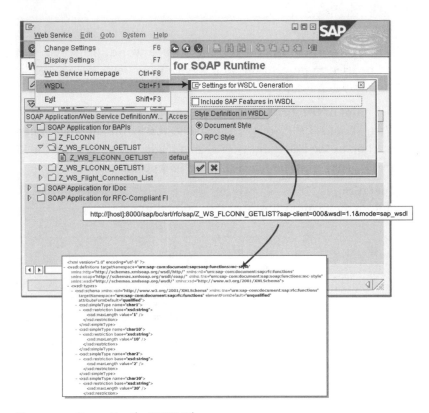

Figure 2.47 Generating the WSDL File

The web service or the WSDL file of the web service is now addressed via the following URL:

http://[host]:[port]/sap/bc/srt/rfc/sap/Z_WS_FLCONN_GETLIST?
sap-client=[client]&wsdl=1.1&mode=sap_wsdl

where:

▸ *[host]* represents the name of the SAP server.

▸ *[port]* refers to the channel. In a standard installation, this is port 8000.

▸ *[client]* stands for the number of the SAP client.

How this SAP flight connection web service can be used or integrated by a Microsoft .NET application is illustrated by the following simple application.

Use the **Add Web Reference** function to make the URL of the SAP flight connection web service, which is used as the client known to a VB.NET console application project. Figure 2.48 illustrates this process. The relevant web service proxy classes are automatically generated by Visual Studio.

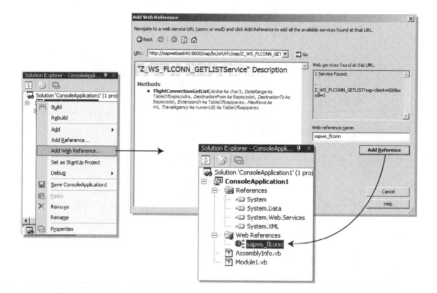

Figure 2.48 Adding the SAP Web Service to the .NET Client

The web service and its methods are now available to the project, and can be addressed in the code.

The Main could read as follows:

```
Sub Main()
Dim airline As String
Dim agency As String
Dim wait As String
Dim oExtOut() As Object
Dim oExtin() As Object
Dim oDateRange() As Object
Dim oDest_To As Object
Dim oDest_From As Object
Dim oList() As sapws_flconn.Bapiscodat
Dim oReturn() As sapws_flconn.Bapiret2
```

```
Dim iMaxRows As Integer = 20
Dim i As Integer = 0
Console.WriteLine("Airline:")
airline = Console.ReadLine()
Console.WriteLine("Travel agency:")
agency = Console.ReadLine()

Dim ws As New sapws_flconn.Z_WS_FLCONN_GETLISTService
Try
   ws.Credentials=New
     System.Net.NetworkCredential("BCUSER",
   "MINISAP")
   ws.FlightConnectionGetList(airline, oDateRange, _
     oDest_From, oDest_To, oExtin, iMaxRows, True, _
     agency, oList, oReturn)
   Catch ex As Exception
      Console.WriteLine(ex.ToString)
      Return
 End Try
 Console.WriteLine("Connections:")
 For i = 0 To oList.Length - 1
   Console.WriteLine(oList(i).Flightdate & " | " & _
   oList(i).Flighttime & " | " & oList(i).Cityto _
     & " (" & oList(i).Airportto & ") to " & _
     oList(i).Cityfrom & " (" & oList(i).Airportfr _
     & ") [" & oList(i).Deptime & " - " & _
     oList(i).Arrtime & "]")
 Next
 Console.WriteLine("Close .......")
wait = Console.ReadLine()
End Sub
```

The results should appear as illustrated in Figure 2.49.

Figure 2.49 Results Display of the Console Application

Note: Chapter 3 also shows an example of how the SAP flight connection web service can be addressed by a Microsoft Excel-based application.

2.3.4 SAP NetWeaver Application Server as a Web Service Client

After describing how a web service can be generated and provided using SAP NetWeaver AS, we will now look at the possibility of calling and using a .NET web service (ASMX) from an ABAP function.

Calling a .NET web service from ABAP

At first, a .NET web service (ASMX) is created that adds up two transferred values and returns the result:

```
Imports System.Web.Services
<System.Web.Services.WebService
(Namespace:="http://tempuri.org/wsCalc/CalcService")>
Public Class CalcService
    Inherits System.Web.Services.WebService
    <WebMethod()>
    Public Function Add(ByVal a As Integer, ByVal b _
      As Integer)
      As Integer
        Return (a + b)
    End Function
End Class
```

Figure 2.50 shows the test and the WSDL description file of the Microsoft .NET web service (ASMX).

To be able to use this external web service from ABAP, an ABAP proxy must be created in SAP NetWeaver AS. It allows message exchange with the external web service. An ABAP proxy is based on the ABAP Objects[10] language extension, but this proxy uses the Web Service Framework of SAP NetWeaver AS 6.40 as a runtime environment.

ABAP proxy

---

10 Recommended reading: *ABAP Objects. ABAP Programming in SAP NetWeaver* by Horst Keller and Sascha Krüger, Third Edition, SAP PRESS, 2007.

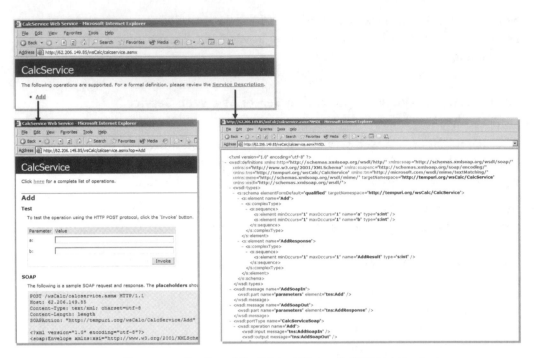

Figure 2.50 Creation of the External Microsoft .NET Web Service

To create an ABAP proxy you need to select **Edit Object** in the Object Navigator (Transaction SE80). In the dialog displayed, select the **Enterprise Services** tab and then the option **Client Proxy · Create**. The following dialog specifies the address of the Microsoft .NET web service previously created:

http://[host]/wsCalc/calcsevice.asmx?WSDL

Figure 2.51 illustrates this process.

ABAP proxy class   Like with the Microsoft .NET web service, an ABAP proxy class (ZCO_ CALC_SERVICE_SOAP) is created with the structures ZADD_SOAP_IN and ZADD_SOAP_OUT. Figure 2.52 shows the generated properties of the proxy class.

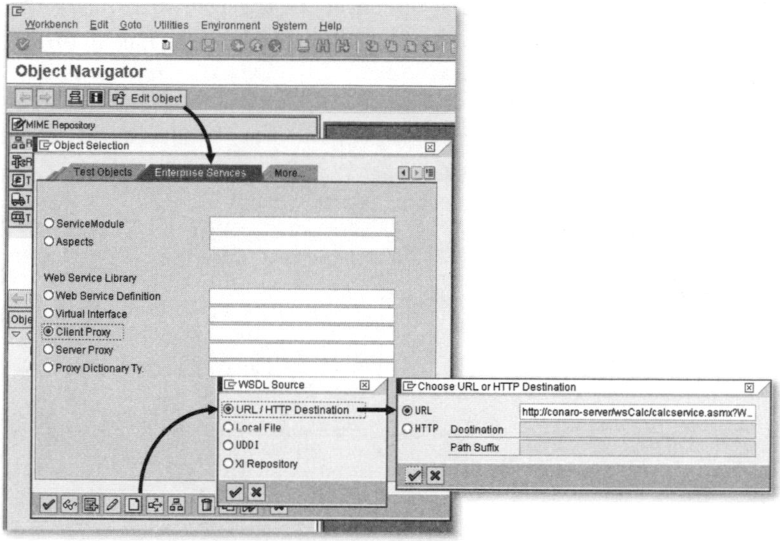

Figure 2.51 Creating the ABAP Client Proxy

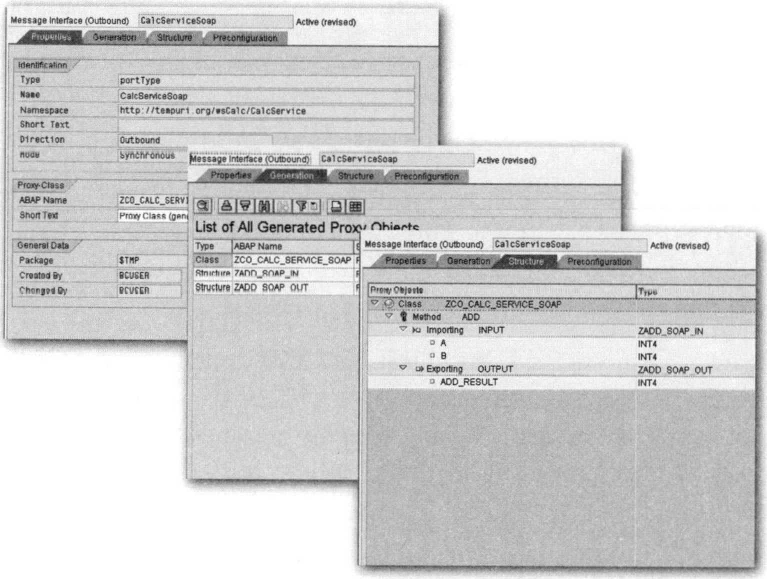

Figure 2.52 Properties of the ABAP Proxy Class

Now a logical port must be created for this ABAP proxy class. A logical port is created using Transaction LPCONFIG.

After the proxy class has been specified in the relevant dialog (see Figure 2.53), a logical port is created automatically based on the proxy class properties.

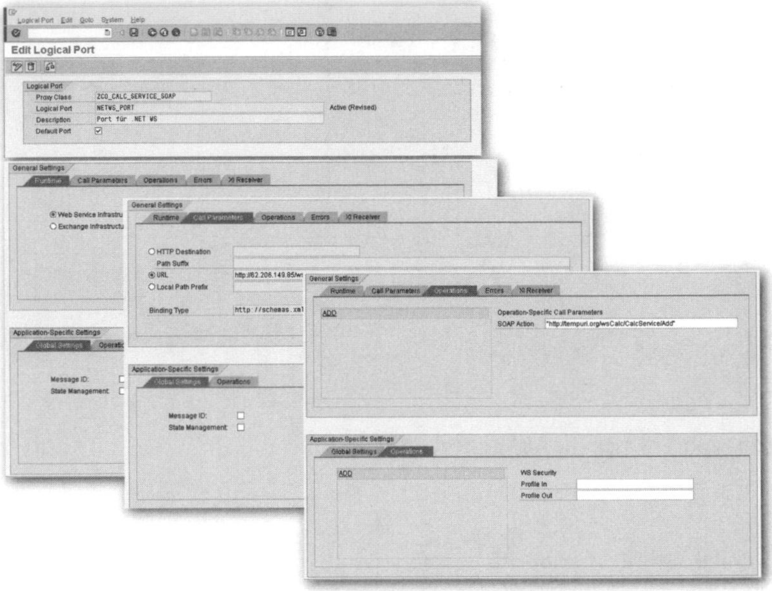

Figure 2.53 Creation and Parameters of the Logical Port

Testing the interface

To check all these settings you need to go back to the Object Navigator. Press the F8 key or select the menu option **Proxy • Test Interface** to check the availability of the external web service. However, you must first activate the proxy.

Figure 2.54 shows a successful test. The XML code must include the message Service has been processed without errors. Now the ABAP proxy can be addressed. The following listing shows a sample report (Z_WS_ADD_TEST) for using the ABAP proxy class ZCO_CALC_SERVICE_SOAP:

```
REPORT  Z_WS_ADD_TEST.
PARAMETERS INPUT_A TYPE I OBLIGATORY.
PARAMETERS INPUT_B TYPE I OBLIGATORY.
DATA:
  lo_clientproxy     TYPE REF TO zco_calc_service_soap,
  lo_sys_exception   TYPE REF TO cx_ai_system_fault,
  ls_request         TYPE zadd_soap_in,
```

```
   ls_response          TYPE zadd_soap_out.
 ls_request-a = INPUT_A.
 ls_request-b = INPUT_B.
 CREATE OBJECT lo_clientproxy.
 TRY.
    CALL METHOD lo_clientproxy->add
      EXPORTING
        input  = ls_request
      IMPORTING
        output = ls_response.
   CATCH cx_ai_system_fault INTO lo_sys_exception.
 ENDTRY.
 COMMIT WORK.
 WRITE: / 'Result:', ls_response-add_result.
```

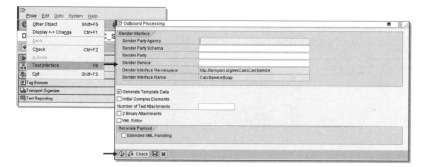

Figure 2.54 Successful Test of the ABAP Proxy

A test run (F8) should display a correct sum after entering the input parameters INPUT_A and INPUT_B, as shown in Figure 2.55.

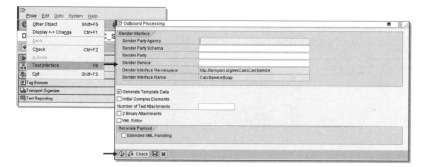

Figure 2.55 Successful Test of the ABAP Report

2.3.5   SAP NetWeaver Exchange Infrastructure (SAP XI)

In the following, we will describe an integration example in which a .NET-based web service client uses the SOAP adapter to call a web

Integration example

service provided by the XI Integration Server that checks the availability of flights in the connected business systems of the airlines.

The integration example is configured based on the integration scenario CheckFlightSeatAvailability used in the SAP flight data example. The design objects necessary for integrating the travel agency and airline applications were defined by SAP and are delivered with SAP XI 3.0. The application systems TravelAgency, Airline_LH, and Airline_UA communicate via the Integration Server of the XI system. This is illustrated in Figure 2.56.

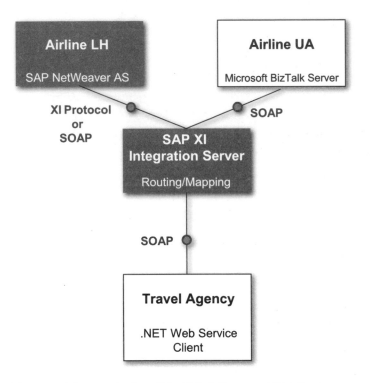

Figure 2.56 Communication of XI—BizTalk Server and Web Service

Communication process

Deviating from the SAP standard example, a .NET-based web service client will represent the travel agency. The SOAP message is converted to the XI message protocol and processed by the Integration Server. Depending on the airline for which the availability of flights is to be determined, the relevant recipient is identified:

▶ A web service provider as an external partner

▶ An SAP business system as an internal partner

In this example, the external partner (the airline UA) uses the Microsoft BizTalk Server as an EAI tool. The availability check is published as a web service via an orchestration. This simulates a web service-based scenario. The configuration of the XI integration scenario is shown in Section 5.3.1.

In the following, we will describe the configuration steps necessary to publish the XI scenario as a web service and to use it with a .NET web service client. It is configured with these steps:

1. Create a WSDL description for the XI scenario

2. Create a .NET-based console application that consumes the web service

To create a WSDL description of the XI web service, you need to perform the following steps:

Creating a WSDL description

1. In the Integration Builder (Integration Directory) menu bar, select **Tools** and then **Define Web Service ....** This opens the wizard for defining web service documents.

2. Select **Continue**.

3. Enter the URL of the web server to receive the web service.[11] The URL must be specified in the following format:

   http://host:port/XISOAPAdater/MessageServlet?channel=party:service:channel

   In this example the following URL was used:

   http://patos063.fres.sap.corp:50000/XISOAPAdapter/MessageServlet?channel=:FlightAgency:CC_FlightSeatAvailabilityQuery

4. Select **Continue**.

5. Now specify the synchronous message interface from the integration repository for which the web service document should be created (input help).

   ▸ Name: **FlightSeatAvailabilityQuery_Out**

   ▸ Namespace: **http://sap.com/xi/XI/Demo/Agency**

   ▸ Software component version: **SAP Basis 6.40**

6. Select **Continue**.

---

11 In the version XI 3.0 SP16 that is used here, you should not use the toolbar button **Suggest URL** ▥ because it does not produce a correct URL in this release.

7. Specify the sender of the message (partner, service, and outbound interface). This specification is not used in this sample scenario.

   ▶ Service: **FlightAgency**

   ▶ InterfaceName: **FligFlightSeatAvailabilityQuery_Out**

   ▶ Interface namespace: **http://sap.com/xi/XI/Demo/Agency**

   The information concerning the sender of the message (partner, service, and outbound interface) is required by the integration server to process the message header.

8. Select **Continue**.

9. In the last step, all information based on which the web service document will be created is displayed in an overview.

10. Select **Finish**.

11. Select **Save** to save the WSDL file.

Editing the WSDL file

The WSDL file still needs to be edited before it can be added to the .NET console application as a web reference. In the namespace declaration, the following entry must be added:

```
xmlns:xsd="http://www.w3.org/2001/XMLSchema"
```

After it has been inserted, the corresponding section of the WSDL file reads as follows:

```
<wsdl:definitions
name="FlightSeatAvailabilityQuery_Out"
targetNamespace="http://sap.com/xi/XI/Demo/Agency"
xmlns:p2="http://sap.com/xi/XI/Demo/Airline"
xmlns:p1="http://sap.com/xi/XI/Demo/Agency"
xmlns:wsdl="http://schemas.xmlsoap.org/wsdl/"
xmlns:xsd="http://www.w3.org/2001/XMLSchema">
```

Creating a console application

For calling the web service, we will create a console application, just like for NetWeaver Application Server (see above). The **Add Web Reference** function is used to make the URL of the XI flight connection web service known to a C# console application project. This procedure is the same as the one shown in Figure 2.48. The source code of the console application as follows:

```
using System;
using System.Collections.Generic;
using System.Text;
using System.Net;
using System.Web.Services.Protocols;
namespace ConsoleApplication2
{
class Program
{
static void Main(string[] args)
{
FlightSeatAvailabilityQuery myQuery = _
  new FlightSeatAvailabilityQuery();

FlightSeatAvailabilityQuery_OutService req = _
  new FlightSeatAvailabilityQuery_OutService();

FlightSeatAvailabilityResponse FlightList = _
  new FlightSeatAvailabilityResponse();
FlightID myFlightID = new FlightID();
int intYear = 2005;
int intMonth - 7;
int intDay = 20;
myFlightID.AirlineID = "AA";
myFlightID.ConnectionID = "0017";
myFlightID.FlightDate = new DateTime(intYear, _
  intMonth, intDay);
myQuery.FlightID = myFlightID;
try
{
req.Credentials = new
NetworkCredential("D041615", "secret");
FlightList =
  req.FlightSeatAvailabilityQuery_Out(myQuery);
Console.WriteLine("BusinessFreeSeats=" +
FlightList.BusinessFreeSeats.ToString());
Console.WriteLine("BusinessMaxSeats=" +
FlightList.BusinessMaxSeats.ToString());
Console.WriteLine("EconomyFreeSeats=" +
FlightList.EconomyFreeSeats.ToString());
Console.WriteLine("EconomyMaxSeats=" +
FlightList.EconomyMaxSeats.ToString());
Console.WriteLine("FirstFreeSeats=" +
FlightList.FirstFreeSeats.ToString());
Console.WriteLine("FirstMaxSeats=" +
```

```
FlightList.FirstMaxSeats.ToString());

}
catch (SoapException XISOAPError)
{
Console.WriteLine("SOAP Exception:");
// Fault Code Namespace
 string error = XISOAPError.Code.Namespace;
//Fault Code Name
string code = XISOAPError.Code.Name;
//SOAP Actor that threw Exception",
string actor = XISOAPError.Actor;
// Detail
string soapMessage =  XISOAPError.Detail.OuterXml;
Console.WriteLine("Error=" + error);
Console.WriteLine("Code=" + code);
Console.WriteLine("Actor=" + actor);
Console.WriteLine("SOAP Message=" +
soapMessage);
}
catch (Exception ex)
{
// General Exception Message
string msgException = ex.Message;
}
}
}
}
```

If you execute this console application using valid flight data, you receive the following output:

```
BusinessFreeSeats=1
BusinessMaxSeats=31
EconomyFreeSeats=13
EconomyMaxSeats=385
FirstFreeSeats=1
FirstMaxSeats=21
Press any key to continue . . .
```

SOAP exception   If the web service is called with invalid flight data, SAP XI generates a SOAP exception that can be validated by the web service client application. The program code contains a catch block to which the SOAP exception is transferred via the variable SOAPError.

The output for a faulty call looks as follows:

```
SOAP Exception:
Error=http://schemas.xmlsoap.org/soap/envelope/
Code=Server
Actor=
SOAP Message=<detail><ns0:FlightNotFound
  xmlns:ns0="http://sap.com/xi/XI/Demo/Airline">
  <standard><faultText>FLIGHT_NOT_FOUND</faultText>
  </standard></ns0:FlightNotFound></detail>
Press any key to continue . . .
```

2.4 Enterprise Service-Oriented Architecture

SAP relies on web services technology, or enterprise services to be the interface technology of the future. They are supposed to completely replace the integrations via RFC and BAPI in the mid-term. SAP is currently building a repository of all enterprise services. The *Enterprise Services Repository* (ESR) is a natural enhancement of the SAP XI integration repository. It will describe the respective *enterprise services* and contain detailed information regarding the processes, objects, and the mapping. Figure 2.57 shows the classification of the ESR.

Enterprise Services Repository

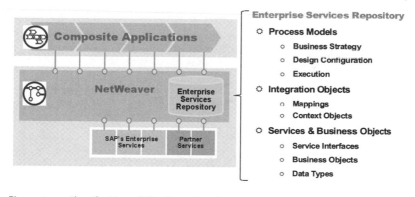

Figure 2.57 Classification of the Enterprise Services Repository (ESR)

Interested developers can already obtain detailed information about enterprise services. One source is the *ESA Preview System* that is accessible via the following SDN URL (see Figure 2.58):

http://www.sdn.sap.com/irj/sdn/esapreviewsystem

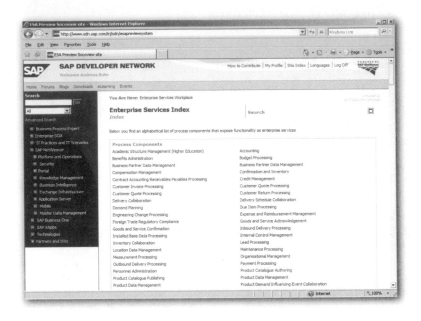

Figure 2.58 ESA Preview System in SDN

Visual Studio As far as Visual Studio is concerned, you can easily add the web services generated using SAP NetWeaver AS or the enterprise services of the incoming Enterprise SOA level as a web reference to the respective VS development project, as described above in the programming examples presented in this chapter (see Figure 2.59).

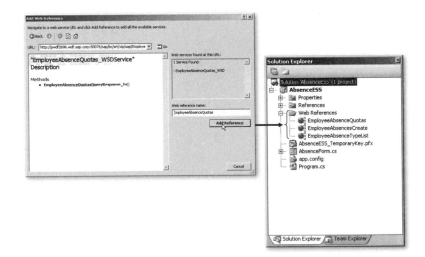

Figure 2.59 Integration of the Enterprise Services in Visual Studio 2005

Currently, SAP is considering providing a plug-in for Visual Studio 2005. Similar to the SAP Connector for Microsoft .NET, it would enable the developer to integrate an SAP system via the Server Explorer and to select an enterprise service from the Enterprise Services Repository and integrate it in the VS 2005 project. Thus, SAP will continue to support the option of developing SAP integration solutions using Microsoft Visual Studio and the new versions of Microsoft .NET Framework. According to SAP, this extension will be called Enterprise Services Explorer for .NET.

In this chapter, we will discuss the possibilities of user integration at the user interface level of various applications used in the enterprise. As an example, we will describe the integration options of the SAP NetWeaver Portal and the Microsoft Office products. Additionally, we will present the joint Microsoft and SAP project, Duet (initially announced under the codename Mendocino).

3   User Integration

The SAP NetWeaver layer of *People Integration* has a mistakable name. It refers to the integration at presentation level, i. e., the integration at the user interface level of applications used in the enterprise. Therefore, it is not the integration of users but a frontend integration. A continuous switching between applications should be avoided. The aim is to provide virtually all information relevant to the user and all required functions from the integrated user interface.

A frontend integration can be divided into two variants: the desktop integration that extends an application residing locally on the work center system so that it can display data from other source systems, and, depending on the integration depth, enable this data to be further processed. An extension of a desktop application is always based on the extension possibilities provided for by the application vendor. Often, function libraries (APIs) and development tools (SDKs) are provided for that purpose. These vary from vendor to vendor and from product to product. The development tools enable the extension, as well as they define clearly what is possible and what is not. The extension created using these tools (add-on, add-in or plug-in) must be installed locally, just like the application to be extended. Therefore, apart from the development effort, the topic of software distribution may not be neglected or underestimated during the desktop integration when determining the required effort. This

Desktop integration

becomes clear if you consider version control, installation dependencies, installation status, operating system versions, etc.

As far as desktop integration is concerned, we will focus on Microsoft Office and the joint SAP/Microsoft project of Duet.[1] In the desktop area, Microsoft Office is an indispensable tool that is used on a daily basis. It is possible to have a scenario in which the user is spared the frequent switching between the Office applications and the SAP system. The information required from the SAP system could be provided via a unified Office user interface. After a short historical look at the development of SAP-Office integration, this chapter explains the current possibilities of Office integration, particularly based on the usage of web services.

Portal integration   The second variant of the frontend integration is the portal integration. In contrast to the desktop integration, it is server-based. Appropriate extensions or modifications enable the portal application existing on the (web) server to present or edit data together with the previous contents depending on the integration depth and the technical possibilities. Portals are innately prepared for extensions. Actually, the extension or integration of further and new contents is the main function of portals. With the appropriate tools and their modular structure in portlets (*iViews* for SAP and *Webparts* for Microsoft), portals favor these extensions by new contents. Enterprise portals in general and the SAP NetWeaver Portal[2] in particular should gradually become the main tool for the enterprise's employees. More and more functions should be merged in this program. The aim is to provide virtually all information relevant to the user and all required functions from the portal as the user interface.

In the area of portal integration, the integration possibilities for the SAP NetWeaver Portal and the tools available for that purpose are described and explained in detail in the following examples (see Figure 3.1).

---

1 This project was first announced under the name Mendocino. In this book, we will present this product according to its current development state in Duet Preview Version 1.0.
2 Previously known as SAP Enterprise Portal (SAP EP).

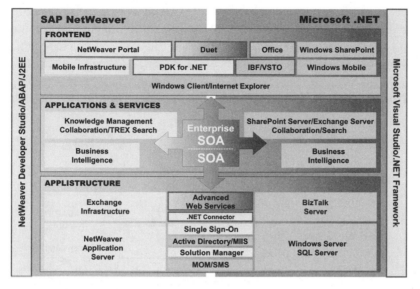

Figure 3.1 SAP/Microsoft User Integration

3.1 Desktop Integration with Microsoft Office

In a desktop integration, two or more applications are merged in one desktop user interface. If you look at the Microsoft Office and SAP applications from this point of view, there are two variants of desktop integration:

1. Microsoft Office (or individual parts) within an SAP interface

2. SAP contents within a Microsoft interface

Both variants are discussed in detail next, focusing on variant 2.

3.1.1 Microsoft Office Within an SAP Interface

For variant 1, Desktop Office Integration has been the solution for quite a while. Within the SAP user interface (SAP GUI) the respective Office application is presented as embedded. What is not visible at first is the fact that the integration goes much deeper than the user might think. The Office application is not only displayed but can be controlled and provided with data from the SAP system.

Desktop Office Integration

Technologically, the DOI is an OLE2 integration. The *SAP Document Container Control* is used for this purpose. This is one of the SAP GUI controls that are installed locally on the client during the installation of the SAP GUI. On the SAP ABAP side, the developers can use some ABAP Objects classes for the dynpros, like CL_GUI_CUSTOM_CON-TAINER, or interfaces like I_OI_SPREADSHEET, to address the Office applications (e. g., Microsoft Word or Microsoft Excel) and to be able to integrate them in the dynpros. This is illustrated in Figure 3.2.

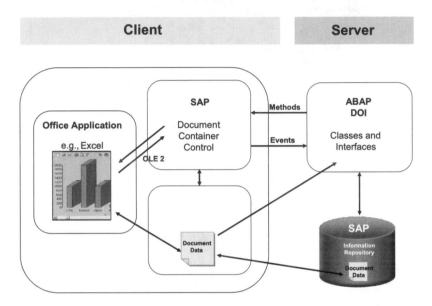

Figure 3.2 Functionality of the Desktop Office Integration

Thus, a client/server communication takes place between the SAP Document Container Control stored locally on the desktop and the ABAP function modules or dynpros on the SAP server. This is not transparent to the user. To him, the SAP GUI and the Office application are apparently merged to one working system, as shown in Figure 3.3.

The most current variant of integration solutions developed in the course of time, however, is the possibility of integrating Microsoft Office in Web Dynpro applications. This is another mix between desktop and server integration because Web Dynpro applications are not local desktop applications.

Office integration can also happen for Web Dynpro applications based on ABAP, as well as those based on Java. Figure 3.4 shows the development environment (Java), Figure 3.5 illustrates the integration of a Web Dynpro application at runtime.

Figure 3.3 Microsoft Excel 2003 in SAP GUI

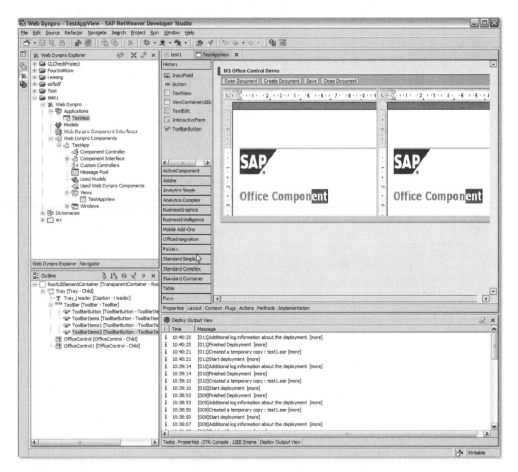

Figure 3.4 Integration of Microsoft Office in a Web Dynpro Application (Java Development)

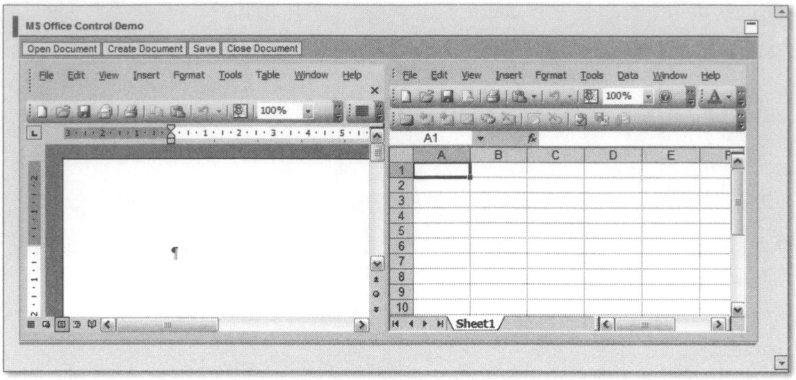

Figure 3.5 Integration of Microsoft Office in a Web Dynpro Application (Runtime)

3.1.2 SAP Within Microsoft Office 2003

Let's now look at variant 2 where SAP contents are integrated within a Microsoft interface. One question first: What is the added value of a solution providing SAP contents within a Microsoft Office user interface, and it is possible to use the SAP DOI solution described above?

Microsoft Office

Enterprise employees have used Microsoft Office for a very long time. In almost all enterprises, the majority of enterprise correspondence is with Microsoft Word. The same can be said for the financial accounting or controlling departments of most corporate groups. Without Excel as their main tool, many of these employees could hardly do their work.

Therefore, you can assume that both Microsoft Word and Microsoft Excel are well-known to employees—they are familiar with its user interface. You can assume that the training period for a Microsoft Office/SAP solution should be shorter than that for a similar new solution with a completely unknown user interface. Additionally, you can assume that it is an advantage to the user if he does not have to perform his processes in different applications. He would not have to screen hop and could thus work in a quicker and more concentrated way.

Standard scenarios

Now, the amount of development effort that is involved in each integration solution in relation to its added value needs to be considered. The development effort is often underestimated, and it is not always worthwhile. Even though standard products are used, there is an individual solution for a specific scenario. To solve this dilemma, SAP and Microsoft decided to deliver out-of-the-box solutions for defined scenarios; both enterprises assumed that these solutions be used by a large number of their customers. These solutions are provided in Duet.

If SAP contents need to be integrated within the Microsoft Office user interface, there are three blocks of questions that need to be further investigated:

Questions

1. **Microsoft Office enhancements technologies**
   How could Microsoft Office applications generally be extended? Which technologies are provided by Microsoft for this purpose, and which might present themselves for the implementation of the Microsoft .NET Framework?

2. **SAP integration**
   How can the respective technology address the SAP system? How are data and contents from the SAP system displayed in the Microsoft Office user interface?

3. **Consequences and general conditions**
   What are the conditions of the respective solution? Which consequences are to be expected? How can, for example, the distribution of such a solution be implemented?

These aspects will be examined for every technology in the following sections.

Integration with Visual Basic for Applications (VBA)

The first possibility of extending Microsoft Office applications by own functions to use macros. Their purpose was primarily to automate the Office interface by recording typical command sequences and operations in the form of an integrated macro programming language using a macro recorder. This macro language, which in part strongly varied from one Office application to another, was soon replaced by the interpreter language Visual Basic for Applications (VBA). Compared to its bigger pendant *Visual Basic*, the functionality of VBA is reduced, and the development environment (VBA Editor) is integrated in the respective Office application. Figure 3.6 shows an example of the VBA Editor user interface.

VBA VBA contains methods of object orientation, e. g., class modules, but is a procedural programming language. It does not know inheritance or the overloading of operators. On the other hand, it enables the access to the *application object* and thus to the host application running the VBA program. VBA can open up numerous methods and functions of the host application to the developer that can be addressed and used.

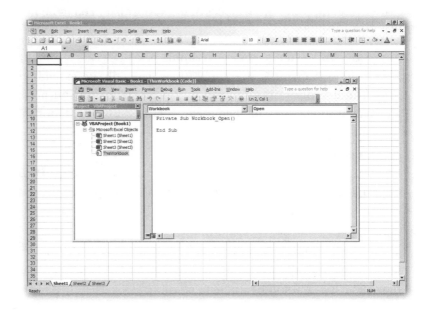

Figure 3.6 VBA Editor

However, VBA is not a .NET programming language and thus does not use the .NET Framework. Since Microsoft is planning to bring Microsoft Office and the .NET Framework closer together, *Visual Studio Tools for Office* will take over the VBA tasks. As far as the integration of SAP content is concerned, there are several ways to accomplish it within a VBA application. Two of these possibilities are presented as examples:

▶ Using the SAP RFC Components

▶ Using web services via the Web Services Toolkit

VBA and the SAP RFC components To address an SAP system from a VBA solution, you can use the *SAP RFC components* already mentioned in Chapter 2. These ActiveX controls encapsulate the functions of the SAP function library *librfc32.dll.* The usage of SAP RFC components within a VBA solution is similar to that described in Chapter 2, although in this case the ActiveX controls do not necessarily have to be integrated as a reference. It is also possible to use the CreateObject() method to create an object that references the SAP control. However, this requires is an appropriate entry in the Windows Registry.

In the following sample code, the click event of one of the buttons placed on the user interface addresses the SAP Function Control wdteuncs.ocx.

At first, the routine is started with a definition of the required objects:

```
Private Sub CommandButton1_Click()
Dim sapFunctions As Object
Dim sapConnection As Object
Dim func As Object
```

Then the wdtfuncs.ocx is addressed:

```
Set sapFunctions = CreateObject("SAP.Functions")
Set sapConnection = sapFunction.Connection
```

And then the logon to the SAP system takes place:

```
If Not sapConnections.Logon(0, False) Then
    MsgBox "Logon failure!"
    Exit Sub
End If
```

This is followed by the specification of the RFC to be addressed. In this case, this is the function module RFC_READ_TABLE.

```
Set func = sapFunctions.Add("RFC_READ_TABLE")
```

The export parameters are set ...

```
func1.Exports("...") = "..."
```

... followed by the function call ...

```
If Not func.Call Then
    If func.exception <> "" Then
        MsgBox "An error occurred during the communication_
        with SAP: " & func1.exception
    End If
Else
    ...
```

... and the reading of the event table:

```
For Each oData In func.tables("DATA").Rows
...
    Next oData
End If
```

Finally, the routine logs off from the SAP system:

```
sapConnection.Logoff
End Sub
```

For distributing such a VBA solution you need to consider that the implementation of the SAP RFC components requires the corresponding components, including the *librfc32.dll,* to be available on the desktop system. Otherwise, the solution is not operable.

VBA with Web Services Toolkit (WST) If the SAP RFC components and the *librfc32.dll* are not available to the developer or they are deliberately left out, there is the option of working with the web service technology.

Microsoft Office products like Microsoft Excel 2003, however, cannot immediately access web services. This can be changed using the *Microsoft Office 2003 Web Services Toolkit 2.01,*[3] which is an extension of the VBA Editor. The Web Services Toolkit (WST) enables the use of web services via VBA.

Figure 3.7 shows how the Web Services Toolkit can be used in the interoperability with SAP. It could address both the web services provided by SAP via the SAP Web AS or SAP XI and the ASP.NET

---

3 Microsoft Office 2003 users can download this toolkit from the Microsoft website. However, it only works with Office 2003. For older versions, there are the corresponding predecessors.

web services (ASMX) that connect to the SAP system via the *SAP Connector for .NET* (NCO).

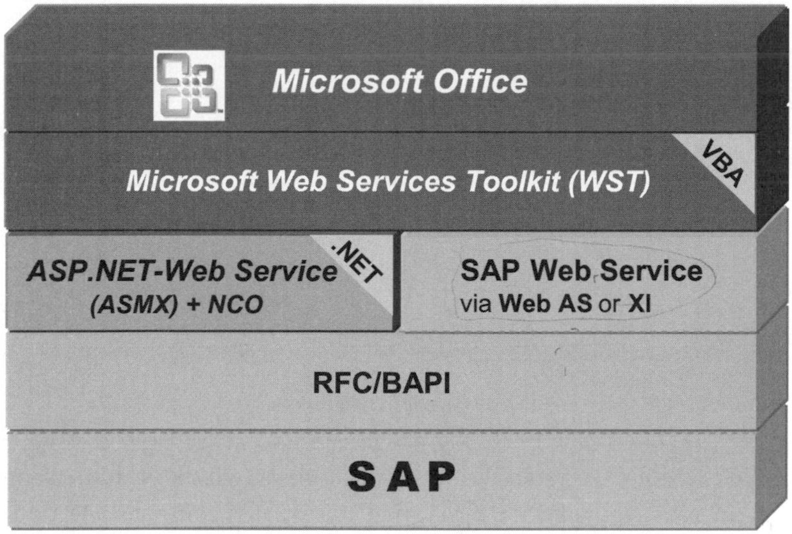

Figure 3.7 Microsoft Office, Web Services Toolkit, and SAP

After the Web Services Toolkit has been installed on the developer system, changes are not apparent at first. However, if you open the VBA Editor as shown in Figure 3.8, you will notice that the **Tools** area now includes an entry **Web Service References**. It is now possible to add a web service as a reference to a VBA project. After selecting the corresponding menu option, a dialog is displayed that queries the web service and the method requested.

Web service references

Here we have the most significant drawback of the Web Services Toolkit in conjunction with SAP web services. The SAP Web AS 6.40 requests an authentication, which is a problem for the Web Services Toolkit because the user and password can only be transferred in the notation *http://user:pwd@host:port/../..*, which is in clear text format. Otherwise, the WST is not even admitted to the SAP Web AS 6.40. The reader can decide for himself if the transfer of logon information in clear text format is desirable.

Authentication

Additionally, asynchronous access is not possible using the Web Services Toolkit, and the exact address (URL) of the web service must be known.

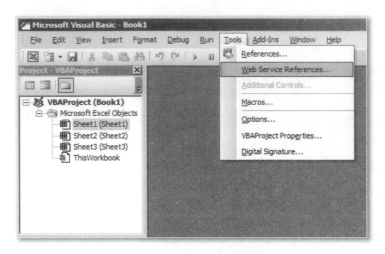

Figure 3.8 VBA Editor and the Web Service References

In the example, we avoid the authentication drawback by addressing the ASP.NET web service (ASMX) that was created using the SAP Connector for .NET (see Section 2.3) SAPWS_BAPI_FLCONN_GETLIST.asmx (see Figure 3.9). Already during the generation of the web service, we stored a user name and a password for the SAP system.

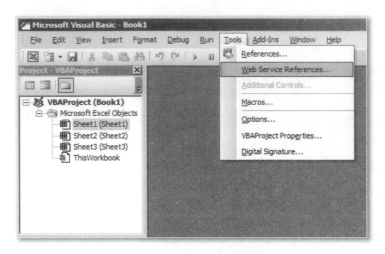

Figure 3.9 Integration of the Web Service in WST

After selecting the web service, the Web Services Toolkit sets a reference to the Microsoft SOAP Type Library v3.0 (*mssoap30.dll*) and generates the appropriate classes. In this case, there is one class for the web service, one for the SAP table structure BAPISCODAT and one for the generic SOAP functionalities, as shown in Figure 3.10.

Class generation

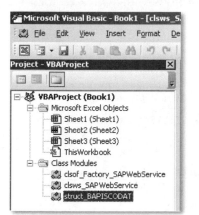

Figure 3.10 Web Services Toolkit Classes in VBA Editor

The generated classes can now be addressed in a VBA program. In this example, the airline and the travel agency are queried in the Excel spreadsheet, and the result of the web service is entered in the subjacent rows. The following function WS_Laden() calls the SAP web service previously integrated by the Web Services Toolkit. The WS_Laden() function could, in turn, be called from other routines, e.g., a click event.

At the beginning, the routine needs to be started with a definition of the required objects:

```
Sub WS_Laden()
    Dim ws As New clsws_SAPWebService
    Dim result() As struct_BAPISCODAT
    Dim sheet As Excel.Worksheet
    Dim rowStr As String
    Dim strAirline As String
    Dim strAgency As String
    Dim i As Integer
    Dim row As Integer
    i = 0
    row = 9
```

This is followed by Excel-specific parameter settings:

```
Set sheet = ThisSpreadsheet.ActiveSheet
ActiveCell.Offset(0, 1).Activate
```

The export parameters are queried by input:

```
strAirline = sheet.Range("C4").Value
strAgency = sheet.Range("C6").Value
```

The web service is called:

```
result = ws.wsm_sapws_BAPI_FLCONN_GETLIST(strAirline, _
  strAgency)
```

The result is entered in the Excel worksheet:

```
For i = LBound(result) To UBound(result)
  row = row + 1
  rowStr = CStr(Zeile)
  sheet.Range("B" & rowStr).Value = _
    result(i).AGENCYNUM
  sheet.Range("C" & rowStr).Value = _
    result(i).FLIGHTCONN
  sheet.Range("D" & rowStr).Value = _
    result(i).FLIGHTDATE
  sheet.Range("E" & rowStr).Value = _
    result(i).AIRPORTFR
  sheet.Range("F" & rowStr).Value = _
    result(i).CITYFROM
  sheet.Range("G" & rowStr).Value = _
    result(i).AIRPORTTO
  sheet.Range("H" & rowStr).Value = _
    result(i).CITYTO
  sheet.Range("I" & rowStr).Value = _
    result(i).NUMHOPS
  sheet.Range("J" & rowStr).Value = _
    result(i).DEPTIME
  sheet.Range("K" & rowStr).Value = _
    result(i).ARRTIME
  sheet.Range("L" & rowStr).Value = _
    result(i).ARRDATE
  sheet.Range("M" & rowStr).Value = _
    result(i).FLIGHTTIME
```

```
    Next i
End Sub
```

Figure 3.11 shows a successful call of the web service.

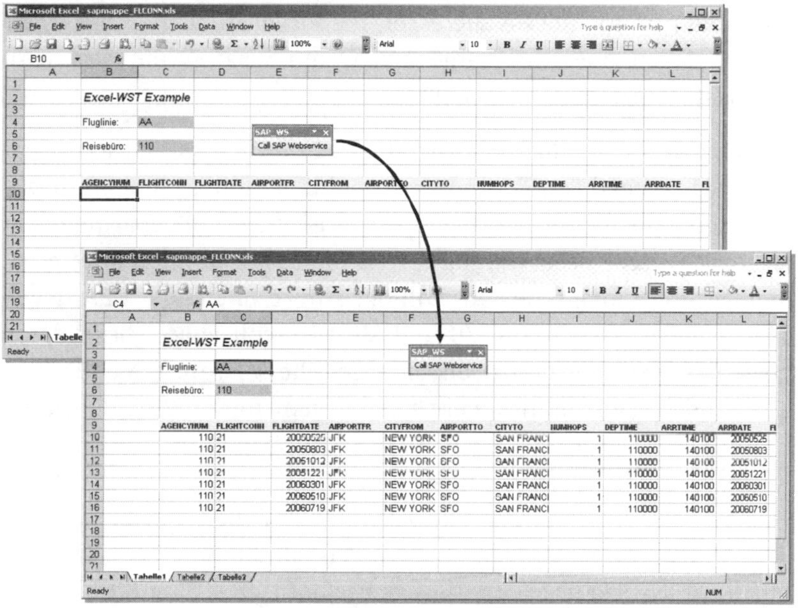

Figure 3.11 Calling the SAP Web Service Using WST

The Excel file can relatively smoothly be distributed to computers running Microsoft Office 2003. The Microsoft SOAP Type Library 3.0 should also be included on the system because it is installed with Microsoft Office 2003.

For using this Excel file, however, it is required that the web service be available to the respective user. If the web service is only available in the enterprise network, the Excel file can only address the web service within the network to update its data. Otherwise, the calling of the web service would not get anywhere.

Availability of the web service

If you compare both VBA variants, note that the implementation of the Web Services Toolkit relieves the developer of having to use SAP-specific desktop components. At first, this simplifies the distribution of the solution. However, an appropriate web service must be available that can be addressed. Because WST has security problems using

SAP web services or web services that require an authorization, there are some obstacles involved in this method, too.

Integration With Visual Studio Tools for Office (VSTO)

Let's now turn to the VBA successor, the *Visual Studio Tools for Office* (VSTO). What does this name mean, and what is the deal with Microsoft Office in this context?

New possibilities with VSTO

It has become clear that the programming of Microsoft Office extensions has reached large proportions and is no longer limited to private users. The concerned developers or engineering departments in enterprises have been waiting for an improved development environment for a long time. Not without a trace of envy, a VBA developer glanced over at his VB and VB.NET colleagues, begrudging them Visual Studio and its convenience. The Microsoft .NET Framework and its possibilities were not relevant to the VBA developer and, at best, usable via third-party products (e. g., Add-in Express by Afalina Co. Ltd.). However, those times are now over with the Visual Studio Tools for Office. The VSTO enables an Office developer to create his extensions or solutions in Visual Studio, based on the Microsoft .NET Framework—he can use both VB.NET and C# as programming languages. In other words, VSTO enables the development of .NET applications using Microsoft Word and Excel as user interfaces.

Three versions of the VSTO

Before we discuss the details of VSTO we must point out that developments in this area are happening so fast that there is currently two versions of VSTO. And a third one has just been released as a preview for beta testers. Now, why are there three versions of VSTO?

Essentially, this has to do with the following factors: The Microsoft .NET world is currently experiencing a version leap of the Framework from 1.1 to 2.0. On the other hand, a similar thing is planned for Microsoft Office. Microsoft Office 2007, also known under the project name "O12," is already announced, and a handful of selected beta testers could review the innovations of the latest version. What does this have to do with the versions of VSTO? Simple:

▶ VSTO 1.0 (also referred to as VSTO 2003) runs in Visual Studio 2003, thus uses .NET Framework 1.1 and enables extensions for Microsoft Office 2003.

▶ VSTO 2.0 (also referred to as VSTO 2005) runs in Visual Studio 2005, thus uses .NET Framework 2.0 and enables extensions for Microsoft Office 2003.

▶ VSTO "V3" CTP[4] also runs in Visual Studio 2005 and uses .NET Framework 2.0, but enables extensions for Microsoft Office 2007 (O12), which is still being developed.

Figure 3.12 illustrates this in an overview.

	.NET 1.1 & VS2003	.NET 2.0 & VS2005	Office 2003	Office 2007
VSTO 1.0/2003	◎	◉	◎	◉
VSTO 2.0/2005	◉	◎	◎	◉
VSTO "V3" CTP	◉	◎	◉	◎

Figure 3.12 Overview of the VSTO Variants

Because Microsoft Office 2007 is still being developed and the beta version will not have spread very widely, we will focus on the two current VSTO versions.

Version 1.0 of Visual Studio Tools for Office primarily consists of project templates for Visual Studio 2003 (see Figure 3.13) and an *assembly loader*. This loader ensures that the assembly created using VSTO is loaded along with the Word document or Excel spreadsheet that was extended via VSTO. In the Microsoft .NET environment, *assemblies* are program classes that are merged and provided in executable programs (EXE or DLL). They can be compared with Java packages.

VSTO 1.0/ VSTO 2003

A VSTO project starts with selecting the respective template. The developer can use project templates for both Microsoft Word 2003 and Microsoft Excel 2003, each in a Visual Basic .NET and a C# variant.

Selection of the project template

---

4 CTP stands for *Community Technology Preview*. This is what Microsoft calls the partially public testing phase before a beta version is released.

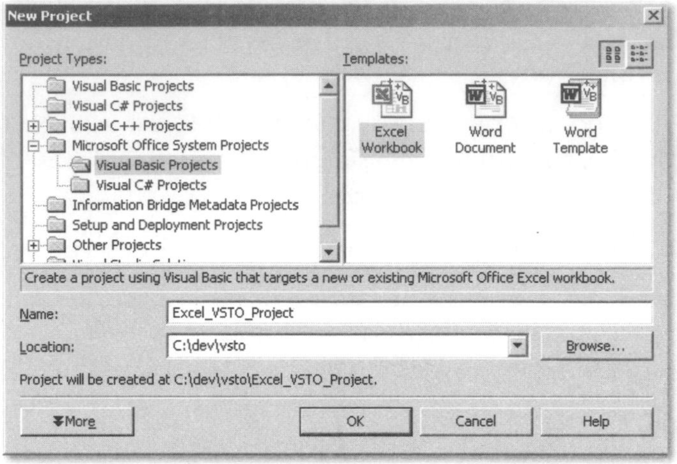

Figure 3.13 VSTO 1.0 Project Templates

After the required template has been selected, a wizard opens (as shown in Figure 3.14) asking the developer if a new Office file or an existing Office file is to be used.

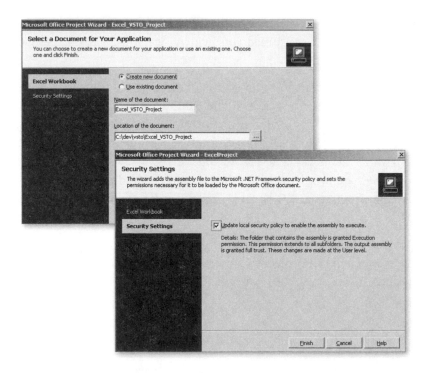

Figure 3.14 VSTO 1.0 Wizard

Finally, the wizard asks if you want to update the local security policy. This will be further explained at the end of this section.

After the wizard has been completed, the following imports have been created via the project template:

```
Imports System.Windows.Forms
Imports Office = Microsoft.Office.Core
Imports Excel = Microsoft.Office.Interop.Excel
Imports MSForms = Microsoft.Vbe.Interop.Forms
```

The framework for a class named OfficeCodeBehind has been created as well. This class defines the variables ThisWorkbook (EXCEL) or ThisDocument (Word) and ThisApplication. Additionally, this class contains the methods Open and BeforeClose that are intended for the corresponding events.

Variable definition

```
Public Class OfficeCodeBehind
    Friend WithEvents ThisWorkbook As Excel.Workbook
    Friend WithEvents ThisApplication As _
        Excel.Application
    Private Sub ThisWorkbook_Open() Handles _
        ThisWorkbook.Open
        ...
    End Sub
    Private Sub ThisWorkbook_BeforeClose(ByRef Cancel _
        As Boolean)
    Handles ThisWorkbook.BeforeClose
        Cancel = False
    End Sub
End Class
```

The actual application can be created either in ThisWorkbook_Open() or in separate event routines.

Now that developers can use Visual Studio 2003 and the .NET Framework, they have the same options discussed in Chapter 2, such as the SAP Connector for .NET. This is recommended for older SAP systems. Or a developer can integrate SAP web services as a web reference in his Microsoft .NET project. Figure 3.15 presents an overview of these possibilities.

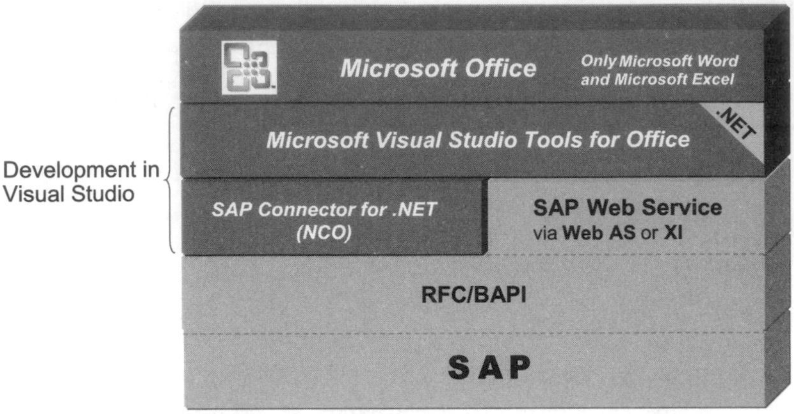

Figure 3.15 VSTO and SAP

Adding a web
service

In this example, we will select variant 2. The SAP web service Z_WS_
FLCONN_GETLIST introduced in Chapter 2 should be accessed. It is
added to the VSTO project via the Web Service Wizard in Visual Studio, as shown in Figure 3.16.

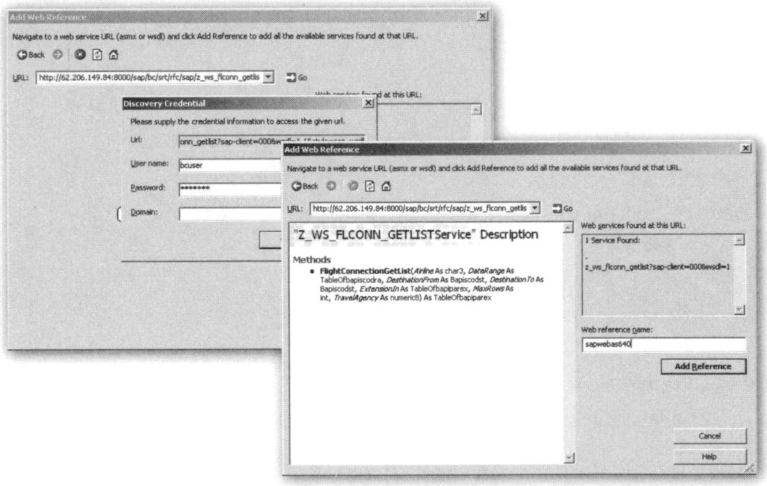

Figure 3.16 Integration of SAP Web Services in the VSTO 1.0 Project

The Web Service Wizard in Visual Studio also enables the authentication with a web service in a better way than the WST variant.

Now we will call the web service and display the result in the Excel
worksheet.

The SAP web service in the Excel worksheet is called via a custom menu. The selection of the menu entry triggers an event and executes the following program code which, by the way, strongly resembles the VBA code of the previous example:

Calling the web service

```
Private Sub GetSAP_WS(ByVal Sh As Object)
   Dim sheet As Excel.Worksheet = _
     CType(Sh, Excel.Worksheet)
   Dim ws As sapwebas640.Z_WS_FLCONN_GETLISTService
   Dim result() As sapwebas640.Bapiscodat
   Dim return() As sapwebas640.Bapiret2
   Dim strZeile As String
   Dim strAirline As String
   Dim strAgency As String
   Dim i As Int32 = 0
   Dim row As Int32 = 9
   Dim ExtOut As Object
   Dim Extin As Object
   Dim DateRange As Object
   Dim Dest_To As Object
   Dim Dest_From As Object
   Dim iMaxRows As Integer = 20
```

The Excel input fields are queried:

```
strAirline = sheet.Range("C4").Value
strAgency = sheet.Range("C6").Value
```

The web service is called:

```
ws.FlightConnectionGetList(strAirline, DateRange, _
   Dest_From, Dest_To, Extin, iMaxRows,False, _
   strAgency, result, return)
```

The confirmation and the result are displayed:

```
   For i = 0 To (result.Length - 1)
     row = row + 1
     strZeile = CStr(row)
     sheet.Range("B" & strRow).Value = _
       result(i).AGENCYNUM
     sheet.Range("C" & strRow).Value = _
       result(i).FLIGHTCONN
     sheet.Range("D" & strRow).Value = _
```

```
        result(i).FLIGHTDATE
    sheet.Range("E" & strRow).Value = _
        result(i).AIRPORTFR
    sheet.Range("F" & strRow).Value = _
        result(i).CITYFROM
    sheet.Range("G" & strRow).Value = _
        result(i).AIRPORTTO
    sheet.Range("H" & strRow).Value = _
        result(i).CITYTO
    sheet.Range("I" & strRow).Value = _
        result(i).NUMHOPS
    sheet.Range("J" & strRow).Value = _
        result(i).DEPTIME
    sheet.Range("K" & strRow).Value = _
        result(i).ARRTIME
    sheet.Range("L" & strRow).Value = _
        result(i).ARRDATE
    sheet.Range("M" & strRow).Value = _
        result(i).FLIGHTTIME
  Next i
End Sub
```

At first, parameters are set and the Excel cells with the input values are read. Then the web service is called together with the read parameters, and the result is written back to the Excel cells defined for that purpose using a For-i loop.

Execution from Visual Studio 2003

If the project is executed from Visual Studio 2003, the relevant Excel file is opened and the functionality can be tested (see Figure 3.17).

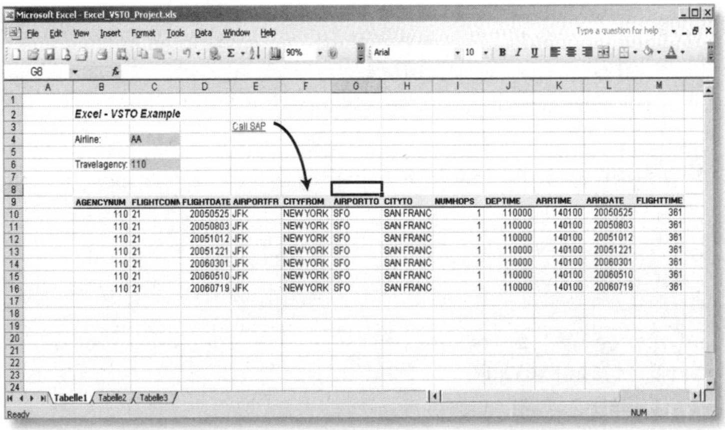

Figure 3.17 Test of the VSTO 1.0 Example

But what is happening in the background? First, an assembly that is separate from the Excel file is created by the VS 2003 in DLL format. Figure 3.18 shows the directories containing the respective files.

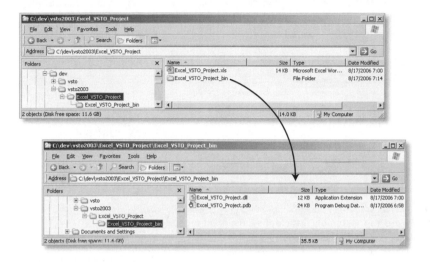

Figure 3.18 VSTO Assembly

In the VSTO assembly, the document and the program code are strictly separated. On opening the Excel file, the created assembly is loaded using the VSTO Loader (*OTKLoadr.dll* in the directory ...*Microsoft Office\Office11\Addins*) and started depending on the implemented function. Figure 3.19 shows where the loader receives the information about which files belong together. The properties of the host file contain the entries for the name and storage location of the assembly.

VSTO assembly

Now that we know where to find the required assembly, it should be easy to distribute the application and its assembly in the enterprise. But hang on! The assembly is a .NET application and requires the .NET Framework as a runtime environment at every workstation. However, the aspect of security policies must be considered. Apart from role-based security, Microsoft .NET also knows the code execution security, which is very important in this context. At the beginning of the project, the VSTO wizard asked for the security policy setting for executing the code. The corresponding specifications are then entered in the Microsoft .NET configuration (see Figure 3.20) in the area **Runtime Security Policy**.

Security policy

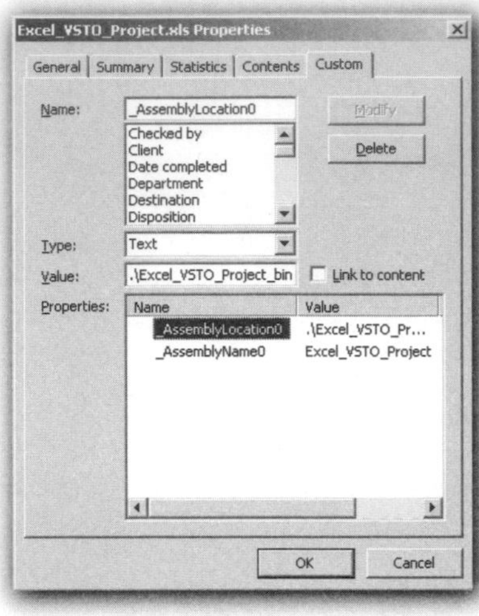

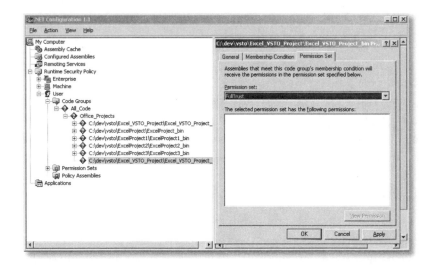

Figure 3.19 Assembly Data in the Document Properties

Figure 3.20 VSTO Assembly Security Settings

These entries contain the exact location of the project files and the security level. For an assembly to be usable it needs the **FullTrust** permission. Local assemblies have this permission. However, if they are to be distributed and moved, the execution is initially denied because by default Microsoft .NET starts this kind of assembly only via **PartialTrust**, which results in an error message. Therefore, these entries first need to be adapted according to the new storage location.

In regard to distribution, however, it is recommended to choose a *strong name* instead of specifying the directory. Using the VS 2003 tool *sn.exe*, the assembly is signed with a key pair consisting of one private and one public key. It is then copied in the *Global Assembly Cache* (GAC) via *gacutil.exe* and becomes directory-independent, which simplifies the distribution throughout the enterprise.

In addition to its support for Microsoft .NET Framework 2.0, VSTO 2005 differs from its previous version because it contains more Office project templates (e.g., for Outlook 2003 and InfoPath) and enables easier application development.

VSTO 2.0/ VSTO 2005

One innovation, for example, is the integration of the Office user interface in Visual Studio 2005. Due to the integration of Visual Designer, an Excel worksheet can be edited directly in Visual Studio 2005 and provided with WindowsForms Controls (see Figure 3.21), for example. The operation method gradually approximates that of WinForm projects.

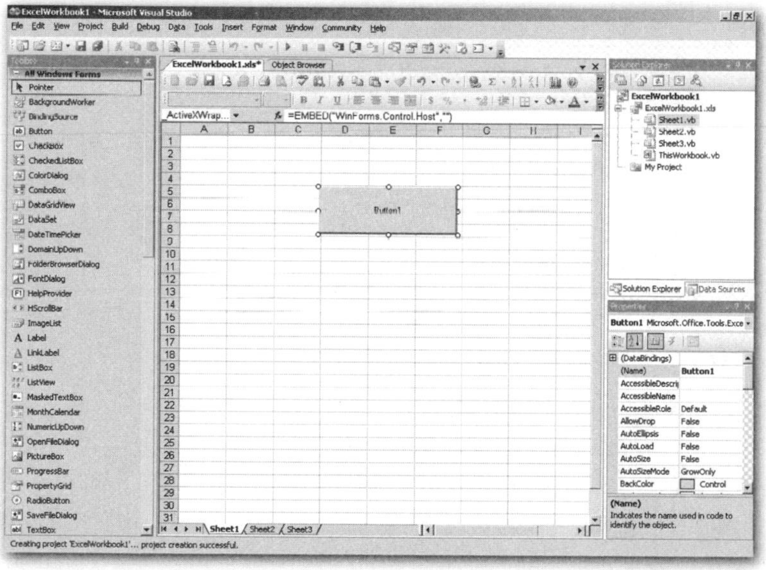

Figure 3.21 Excel in VSTO 2005

In contrast to the predecessor version, Excel solutions based on VSTO 2005 not only have one code file but, similar to a VBA project, a separate code file per worksheet and another code file for the entire project (see Figure 3.22). One frame is created per routine for the startup and the shutdown event of the table or the entire worksheet.

Figure 3.22 Excel VSTO Project Parts

The program code for `ThisWorkbook` looks as follows:

```
Public Class ThisWorkbook
Private Sub ThisWorkbook_Startup(ByVal sender _
  As Object, ByVal e As System.EventArgs) _
  Handles Me.Startup
  ...
End Sub
Private Sub ThisWorkbook_Shutdown(ByVal sender _
  As Object, ByVal e As System.EventArgs) _
  Handles Me.Shutdown
    ...
End Sub
End Class
```

The situation is similar for the individual table sheets (e. g., `Table1`):

```
Public Class Table1
Private Sub Table1_Startup(ByVal sender As Object, _
```

```
    ByVal e As System.EventArgs) Handles Me.Startup
    ...
End Sub
Private Sub Table1_Shutdown(ByVal sender As Object, _
    ByVal e As System.EventArgs) Handles Me.Shutdown
    ...
End Sub
End Class
```

The VSTO 1.0 loader no longer exists either. Instead, VSTO 2.0 provides a VSTO runtime component consisting of the file *vstor.exe*.

What has been added as well is the enhanced support of the *SmartTag* technology and a simplified possibility of developing the work area (*ActionPane*) in Visual Studio 2005. Since *SmartTags* were introduced in Microsoft Office XP, they should recognize a specific defined string and offer the user the corresponding responses. A *SmartTag Recognizer* compares the entered word to a list of stored words and provides the corresponding stored actions.

SmartTag
technology

The SmartTag technology is part of the Microsoft concept of Smart-Documents. These are intelligent documents with an individual user guide depending on the scenario in the task pane, which was introduced with Office XP as well (*TaskPane*). Previously, the development of SmartTags as well as the programming of the Office task pane was a very complex process until VSTO 2005. However, with the integration of the Office user interface in VS 2005 mentioned above the development of the Office TaskPane can be compared to the development of Windows forms. Figure 3.23 shows an example of how a TaskPane consists of a user control. While the TaskPane was previously tightly coupled to the SmartTags, this connection is no longer required.

SmartDocuments

The task pane in VSTO is document-dependent, which means that on closing the document, the individual task pane is also closed. This is going to change again in the upcoming version of VSTO. But we'll get back to that later.

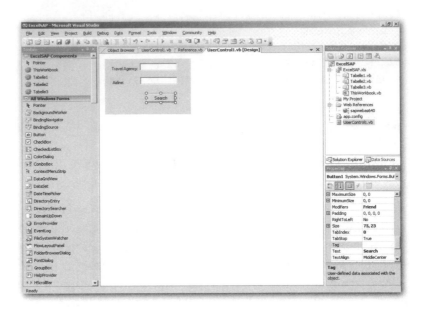

Figure 3.23 Development of a TaskPane Using VSTO 2.0

VSTO 2005/SAP integration

Let's now look at the SAP integration with VSTO 2005. Because VSTO 2005 is based on VS 2005 and Microsoft .NET Framework 2.0, the SAP Connector for .NET cannot be used. Either you encapsulate the SAP proxies created in VS 2003 in a wrapper class and then integrate them in the VS 2005 project, or you need to use web services. However, the first variant is only recommended if it is not possible to access the SAP system via web services. Otherwise, web services are the preferred method.

In our example, we chose the web services variant. To illustrate the difference to the previous solutions, we will use the FlightConnection scenario again. This time, we will use the option of programming the work area of the TaskPane.

User control

For this example, a UserControl is added after the corresponding project template has been selected and the SAP web service has been added as a web reference to the project. This UserControl is assigned the necessary input fields and the **Start** button.

In the program code, the class of the UserControl is assigned both a function for calling the SAP web service and an additional event for filling the Excel table:

```
Public Class UserControl1
Event FillSheet(ByVal list As Object)
Private Sub Button1_Click(ByVal sender As _
  System.Object, ByVal e As System.EventArgs) _
  Handles Button1.Click
Dim airline As String
Dim agency As String
Dim oExtin() As Object
Dim oDateRange() As Object
Dim oDest_To As Object
Dim oDest_From As Object
Dim oList() As sapwebas6401.Bapiscodat
Dim oReturn() As sapwebas6401.Bapiret2
Dim iMaxRows As Integer = 20
agency = Me.TextBox1.Text
airline = Me.TextBox2.Text
Dim ws As New sapwebas6401.Z_WS_FLCONN_GETLISTService
Try
ws.Credentials = _
  New System.Net.NetworkCredential("BCUSER", "MINISAP")
ws.FlightConnectionGetList(airline, oDateRange, _
  oDest_From, oDest_To, oExtin, iMaxRows, True, _
  agency, oList, oReturn)
Catch ex As Exception
  MsgBox(ex.ToString)
  Return
End Try
RaiseEvent FillSheet(oList)
End Sub
End Class
```

But this is not enough. The UserControl still needs to be merged with the Excel document. This is achieved with the class named ThisWork-book. This class was generated during the creation of the project and represents the basic class of an Excel VSTO 2.0 solution. The previously developed UserControl is communicated to the class and added to the startup routine of the ActionPane list of the Excel document:

ThisWorkbook

```
Public Class ThisWorkbook
Private WithEvents myControl As New UserControl1
Private Sub ThisWorkbook_Startup(ByVal sender _
  As Object, ByVal e As System.EventArgs) _
  Handles Me.Startup
      Me.ActionsPane.Controls.Add(myControl)
End Sub
```

Then, a routine is created responding to the F1llSheet event of the user control and filling the Excel worksheet with the result returned from the SAP web service:

```
Private Sub myControl_FillSheet(ByVal oList _
  As Object) Handles myControl.FillSheet
Dim sheet As Excel.Worksheet = Me.ActiveSheet
Dim row As Integer = 1
Dim i As Integer = 0
Dim strRow As String = CStr(row)
For i = 0 To (oList.Length - 1)
    row = row + 1
    strRow = CStr(row)
    sheet.Range("A" & strRow).Value = _
      oList(i).Agencynum
    sheet.Range("B" & strRow).Value = _
      oList(i).Flightconn
    sheet.Range("C" & strRow).Value = _
      oList(i).Flightdate
    sheet.Range("D" & strRow).Value = _
      oList(i).Airportfr
    sheet.Range("E" & strRow).Value = _
      oList(i).Cityfrom
    sheet.Range("F" & strRow).Value = _
      oList(i).Airportto
    sheet.Range("G" & strRow).Value = _
      oList(i).Cityto
    sheet.Range("H" & strRow).Value = _
      oList(i).Numhops
    sheet.Range("I" & strRow).Value = _
      oList(i).Deptime
    sheet.Range("J" & strRow).Value = _
      oList(i).Arrtime
    sheet.Range("K" & strRow).Value = _
      oList(i).Arrdate
    sheet.Range("L" & strRow).Value = _
      oList(i).Flighttime
Next i
End Sub
End Class
```

Figure 3.24 shows the function of the completed VSTO 2.0 solution. After entering the query values and starting the **Search** button, the web service is called and the results are written to the Excel worksheet.

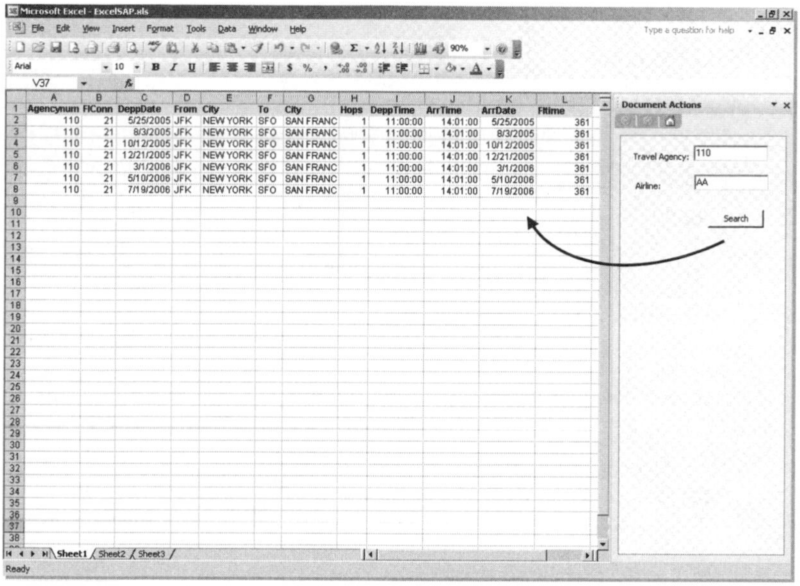

Figure 3.24 Testing the SAP Excel VSTO 2.0 Solution

While VSTO 2005 is still very fresh, its successor is already being   VSTO V3
developed under the working title "V3." Version 3 is designed to
support Office 2007 and will also support the new XML document
format as well as others. Currently, there is a preview version for
Visual Studio 2005 but it can be assumed that the final version of V3
will be based on the successor of Visual Studio 2005.

Not much is known at this time about V3, however, the PDC 2005
provided a first insight. In V3, the currently document-related
ActionPane will be converted into an application-related, cross-doc-
ument CustomTaskPane so that the VSTO solution is completely separated from the document to form a real Office application extension. The VSTO roadmap in Figure 3.25 shows that there is a plan to
offer support for all Office applications (including PowerPoint, for
example).

How an SAP integration could be achieved for VSTO V3 can only be
guessed at this time. Web services or enterprise services will likely
play a significant role.

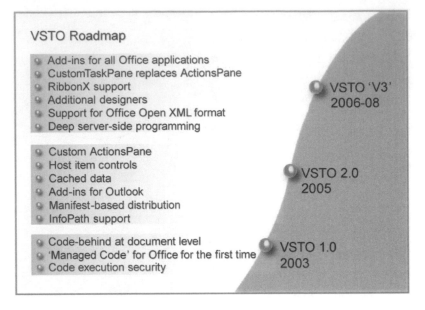

Figure 3.25 VSTO Roadmap

The Special Case of Outlook and COM Add-Ins

Microsoft Outlook Up to now, this chapter primarily mentioned Microsoft Excel and Microsoft Word with regard to an Office extension. One Office application that plays an important role in many enterprises has not been mentioned yet when discussing the extension by .NET components: Microsoft Outlook. There is a reason why.

Microsoft Outlook can only be extended using *Component Object Model* (COM) add-ins. The same applies to Outlook 2003. A COM add-in is a program file based on the *COM* that can be called and used by the host application. This involves accessing the Office Interop libraries provided by Microsoft (the *Primary Interop Assemblies* or short PIAs, at the *COM Interop* level). Within a .NET application, a wrapper must be created around the COM libraries.

Visual Studio 2003 provides the possibility to develop add-ins. However, that was a general add-in in contrast to the specific Outlook add-in in VSTO 2005 that can be developed using VS 2005. Figure 3.26 shows the points of entry for an add-in project in VS 2003 and VS 2005.

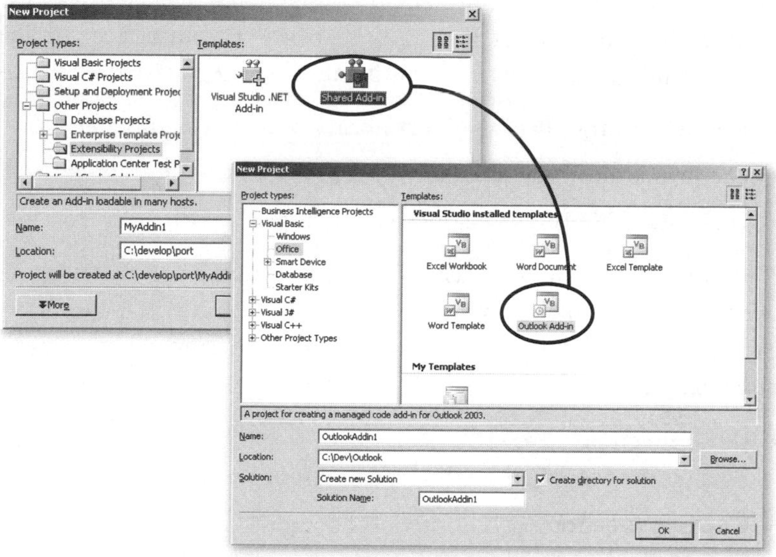

Figure 3.26 Outlook Add-In Project Templates

How is an Office 2003 add-in created in Visual Studio 2003?

After selecting the Visual Studio project template **Shared Add-in**, the Visual Studio Add-in Wizard is started. In four steps, it prompts you for the following information:

Visual Studio
add-in wizard

1. Select the programming language C#, VB .NET, or C++.

2. Select the Office application(s) to be extended.

3. Specify a name and a description.

4. Determine the add-in options:

   ▶ Load the add-in when host application is loaded?

   ▶ Is the add-in available to all users of the respective worksta-
     tion?

After all of this information has been entered and the summary has been confirmed, the VS wizard creates a project folder containing two projects:

▶ The actual Office add-in project

▶ The setup project for the Office add-in

connect.vb   Within the Office add-in project, a connect class (`connect.vb`) was created that implements the `IDTExtensibility2` interface. In this class, the following items were automatically integrated as *reference*:

- The Microsoft Office 11 object library: *Microsoft.Office.Core*
- The primary Interop assembly: *Extensibility*
- The .NET-COM Interop namespace: *System.Runtime.InteropServices*

Additionally, the connect class (`connect.vb`) contains the code frameworks for the following methods of the `IDTExtensibility2` interface that are described in the Microsoft add-in designer type library *msaddndr.dll*:

- **OnConnection**
  This method is called by the load event of the add-in.

- **OnDisconnection**
  This method is called when the add-in is closed.

- **OnStartupComplete**
  This method starts up when the add-in has been fully loaded. This would be the obvious place for implementing the actual functionality of the add-in.

- **OnAddinUpdate**
  This method is called when a COM add-in is installed or removed from the host application; that is, when there are changes to the registered COM add-in.

- **OnBeginShutdown**
  This method is called when the termination of the application is triggered.

Within these code frameworks, the actual functionality of the Office add-in is implemented. The same applies to the SAP integration.

To access the SAP system, it would make sense to add the SAP web service as a web reference to the project and implement the web service call within the methods. Alternatively, it would be possible to use the SAP Connector for .NET in this Visual Studio 2003 project, as illustrated in Figure 3.27.

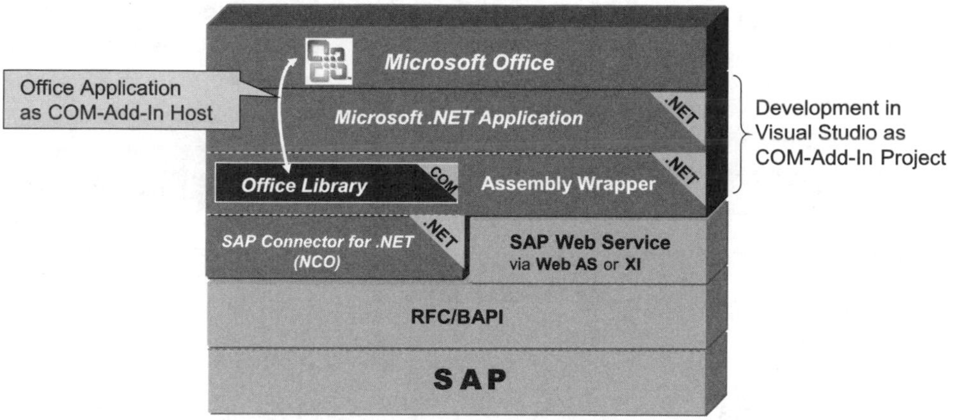

Figure 3.27 SAP Integration With Outlook COM Add-Ins

What is the situation in VSTO 2005? Again, the development of Outlook add-ins has been simplified even more. As shown in Figure 3.26, the developer can use a specific Outlook add-in as a template in VSTO 2005. Just like its predecessor, Visual Studio 2005 creates two projects when this template is selected, one project for the add-in and a setup project.

Outlook add-ins in VSTO 2005

The most important class created in the add-in project is ThisApplication. For this class, the frameworks for the Startup and Shutdown methods are created:

```
public class ThisApplication
Private Sub ThisApplication_Startup(ByVal sender _
  As Object, ByVal e As System.EventArgs) _
  Handles Me.Startup

    ...
    End Sub
Private Sub ThisApplication_Shutdown(ByVal sender _
  As Object, ByVal e As System.EventArgs) _
  Handles Me.Shutdown

    ...
    End Sub
End class
```

Figure 3.28 shows the other possible events and methods of this class. For example, the event handlers ItemSend and NewMail would certainly be interesting for a mail system like Outlook. They enable a reaction to both incoming and outgoing mail.

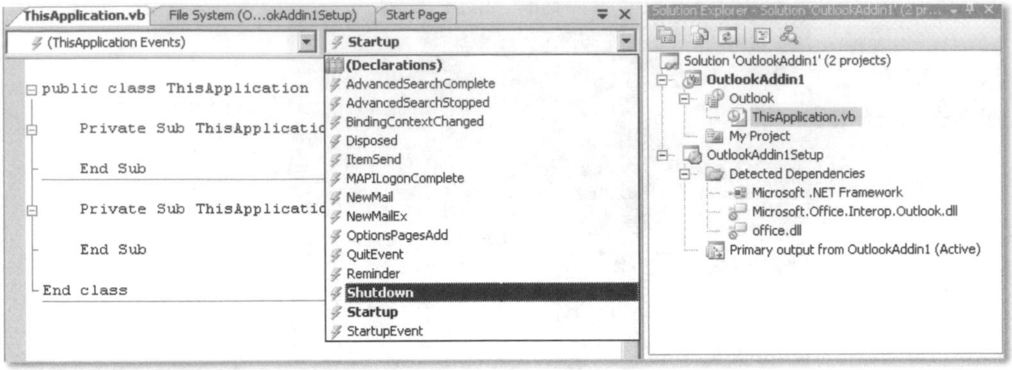

Figure 3.28 More Events of this Application for Outlook

It is recommended to use the events and methods as points of entry for a potential SAP integration. The developer can avail himself of the options provided by a Microsoft .NET 2.0 framework environment and Visual Studio 2005 that have been described above.

The Special Case of InfoPath

Dynamic forms   Microsoft InfoPath is a relatively young member of the Office family[5] that is used for creating and using dynamic forms. These dynamic (entry) forms enable a targeted entry and collection of data or information. This data entry can be integrated into enterprise processes because InfoPath supports XML schemas and the coupling with web services, therefore it can be linked to other systems and applications that support these standards as well.

The InfoPath forms can also be used as standalone user interfaces or frontends for processes of all kinds. Currently, they are infrequently used because the distribution of InfoPath forms always requires an InfoPath runtime on the work center system. This also involves additional license cost.

Because InfoPath plays an important role in the Microsoft strategy in combination with BizTalk and Human Workflows, we will show how an InfoPath form can be coupled to an SAP web service.

---

5 It was sold with Office 2003. As a package, it is currently only included in the Enterprise Edition. Otherwise, it can be obtained separately.

In the following scenario, we will create an InfoPath form listing the possible flight connections after the ID of an appropriate airline and the number of a travel agency have been entered. This InfoPath form uses the `Z_WS_FLCONN_GETLIST` web service as a data source, which was created in Section 2.2.2 using SAP Web AS 6.40. This web service in turn addresses the SAP BAPI `Flight-Connection`. To refresh your memory, please see Figure 3.29.

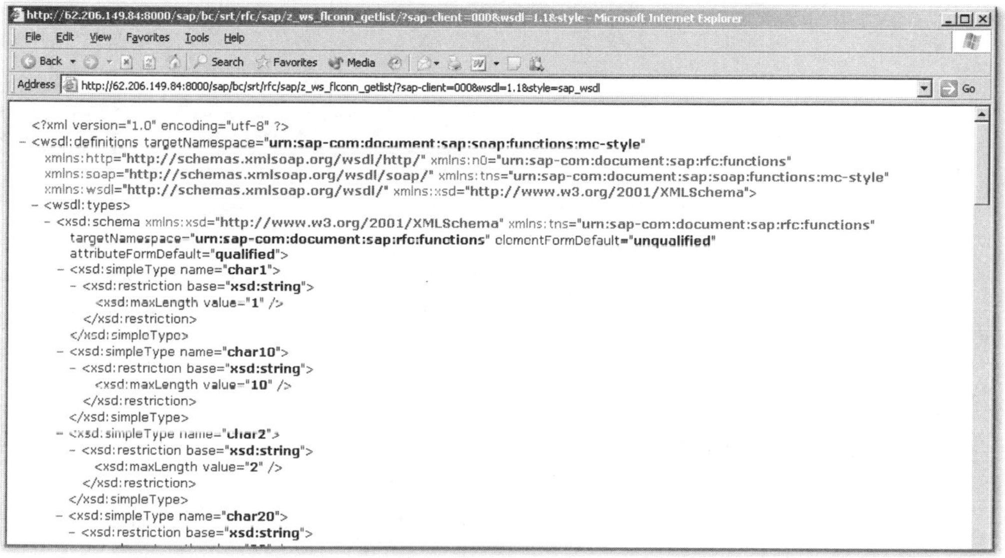

Creating an InfoPath form

Figure 3.29 WSDL File of the Web Service Z_WS_FLCONN_GETLIST

If you want to create a new form, a wizard is displayed after the Microsoft InfoPath application has been started. Its dialogs specify that the data source is a web service. Figure 3.30 illustrates the dialog.

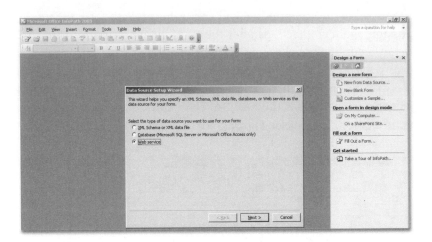

Figure 3.30 First Screen of the Wizard

The wizard then asks which web service is to be addressed, and the desired web service method is selected as shown in Figure 3.31 and Figure 3.32.

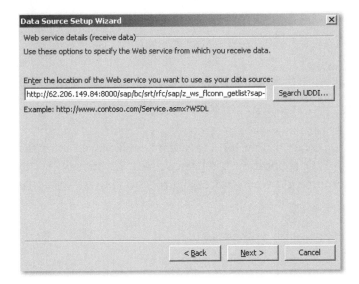

Figure 3.31 Specification of the Web Service

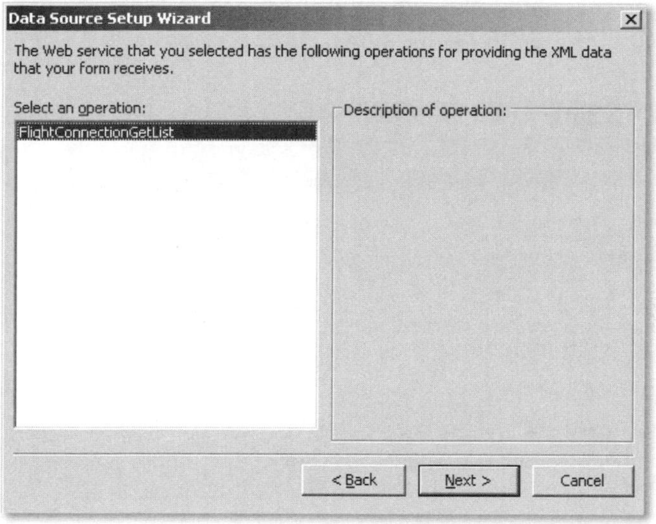

Figure 3.32 Selection of the Web Service Method

The specified web service parameters are then assigned to the Info-Path form (see Figure 3.33).

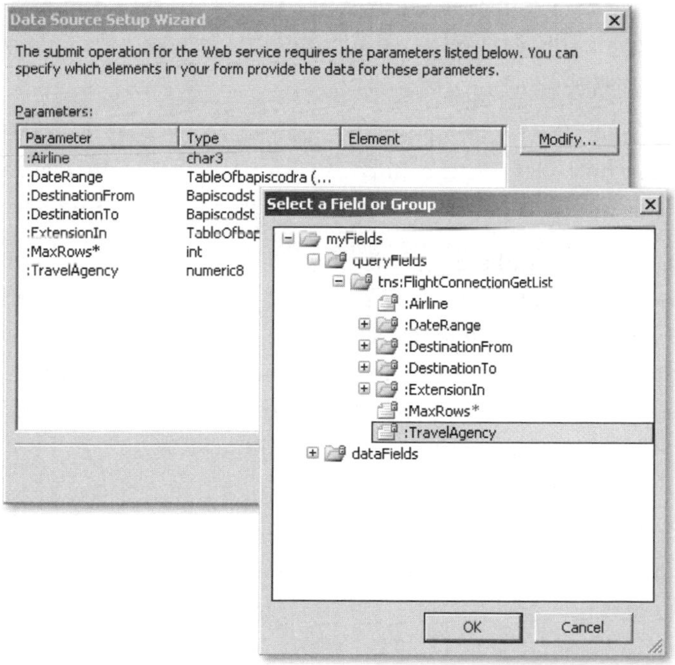

Figure 3.33 Assignment of the Parameters to the Form

Finally, the wizard summarizes which web service and method have been selected, as shown in Figure 3.34.

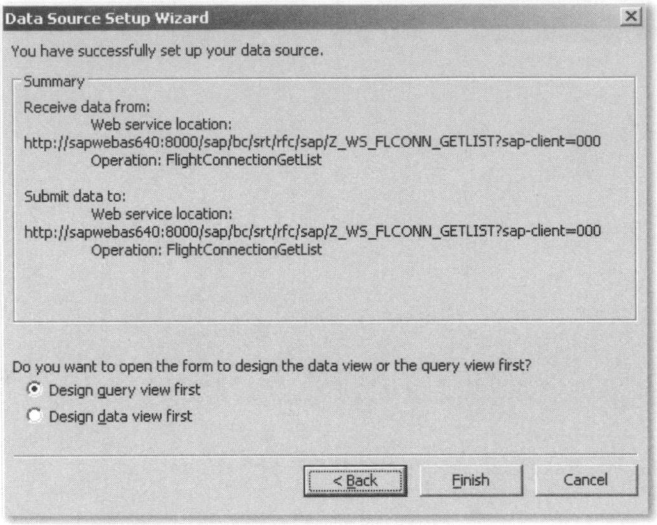

Figure 3.34 Final Wizard Summary

Designing an InfoPath form

The web service data source is thus set up. Now you can design the InfoPath form. In this example, we distinguish between the query view and the data view.

In the query view, the required search parameters are drawn to the design of the entry view of the InfoPath form as shown in Figure 3.35. In this example, these are the fields **Airline** and **TravelAgency**.

The data view of the InfoPath form is then edited. The required data fields of the defined data source are drawn to the form as illustrated in Figure 3.36. In this example, these are the complex type `FlightConnectionList.Item` containing the list of found flight connections and the field `Return.Item.Message` that returns the SAP message concerning the success or failure of the communication.

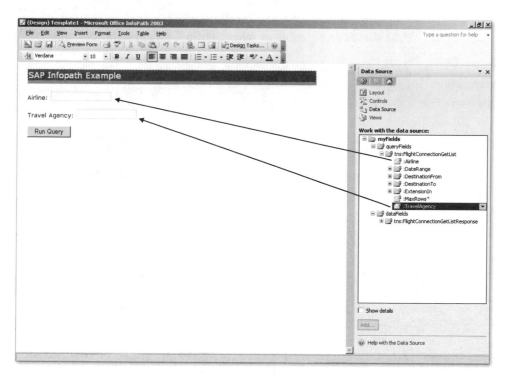

Figure 3.35 Design of the Query View

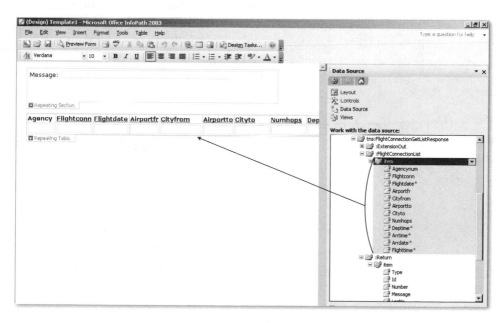

Figure 3.36 Design of the Data View

The form can now be graphically revised, saved and tested. Figure 3.37 shows an example of what the final form might look like.

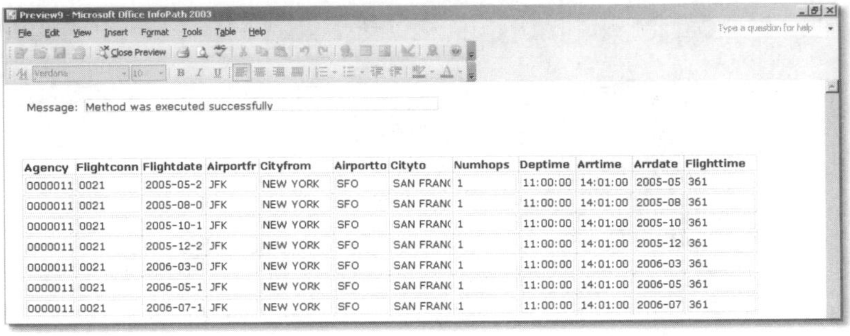

Figure 3.37 Completed InfoPath Form

The form can now be distributed and used in the enterprise as a file. However, important prerequisites are that user has installed the Microsoft InfoPath application and that he can access the web service addressed by the InfoPath form.

Expense Please note that we presented a relatively simple scenario to illustrate this technology. The addressed web service was not complex and the corresponding InfoPath form could be created within a few minutes. However, you may not think that a quick solution like this is also feasible in a real project with more complex interactive applications. For example, the input plausibility checks and the validation of user permissions require a clearly increased effort, particularly for service-oriented applications.

Office Information Bridge Framework (IBF)

A parallel branch to the Visual Studio Tools for Office is the *Microsoft Office Information Bridge Framework* (IBF). This is a relatively recent and fairly unknown technology based on the use of XML metadata and web services.

IBF is not very wide spread and hardly played a role in the context of the SAP Office integration. However, this technology recently increased in importance because in an enhanced version it is part of Duet's technology.

The Microsoft Office Information Bridge Framework primarily differs from the previously mentioned technologies in that it uses a different declarative approach. Although it should allow the access from the document to important data and business processes, these are not written directly to the Word document or Excel spreadsheet in contrast to the previous examples. Instead, the data from the source system is provided on demand in the Office work area (TaskPane) described above. The operation method, however, is completely different from that of VSTO.

IBF approach

For controlling the procurement and the display of this data, metadata is very important. It virtually represents the core of an IBF solution. It is made up of relatively large XML documents containing the relevant data. Metadata is data that provides information about other data. This can be properties of an object, for example, the name of the author, publisher and ISBN, are metadata of a book.

How is this metadata created and transferred to the work area? The IBF does this.

Technologically, an IBF solution consists of the following parts:

IBF components

- ▶ An IBF client component
- ▶ An IBF server component

With regard to the IBF client component, you need to distinguish between user and developer client. For the developer client, the *Metadata Designer* is installed as a plug-in for Microsoft Visual Studio 2003. On the user client, the *IBF Client Engine*[6] needs to be installed.

The IBF server component[7] consists of the *Metadata Service* and the *Metadata Storage*. The Metadata Service includes a read and a write service to the metadata. The metadata in turn is stored in a database[8], the Metadata Repository.

---

6 Prerequisite: Microsoft Office 2003 Professional with support for .NET and the Microsoft .NET Framework 1.1.
7 Prerequisite: Windows 2003 Server as the operating system and Microsoft IIS 6.0 with activated ASP.NET as the Web Application Server.
8 Microsoft SQL Server 2000 installation with current service packs.

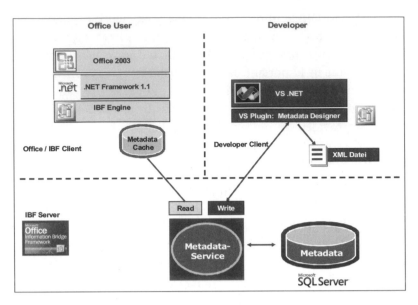

Figure 3.38 Overview of IBF Clients and IBF Server

Defining the scenario and its parts
To develop an IBF solution you first need to define the corresponding scenario and its parts.

The following aspects need to be specified in an IBF solution:

▶ **Entity**
An entity is a business object like a customer or a business partner.

▶ **Views**
To display a business object you need to define at least one default view of the object. These are defined in XML.

▶ **Reference**
This is the primary key of an entity.

▶ **Actions**
Actions define the functions that can be used for the business objects.

▶ **Relationships of Views**
Relationships are connections of views of different business objects.

metadata.xml
These specifications are defined in Visual Studio 2003, the Metadata Designer and its wizard, and stored in the file *metadata.xml*. To simplify the work of a developer, Visual Studio has been extended by the *Metadata Explorer* and the *Metadata Guidance Window*.

The Metadata Explorer shows the current editing status of the *metadata.xml* file, while the Metadata Guidance Window guides the developer through the necessary steps of creating an IBF solution and starts the corresponding wizards, if needed.

While the file *metadata.xml* is being edited, the sources of the data to be later provided in the task area are addressed and the schemas are imported.

After all required specifications have been defined and stored in the *metadata.xml file*, which is published and saved to the IBF server and is available for further use. Figure 3.39 illustrates the runtime architecture of IBF. In future, whenever the IBF SmartTag is addressed in the document, the IBF work area responds and provides the actions defined in the metadata it obtains from the metaservice. The user selects an action, and the IBF Engine uses the metadata to decide which data source or which web service (e. g., from SAP) needs to be addressed and how the data needs to be presented.

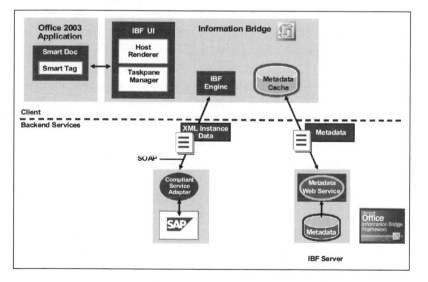

Figure 3.39 IBF at Runtime

With regard to the distribution of IBF solutions, please note that they only run online. You need to be able to access the IBF server and the respective client must have the IBF runtime installed. This significantly increases the distribution effort compared to the variants described above.

3.1.3 Duet

A term often heard in the Microsoft and SAP environment is *Mendocino*, which is the name of a joint Microsoft and SAP development project. It was recently announced that the project has developed into a finished product named *Duet*. What is this about?

Enterprise Services Duet is an integration application between mySAP ERP 2004 and Microsoft Office 2003. Microsoft Office 2003 serves as an alternative user interface for (currently) four employee and management self-services made available as enterprise services. Enterprise services are the communication services of SAP's Enterprise SOA, the SAP implementation of a service-oriented system architecture. Thus, Duet is an example of the integration and use of Enterprise SOA.

Objectives of Duet

The purpose of Duet is to support employees (information workers) who perform the majority of their daily tasks using Microsoft Office 2003 (see Figure 3.40). Microsoft Office is the familiar work environment for these employees, and it is a breach in their workflow to get business data and information from another user mySAP ERP interface (like SAP GUI or NetWeaver Portal) for specific processes; this information must then be manually extracted. This is particularly relevant when the employee does not have access to SAP, and colleagues with the appropriate permission (SAP users) must perform this step and then forward the data back to the employee. In addition to the integration gap and the inefficient workflow, a significant drawback of this situation is the fact that the data obtained might have become obsolete or that parts of the data might have been lost or inadvertently falsified on their way to the employee. Therefore, there is a risk of information inconsistency if the data is kept in two different locations and are not automatically updated.

For a number of SAP business processes, Duet closes this gap between Office user and the mySAP ERP 2004 data source. Users can get access to SAP data from within their familiar work environment and to process this data (see Figure 3.41). The data is provided by mySAP ERP via enterprise services and can be used within the Office application, and the data or information flow is synchronized. The employee works with live data and can directly integrate it into his work processes.

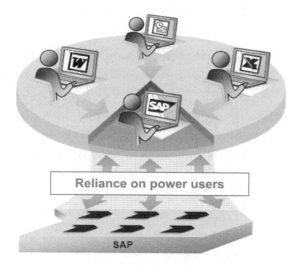

Figure 3.40 Microsoft Office 2003 and SAP Users Today

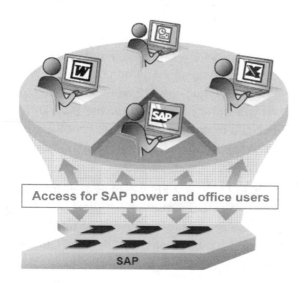

Figure 3.41 Access for Both SAP and Office Duet Users

Duet Technology

There are two very important parts to Duct: For corresponding high-level web services, the *Enterprise Services* must be available or provided for the SAP business processes to be accessed; and a framework is required for the Office client to access these services.

The enterprise services for the first version of Duet come from the SAP HR area and are available as of mySAP ERP 2004.

Duet components

In detail, Duet consists of the following component (see Figure 3.42):

▶ **Duet server**
The Duet server requires Microsoft Windows 2003 SP1, .NET Framework 2.0, and an activated IIS 6.0 with ASP.NET. Additionally, a database, the Microsoft Active Directory 2000, and an Microsoft Exchange Server 2003 with Service Pack 1 are required. If there is no database, e. g., a SQL server is available, then the Express Edition of Microsoft SQL Server 2005 is installed.

Server components

The actual Duet server itself consists of Microsoft and SAP components. The Microsoft components representing the client integration components include the *Metadata Repository*, the *Metadata Storage* and the *Exchange Message Formater* for converting asynchronous messages. The SAP components mainly consist of tools for communicating with the SAP system, like the SAP Service Provider and the SAP Service Mapper.

▶ **Duet client**
The Duet client is a desktop system based on Windows XP and Microsoft Office 2003 Professional. Additionally, the client requires the Microsoft .NET Framework 2.0 and a local database as a data storage. This data storage is needed for the Duet Office add-on. The Duet Office add-on includes the Duet Client Runtime Engine and utilities, services, and tools for the communication and data transfer with the Duet server.

User interface

In the first version of Duet, Outlook 2003 works as a central host application or user interface with distribution list functions. Outlook was the obvious choice because its online/offline capabilities that are supported by the Duet applications. Additionally, Outlook addresses Excel and InfoPath.

▶ **Duet SAP add-ons**
The Duet SAP add-ons complete the SAP system with required business objects (SAP Duet ABAP add-on) and with services for accessing the NetWeaver Enterprise SOA level (SAP Duet Java add-on). Additionally, a local Application Metadata Repository Interface and a local Metadata Storage for exchanging metadata are added to the SAP system.

The SAP system version must at least be mySAP ERP 2004 and provide the SAP Enterprise SOA add-ons.

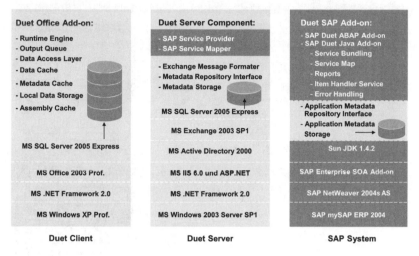

Figure 3.42 Overview of the Duet Parts

We would like to point out that this is Duet's status at the time of this book's printing and that details of the technology might continue to change until it is released to the market.

Duet Functionality

In the first announced Duet version 1.0, SAP business processes that are related to personnel administration and control are supported. These business processes are:

Supported business processes

▶ **Absence management**
   Absence management enables you to administer the absence times of employees (e. g., vacation or illness) using the calendar and appointment function in Outlook. For example, the employee can submit a leave request that the supervisor can either accept or decline. Additionally, both the supervisor and the employee can obtain overviews of requests and appointments. Outlook uses Duet to access the SAP enterprise service *Personnel Absence Processing*. This service reconciles the data with the HR module in mySAP ERP. An example of a leave request is shown in Figure 3.43.

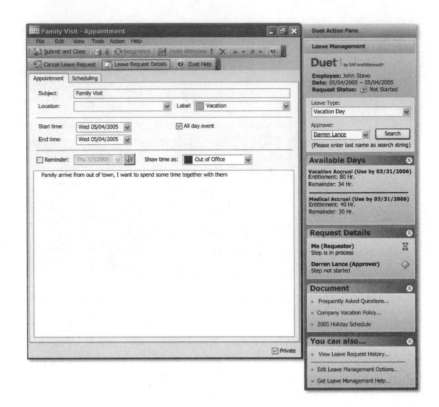

Figure 3.43 Absence Management

▶ **Time management**

The time management reconciles the data from the employee's Outlook calendar with the SAP system. Thus, the employee no longer needs to redundantly record project times. Times and appointments are maintained in Outlook, which uses the SAP enterprise service *Personal Times Management* to transfer this information to the SAP project time management. Additionally, users can display an overview of project times in the Outlook task area (Figure 3.44 shows an example).

▶ **Budget monitoring/reporting**

Duet supports users in controlling costs and budgets in the context of both planning and monitoring. When budget limits are exceeded and strong variances occur, Duet offers an alarm function. Additionally, a link to the related SAP reports is provided. Duet accesses functions of SAP Analytics, and SAP reports can be received and edited both in Outlook and in Excel (see Figure 3.45).

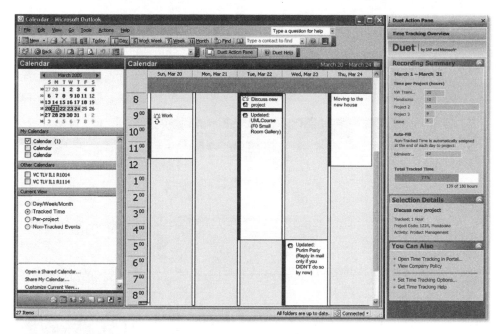

Figure 3.44 Time Management

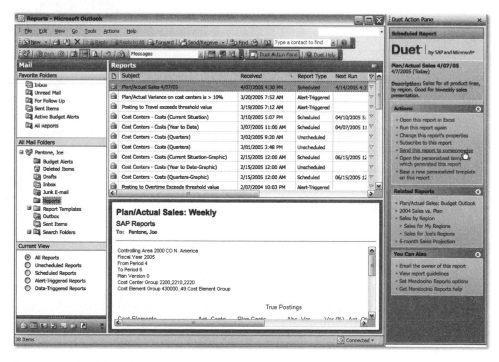

Figure 3.45 Example of Accessing SAP Reports

▶ **Personnel administration/bonuses**

Another function is the possibility of paying bonuses and salary increases. The function *Employee Shift Bonus Create Request Response* of the SAP Enterprise Service Personal Times Management is used from Outlook. Figure 3.46 shows an example.

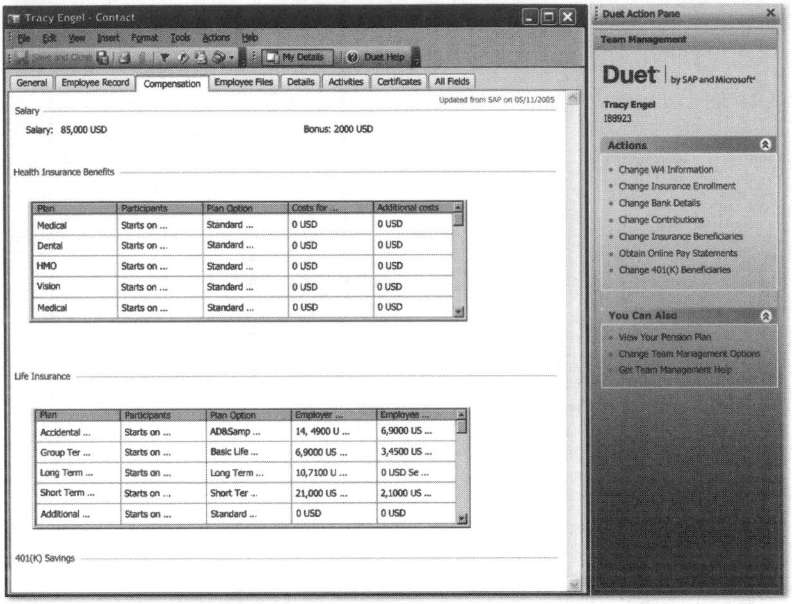

Figure 3.46 Payment of Bonuses

▶ **Personnel administration/personnel file**

Last but not least, a link between the Outlook contacts functionality and the personnel data from the SAP personnel administration was established for the *personnel file* function using the SAP enterprise service, *Personal Management*. Depending on the user permission, further details of the relevant contact can be viewed. Additionally, employees with personnel management function can view and assess the employees' data. Figure 3.47 shows the corresponding access to personnel data.

More Duet functions More functions will be added gradually. Planned features specifically include functions that are to access processes from the mySAP CRM, SRM, and SCM areas.

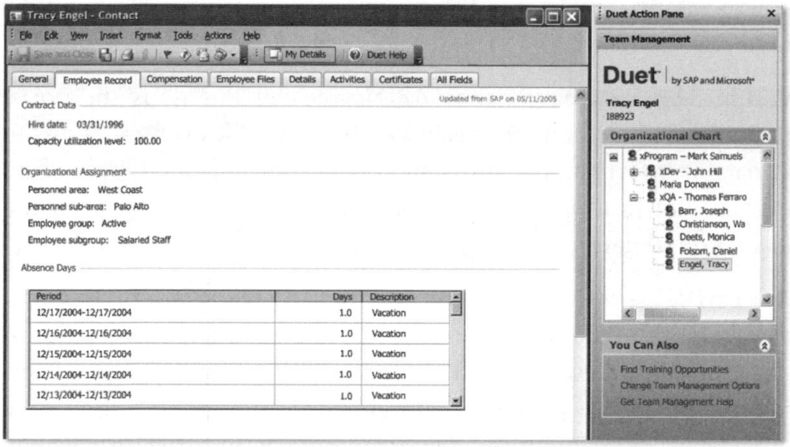

Figure 3.47 Access to Personnel Data

Duet Schedule

According to plan, the first preview version of Duet was delivered to selected customers at the end of 2005. The final Duet version 1.0 was announced for mid-2006.

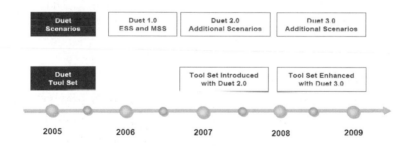

Figure 3.48 Duet Schedule

3.2 Portal Integration: SAP NetWeaver Portal

Like the desktop integration, the portal integration is a frontend integration. However, it is based on a (web) server. The integration takes place within the portal application on the Web Application Server, and the user client is not affected. Users use the web browser as a framework or container and they can hardly detect the source of the respective content.

Within SAP NetWeaver, the SAP NetWeaver Portal[9] is the portal component. Based on web technologies, it enables central access to all data or information sources and applications in an enterprise and can thus function as a central integration platform for structured and unstructured data, providing a unified look and feel.

Portal content As a part of the SAP standard version, the SAP NetWeaver Portal provides a lot of predefined content. For example, SAP provides almost one thousand iViews. These iViews can be integrated, used and customized to the customers' requirements. Additionally, the portal provides the possibility to extend contents by proprietary developments. Apart from the development platforms of Java and ABAP, SAP also enables Microsoft .NET developers to develop portal contents. The main tool for this purpose is the *Portal Development Kit for Microsoft* that is provided by SAP. This tool and its usage are discussed in detail in this chapter. First, however, we will introduce SAP NetWeaver Portal architecture.

Portal components As shown in Figure 3.49, SAP NetWeaver Portal consists of the following components:

▸ the actual portal framework

▸ connectors for different information sources

▸ knowledge management components

▸ unification components

What exactly is displayed in the SAP NetWeaver Portal? A portal is made up of a unified user interface. This user interface presents the content that consists of pages. Figure 3.50 shows that the pages contain *worksets* that, in turn, are made up of portal components that are referred to as *iViews* in SAP NetWeaver Portal and as *webparts* for SharePoint. These iViews are the smallest portal unit in this context and represent the actual content.

---

9   Previously known as SAP Enterprise Portal (SAP EP).

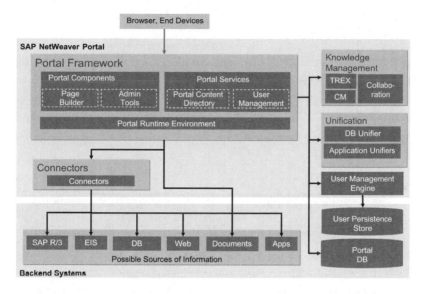

Figure 3.49 Components of SAP NetWeaver Portal, Logical View

iViews provide information and enable the interaction with the user, if applicable. They can be thought of as small web applications. An initial installation of an SAP NetWeaver Portal provides more than 7,000 predefined iViews.

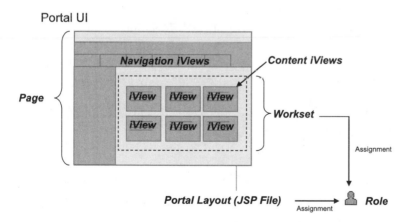

Figure 3.50 Components of the Portal User Interface

For creating these iViews for the portal, SAP provides various tools, which are presented in Figure 3.51. These tools address different users with different abilities. In general, a distinction is made between *creating portal content* and *developing portal content*.

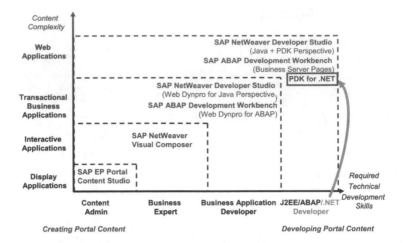

Figure 3.51 Overview of Portal Content Tools

The area of *creating portal content* includes (see Figure 3.52):

▶ **Portal Content Studio**

Within the SAP NetWeaver portal interface, the *Portal Content Studio* enables the quick creation of iViews without program code by using wizards and templates (e. g., navigation iViews and the content iViews). The *Portal Page Builder* is used for this purpose.

▶ **Visual Composer**

The Visual Composer (previously GUI Machine) is an easy to use graphical development tool for portal applications that can be used for creating iViews based on HTMLB. HTMLB stands for *HTML Business* and consists of a set of controls that can be compared to Java Swing.

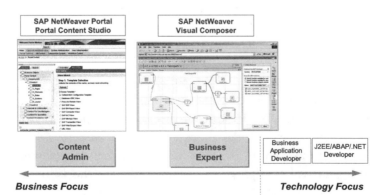

Figure 3.52 Tools for Creating Portal Content

The following tools pertain to the area of developing portal content (see Figure 3.53):

Developing portal content

▶ **SAP NetWeaver Developer Studio**
SAP NetWeaver Developer Studio can be used to create Web Dynpros. Web Dynpros can then be integrated in the portal as iViews.

▶ **ABAP Workbench**
With SAP Web AS 6.10, the ABAP Workbench was extended by the Web Application Builder for creating business server pages applications. Business server pages are web applications that use server-side scripting. ABAP can be used as the scripting language. Like Web Dynpros, business server pages can be integrated in the portal as iViews.

▶ **Portal Development Kit**
This is a programming language-specific development tool for iViews. It is a portal extension in the form of a *portal business package* (*.pkg). There are versions for both Java and Microsoft .NET.

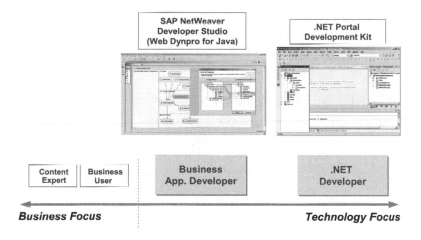

Figure 3.53 Tools for Developing Portal Content

▶ **Portal Content Portfolio**
Although the name iView Studio might suggest it, it was not a developer IDE but an SAP web page that provided an overview of the available business packages. These contained interrelated worksets that were made up of relevant iViews. The business

packages could be downloaded and used. The iViewStudio web page was replaced with the *Portal Content Portfolio*.[10]

Because only the Portal Development Kit (PDK) for Microsoft .NET enables the creation of iViews within a Microsoft .NET environment and by using Microsoft .NET tools, it is discussed in detail in the following chapter.

3.2.1 Portal Development Kit for .NET Development Tool

The SAP Labs in Israel developed the Portal Development Kit for .NET as the ultimate tool for developers who want to or have to create contents for the SAP NetWeaver Portal based on the Microsoft .NET Framework.

ASP.NET

The PDK enables a comfortable development of SAP Portal iViews using the Microsoft Visual Studio 2003 development environment. This applies to both the development of new portal applications and the migration of existing web applications based on ASP.NET.[11] Developers benefit from the fact that the Microsoft .NET iViews structures are similar to those of ASP.NET user controls. This should simplify the first step into iView development, particularly for experienced ASP.NET developers.[12]

The PDK for .NET is an important component in the SAP strategy for developer tools because it easily integrates existing and future Microsoft-based applications into the SAP NetWeaver Portal. Therefore, it is not surprising that the PDK for .NET was presented by SAP together with Microsoft (even though it is an SAP product).

With the PDK for .NET, the SAP NetWeaverPortal can dispose of a large number of possible contents. Thus, enterprises using both SAP and Microsoft web applications gain new integration options.

Components of the PDK for .NET

What is the PDK for .NET (see Figure 3.54)? In version 1.0, patch 3, it consists of the following components:

---

10 The Portal Content Portfolio can be found in the SAP developer forum at *https://www.sdn.sap.com/irj/sdn/developerareas/contentportfolio*.

11 ASP.NET: Active Server Pages .NET. The .NET technology for creating dynamic web applications based on the Microsoft .NET Framework.

12 For this reason, the PDK for .NET could also be suitable for migrating existing ASP.NET applications to the SAP NetWeaver Portal.

▶ **Portal Add-in for Visual Studio 2003**
The extension of Microsoft Visual Studio 2003 which enables Microsoft .NET developers to develop iViews based on Microsoft .NET in Visual Studio.

▶ **Portal Runtime for Microsoft .NET**
A Windows service that enables the operation of Microsoft .NET-based iViews. It directly uses the ASP.NET engine.

▶ **Java/.NET Interoperability Framework**
This framework enables the use of API calls between the Java stack of the SAP systems and the Microsoft .NET development stack.

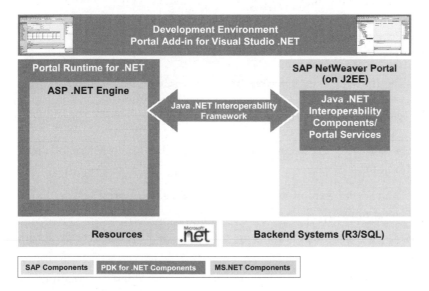

Figure 3.54 Overview of the PDK for .NET Components

To create iViews based on Microsoft .NET, the developer system needs to have SAP NetWeaver Portal, Microsoft Visual Studio 2003, and, optionally, SAP Connector for .NET 2.0 installed. In addition, the PDK for .NET package must be downloaded from the SAP Developer Network (SDN). It consists of two installation packages, one for the Visual Studio 2003 add-in and another one for the SAP .NET runtime engine.

Installation of the PDK for .NET

The add-in needs to be installed on the developer system running Visual Studio 2003, and the runtime engine must be installed on the Windows system hosting the portal. After the add-in has been installed, Visual Studio should be started, as shown in Figure 3.55.

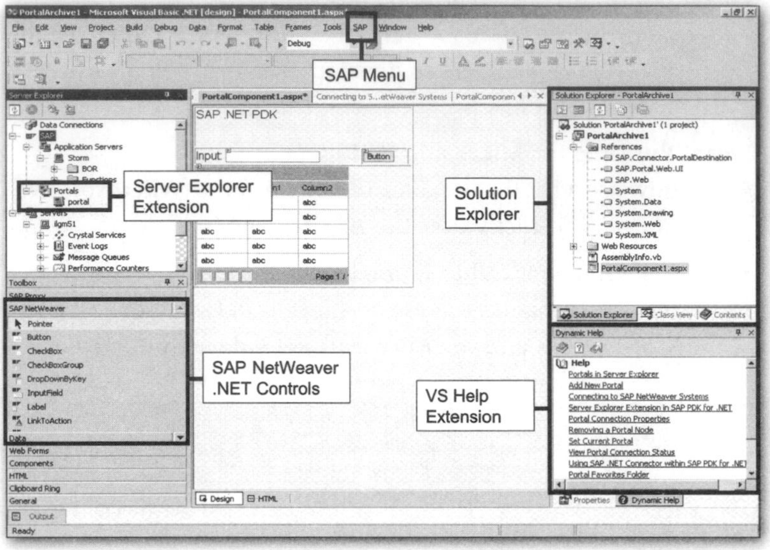

Figure 3.55 Extensions of Visual Studio 2003

Enhancements

The following enhancements are now available to a Microsoft .NET developer:

- The Server Explorer displays SAP NetWeaver portal servers in the local network.

- The VS Toolbox contains an additional SAP NetWeaver area with related SAP NetWeaver .NET controls.

- An SAP menu for deployment has been provided for creating and distributing a Portal Archive (PAR).

- The Visual Studio help has been supplemented with information about the PDK for .NET.

- Additionally, as shown in Figure 3.60, Visual Studio 2003 provides developers with a new project template for Visual Studio 2003 C# and VB .NET Portal Application.

On the server side, after the installation of the SAP .NET Runtime Engine, the following included Software Delivery Archive (SDA[13]) files need to be uploaded from the following sources to the SAP

---

13 SDA files are ZIP-compatible archive files used for distributing SAP development components.

NetWeaver Portal Server using the Software Deployment Manager (SDM), as shown in Figure 3.56:

- *com.sap.portal.dotnet.framework.sda*
- *com.sap.portal.dotnet.services.systems.sda*

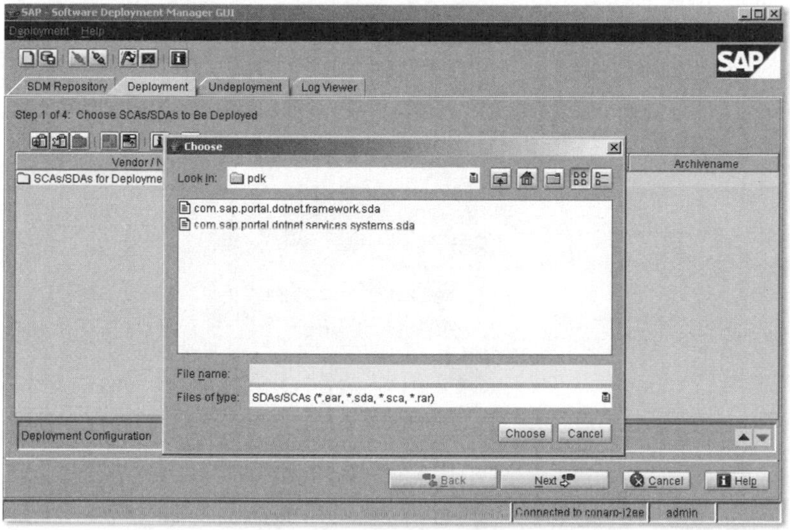

Figure 3.56 Software Deployment Manager

SDA files no longer need to be manually deployed in a portal version higher than 6.0 SPS 15 because these components are already included.

The installation is not yet finished on the Portal Server. You still need to create a user name for the runtime engine that by using the server's control panel obtains an authorization for the following directories:

Assigning authorizations

- Portal Runtime for .NET directory:
  C:\Program Files\SAP\Portal Runtime for Microsoft .NET
- Temporary directory of ASP.NET files:
  %windir%\Microsoft.NET\Framework\v1.1.4322
  Temporary ASP.NET Files
- Temporary Windows directory: *%windir%\Temp*

Figure 3.57 shows an example of assigning the authorization for the directory of temporary ASP.NET files.

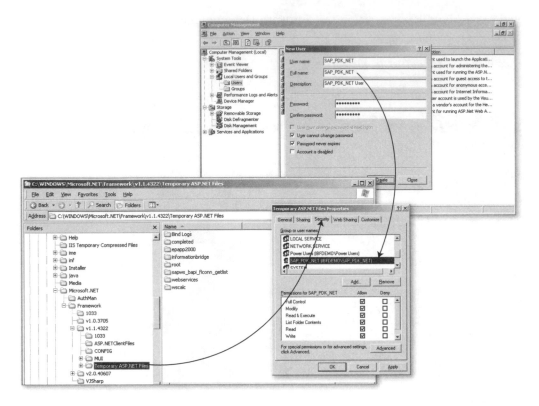

Figure 3.57 Assigning the User Authorizations for the Runtime Engine

Finally, as you can see in Figure 3.58, the portal runtime for Microsoft .NET needs to be started via the management console (*epmmc*).

Figure 3.58 Starting the Runtime Engine

Function of the runtime engine

How does the runtime engine work? The runtime engine contains an ASP.NET engine and uses a Windows system as an operating system. If a .NET iView is addressed from the portal, the *Java .NET Interoperability Framework* forwards a request to the Portal Runtime for

Microsoft .NET, as illustrated in Figure 3.59. The communication protocol used in this case is TCP/IP. The Portal Runtime for Microsoft .NET executes the iView.

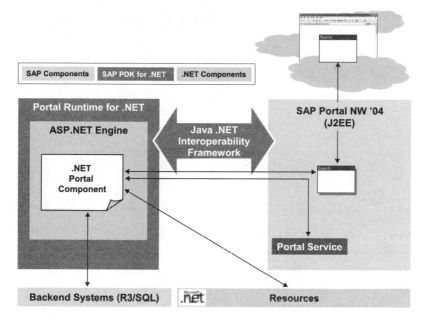

Figure 3.59 Operation of Microsoft .NET iViews

The Microsoft .NET iView addresses the source systems and retrieves data or changes it. However, the iView can also use the Java-based portal services via the Java .NET Interoperability Framework. The responses from the .NET iView are returned via the Java .NET Interoperability Framework back to the SAP NetWeaver Portal.

Let's now look at the creation of an iView based on the Microsoft .NET Framework using the PDK for .NET. When the developer starts up Microsoft Visual Studio 2003 on the developer system to create a new project, he can select the relevant templates for SAP Portal Applications for Visual Basic or C# programming languages (see Figure 3.60). An SAP Portal Application is a web project template designed for creating one or several SAP Portal Components. These SAP Portal Components each correspond to an ASP.NET user control.

Creating an IVIew using PDK for .NET

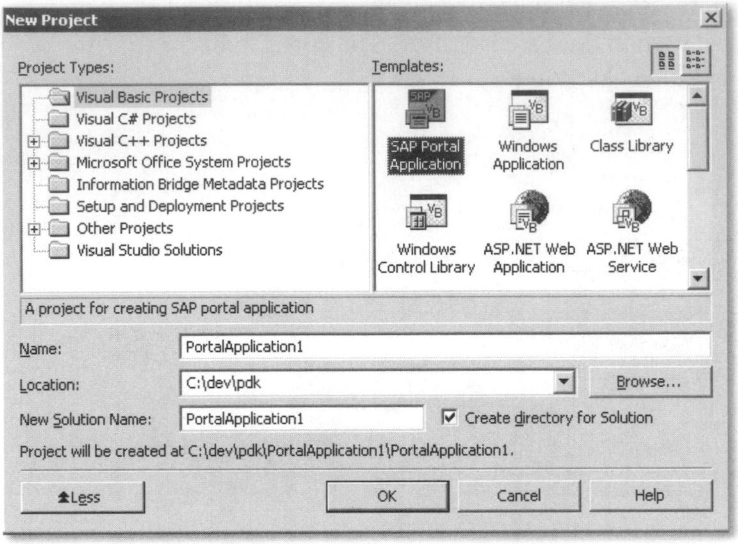

Figure 3.60 VB .NET Project Template SAP Portal Application

Development libraries

If the project template **SAP Portal Application** is selected, the following development libraries of the SAP NetWeaver Portal are automatically integrated as a reference in the product:

- ▶ **SAP.Connector.PortalDestination.dll**
  The destination library contains the helper classes for the connection string to the SAP NetWeaver Portal as well as the corresponding security parameters.

- ▶ **SAP.Portal.Web.UI.dll**
  Contains classes for creating *SAP Portal Components* or the user interface (UI) classes, respectively, as well as their property specifications.

- ▶ **SAP.Web.dll**
  Collection of basic classes for creating the SAP NetWeaver server controls in iViews.

Detailed information about these classes can be found in the PDK for .NET online help, which is part of the VS help system.

Figure 3.61 shows the development libraries in the Visual Studio Solution Explorer.

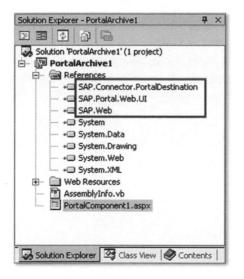

Figure 3.61 SAP Portal Development Libraries

The functionality during the development of an SAP Portal Application based on Microsoft .NET corresponds to the functionality of "normal" ASP.NET applications. The difference is that, for example, SAP NetWeaver controls are implemented that are adapted to the SAP NetWeaver Portal with regard to their presentation and behavior.[14] Otherwise, the required controls are placed on the WebForm and the program code is implemented in C# or VB .NET, depending on the selected programming language.

As an example, we will create a classic "Hello World!" iView using Visual Studio 2003. First, select the **SAP Portal Application** Visual Basic template. From the interface of the portal component, the future iView, an SAP label field, and an SAP button are selected from the group of SAP NetWeaver controls.

Creating a "Hello World!" iView

---

14 They correspond to SAP Unified Rendering, which is implemented across all SAP UI technologies.

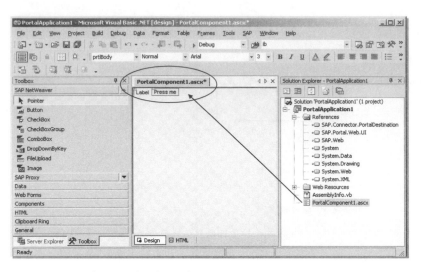

Figure 3.62 Simple Example of PDK for .NET

The implemented functionality has been intentionally kept very simple. After clicking the button, the label is assigned the text "Hello World!".

```
Private Sub Button1_Action()
    Label1.Text = " Hello World !"
End Sub
```

In contrast to the development of ASP.NET applications in Visual Studio 2003, the application can be viewed only in the SAP NetWeaver Portal. For this purpose, it first needs to be published in the SAP NetWeaver Portal. This is done in Microsoft Visual Studio 2003 via the **SAP** menu and the menu item **Deploy current project**, as shown in Figure 3.63.

Adding an iView to the content catalog
Finally, the iView must be added to the *Content Catalog* in the SAP NetWeaver Portal (*http://[host]:50000/irj/portal*). Figure 3.64 illustrates the procedure.

1. In the Content Catalog, right-click the folder where you want to create the iView.

2. Select the Portal Archive (PAR) file using the option **New from PAR/Iview**.

3. Follow the wizard guiding you through the next steps.

4. Click on **OK**.

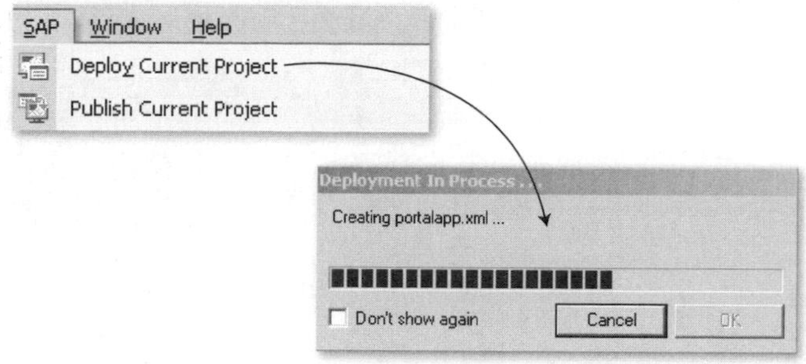

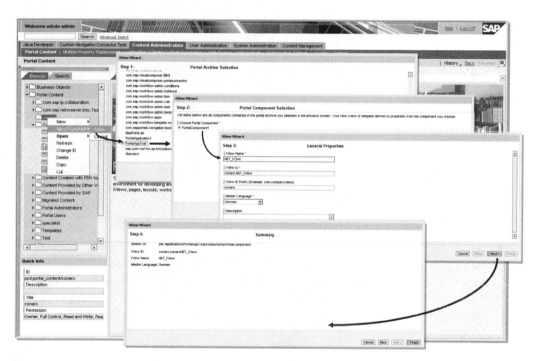

Figure 3.63 Deployment of the SAP Portal Application

Figure 3.64 Creating the Microsoft .NET iView in the Portal

Now you must select the page to assign the iView, and for the last step, specify the page layout.

Now you can test the result via the **Preview** function. If the sample application is executed without errors, clicking on the button in the previously invisible label field should cause the famous words "Hello World!" to be written and displayed, as shown in Figure 3.65.

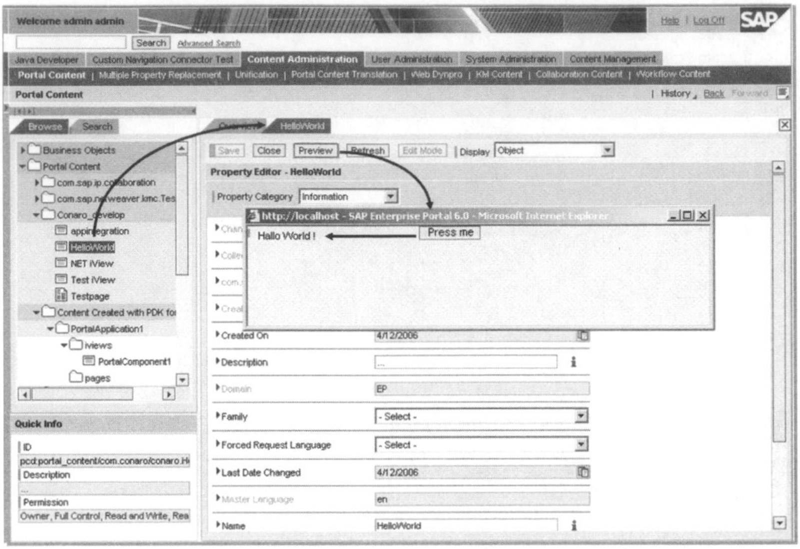

Figure 3.65 Assigning the iView to the Page and Preview of the iView

3.2.2 Innovations in Version 2.0 of the PDK for .NET

New development tools

While the interim version of PDK for .NET 1.0, patch 3, already included some innovations such as enhanced debugging, Intellisense[15], a new portal system template, and a snap-in for the Microsoft Management Console (*epmmc*), the most recent PDK for .NET 2.0 (published by the end of 2005) provided more supplements and improvements. Apart from new and enhanced classes, APIs and new SAP NetWeaver controls, PDK for .NET 2.0 includes new development tools, including:

▶ **Portal Page Designer**
While the *portal pages* were always designed in SAP NetWeaver Portal in the previous versions, you can now use the Portal Page Designer as a graphical tool to design portal pages without having to leave the Microsoft Visual Studio development environment, as shown in Figure 3.66. Even a page preview is now available.

---

15 IntelliSense is a feature in Visual Studio for displaying helpful additional information in the code editor, like properties and methods of an object whose name is written to the editor.

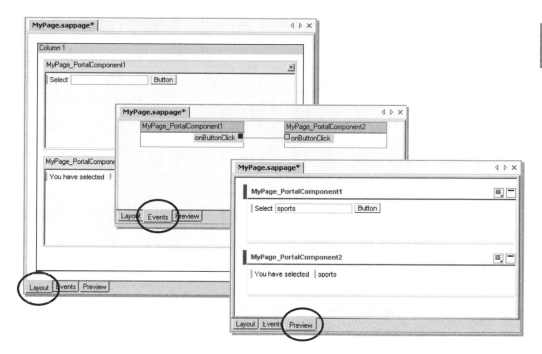

Figure 3.66 PDK 2.0—Portal Page Designer

▶ **Portal Style Designer**
The Portal Style Designer is another graphical tool that is embedded in the Microsoft Visual Studio development environment to adapt user interface controls that don't originate from SAP to adopt the look and feel of the SAP NetWeaver Portal. Figure 3.67 shows the Designer user interface. Using the Portal Style Designer, you can use and edit the CSS classes and the style definitions of the SAP NetWeaver Portal.

▶ **Object-based navigation**
The *object-based navigation* (OBN) is a new function for developing a role- and user permission-related usage of content. Version 2.0 of the PDK for .NET is delivered with tools like *OBNAdapter* and *OBNView Control* based on the OBN service API.

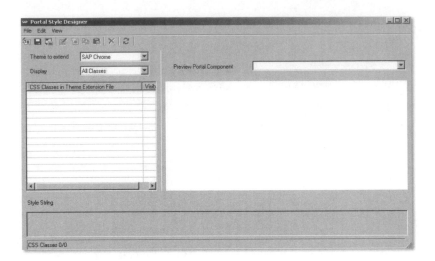

Figure 3.67 PDK 2.0—Portal Style Designer

▶ **Deployment**

The deployment has been extended in PDK for .NET version 2.0. Apart from the Portal Archive files (PAR) used, it is now also possible to create and distribute SDA or Cabinet files (CAB).

Publish Project function The ability to create an automated, full SAP Portal Application project in the requested SAP NetWeaver Portal will be a particular favorite. The corresponding subfolders, pages, and iViews are created in the SAP NetWeaver Portal Content Catalog. Therefore, the manual steps previously required are no longer necessary.

Additionally, there is the possibility to generate and deploy the applications created via PDK for .NET 2.0 as a web part for a Microsoft SharePoint Portal Server instead of as an iView for the SAP NetWeaver Portal. This possibility is hidden in the options of the PDK for .NET 2.0 add-in in Visual Studio 2003, as shown in Figure 3.68. However, this requires the SAP Portal Runtime for Microsoft .NET to be installed on the SharePoint Server.

Therefore, it's possible to use the PDK to create web applications for both the SAP NetWeaver Portal and the SharePoint Portal Server without having to change the code.

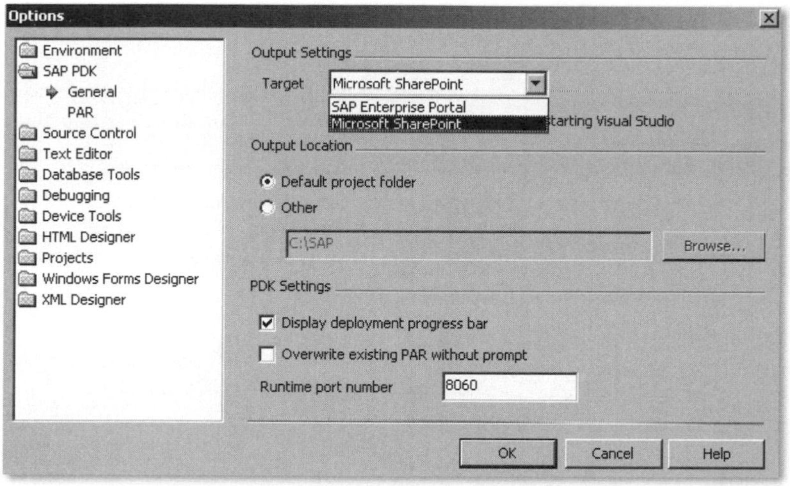

Figure 3.68 SAP PDK Options in Visual Studio 2003

Runtime Service Configuration Editor

The Microsoft .NET Runtime Service Configuration Editor in the SAP NetWeaver Portal provides a comfortable possibility of configuring the portal-side settings of the .NET runtime services, as shown in Figure 3.69. Starting with SAP NetWeaver Portal version 6.0 SPS 15, the Microsoft .NET Runtime Service Configuration Editor is already included in the standard installation.

Configuring portal-side settings

MapPointLab Sample Application

Using a comprehensive development example, we will demonstrate development using version 2.0 of the PDK for .NET. This is a sample application created by the SAP development lab in Israel that has already been published in a similar version in the SDN. We are referring to the *MapPointLab Portal Application*. The creation of this application shows how two different data sources can be combined within a PDK for .NET application and integrated in the SAP NetWeaver Portal. Specifically, this means that the sample application displays a customer list from a SQL Server table within an iView, and that the Microsoft MapPoint web service is addressed based on this data to get interesting locations near a customer's address, which can also be displayed in a map.

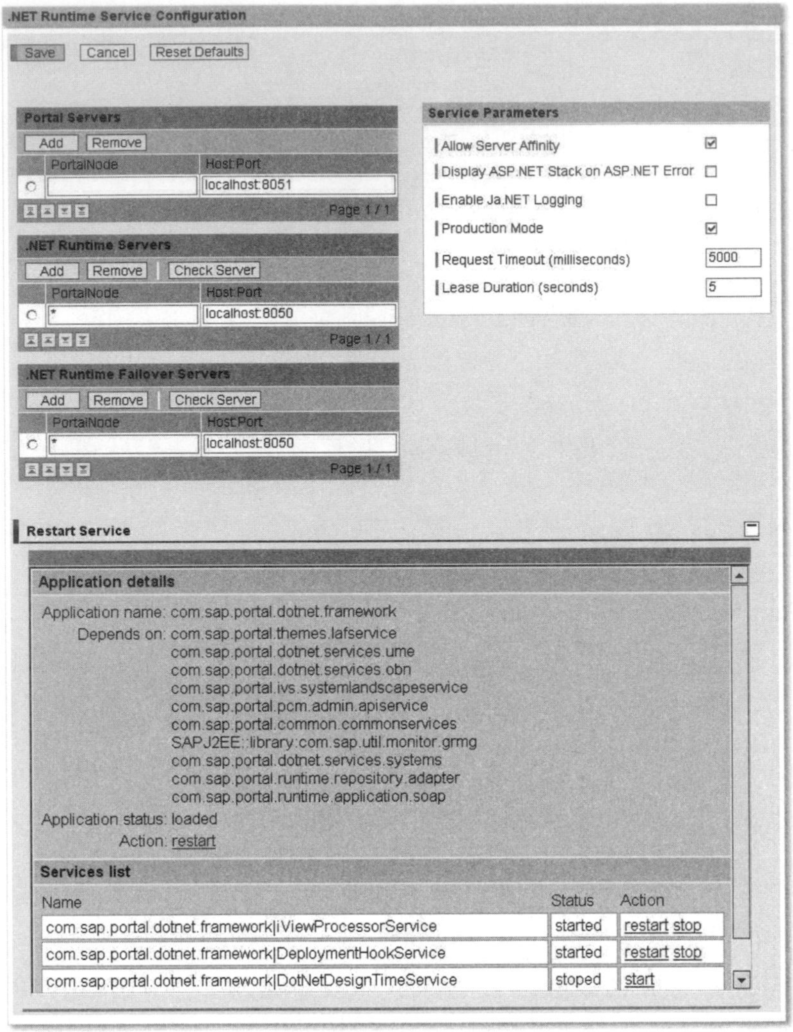

Figure 3.69 PDK 2.0 Runtime Service Configuration Editor

Prerequisites Apart from a functioning PDK for .NET infrastructure, the following requirements must be met to create this application:

▶ A SQL server with a database containing the customer table (Customer). A relevant script is included in the sample application.

▶ A MapPoint web service developer access.[16]

---

16 Available for free at the MapPoint web service web page: *http://www.microsoft.com/mappoint/products/webservice/default.mspx.*

► A Microsoft IIS for installing the MapPoint WebService proxy (`SAP.Demo.WebService.Maps`). This proxy is included in the sample application and must initially be created as a virtual directory in the IIS.

Once these data sources have been created, the SAP Portal Application project can be created in Visual Studio 2003 based on the corresponding project template, as shown in Figure 3.70.

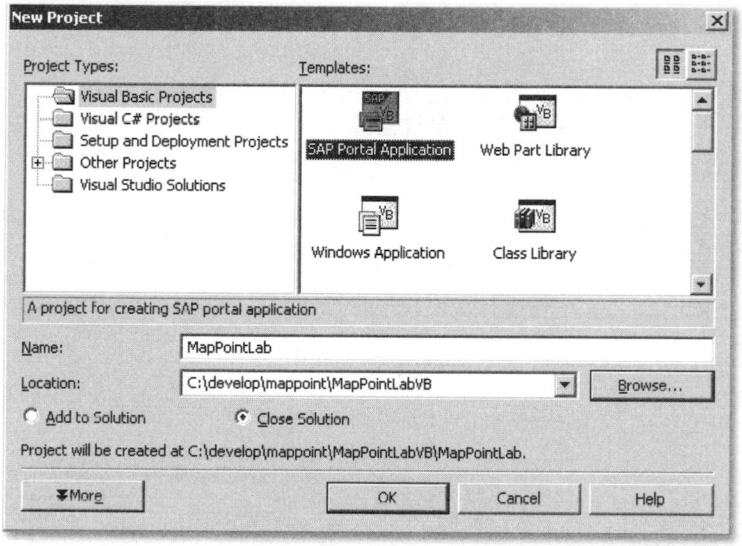

Creating the portal project

Figure 3.70 Creating an SAP Portal Application Project

You need to delete the *PortalComponent1.ascx* file that was automatically created (see Figure 3.71), and add an SAP Portal System Template to the project instead, as shown in Figure 3.72. This file is added to the project as *MapPointSystem.VB*.

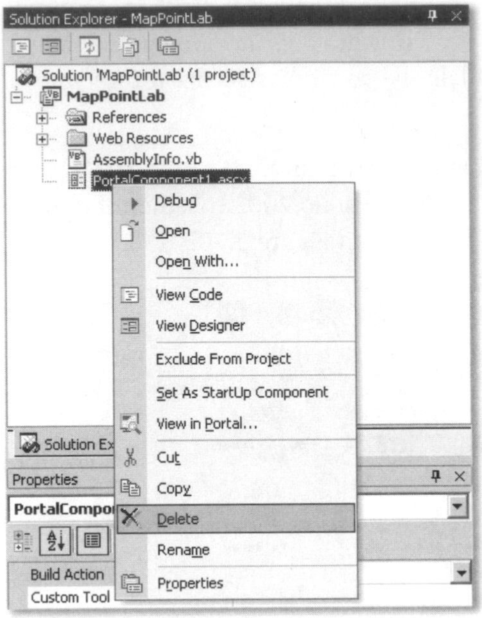

Figure 3.71 Deleting PortalComponent1.ascx

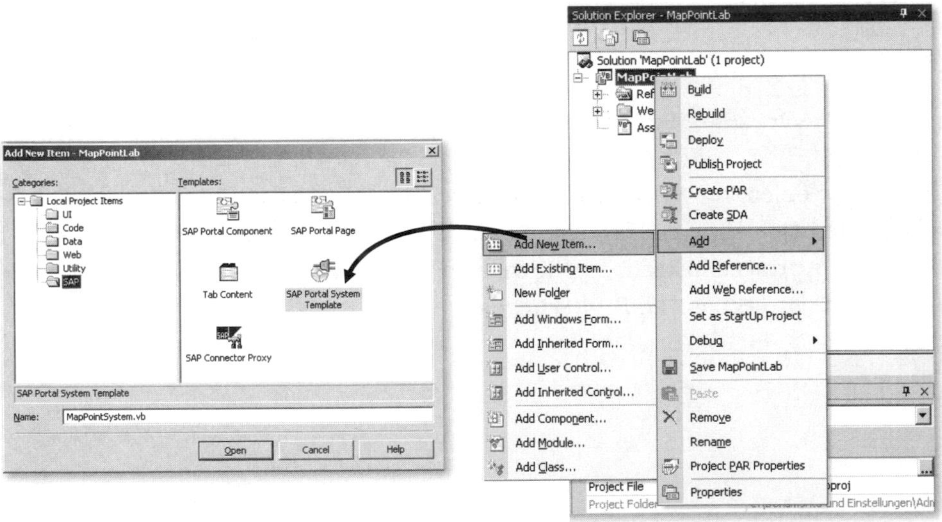

Figure 3.72 Adding the SAP Portals System Template

Code additions

The program code of this file is extended by the following additions that are needed for the Portal System Profile at a later stage:

```
<PortalComponentFieldProperty(PlainDescription:= _
  "SQLConnection String",
PropertyType:=PropertyValueType.String, LongDescription:= _
  "The SQL Connection String",
AdminPersonalization:=PersonalizationType.Dialog, _
  Category:="Application Settings"),
DefaultValue("Server=[host]:[port]; _
  Database=[DB-Name]; Trusted_Connection=False;User _
  ID={0};Password={1}")>
Public ReadOnly Property ConnectionString() As String
 Get
      Return String.Format(Me.GetValue("ConnectionString"),
      Me.MappedUser, Me.MappedPassword)
 End Get
End Property
```

The project must then be created on the SAP Portal for the first time, as illustrated in Figure 3.73. For this purpose, you need to select the **Deploy** menu item.

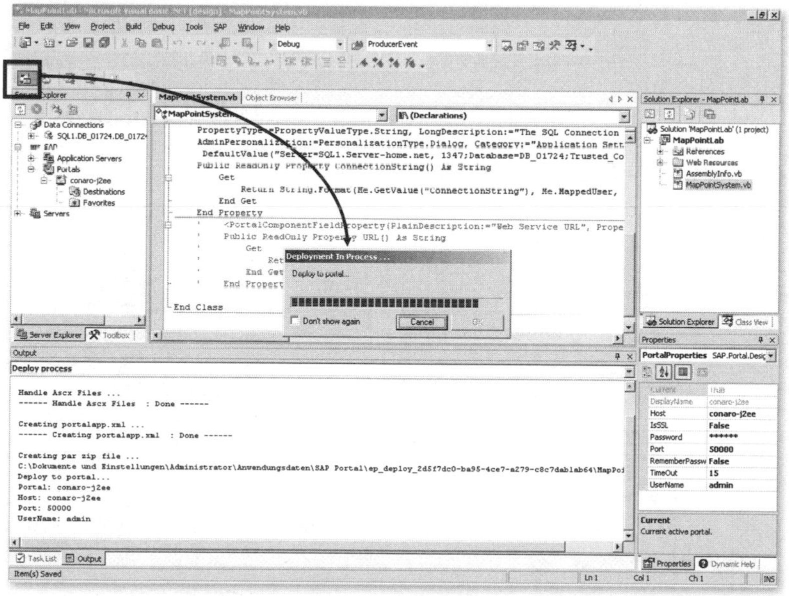

Figure 3.73 Initial Creation of the Mappoint Project in the Portal

Now you need to configure the Portal system that was previously created in the SAP NetWeaver Portal. For this purpose, the Map-PointSystem is created in the **Portal Content Catalog,** which is acces-

Configuring the system

sible via the menu options **System Administration • System Configuration**. Figure 3.74 shows the corresponding entry point.

In the **Portal System Wizard** now displayed, properties like Name (**MapPointSystem**) and System ID (ditto) are created. Figure 3.74 and Figure 3.75 show the individual steps of the Portal System Wizard.

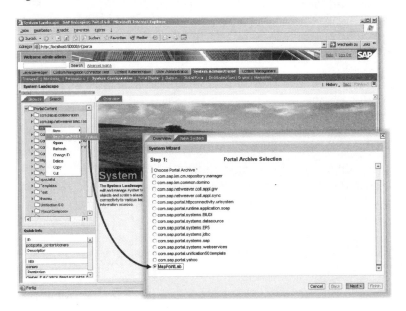

Figure 3.74 Starting the Portal System Wizard

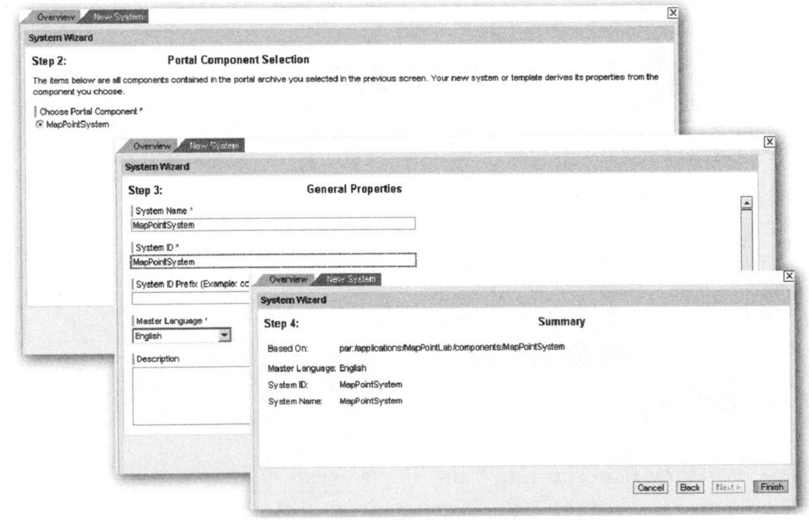

Figure 3.75 Individual Steps of the Portal System Wizard

When installation of Portal System Wizard is complete, the properties of the newly created MapPointSystem can be reviewed. In the **Application Settings** area, for example, the SQL Connection String that was initially created as a property of the system in the file *MapPointSystem.VB* is displayed automatically (see Figure 3.76).

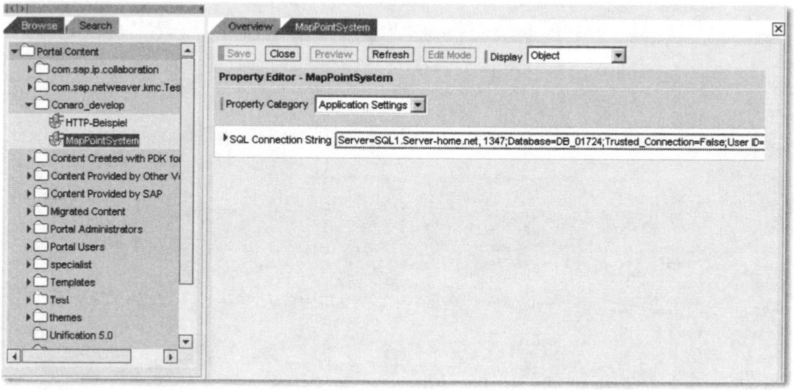

Figure 3.76 Display of the Application Settings

In the next step, a user mapping must be created for the SQL Server data connection in addition to the SQL Connection String that has already been created. For this purpose, you select the User Mapping property. Select the **User Mapping** option in the **Property Category** list, and then select **admin, user** in the **User Mapping Type** list, as shown in Figure 3.77.

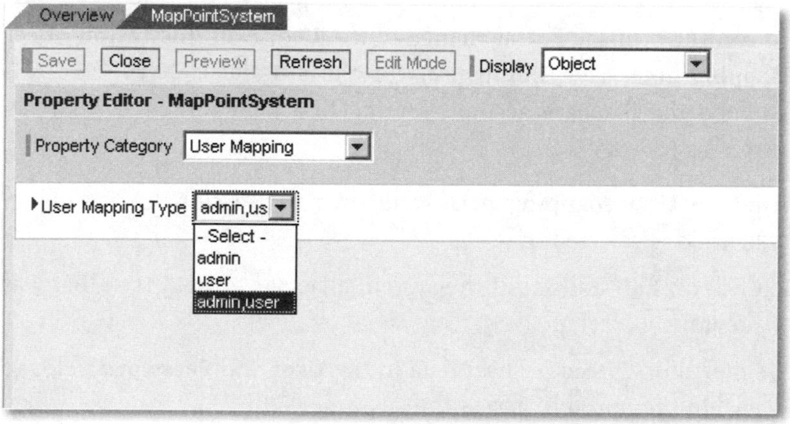

User mapping

Figure 3.77 Assigning a User Mapping Type

System alias   Figure 3.78 shows the next step related to the user mapping: the definition of a system alias. To create it, select **System Alias** from the **Display** list. In this example, the system alias is named `MapPointSystem`. It is added to the Alias list.

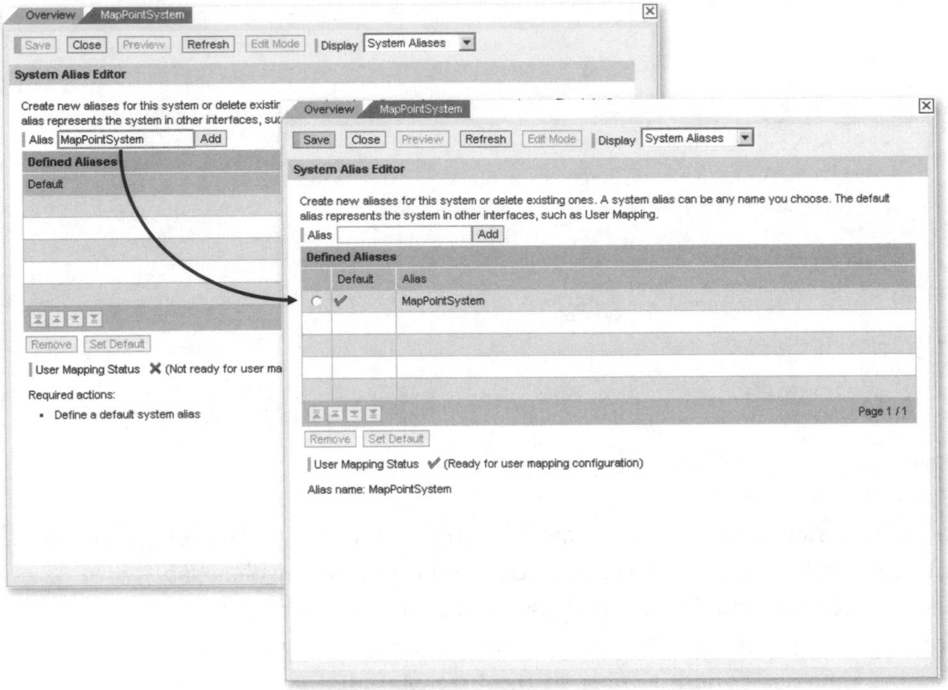

Figure 3.78 Creating a System Alias

To continue, in the Portal change to the **User Administration • User Mapping** area. The Admin user for the system `MapPointSystem` is assigned the database account for the first data source. The procedure is as follows:

1. In the **User Mapping** mask, the user permission to be supplemented is selected.

2. Click on **Edit** and select the system alias `MapPointSystem` that was previously created.

3. Enter the SQL Server user data in the **User** and **Password** fields to enable the portal to access the customer DB.

4. Save the process by clicking on **Save**.

Figure 3.79 shows this procedure.

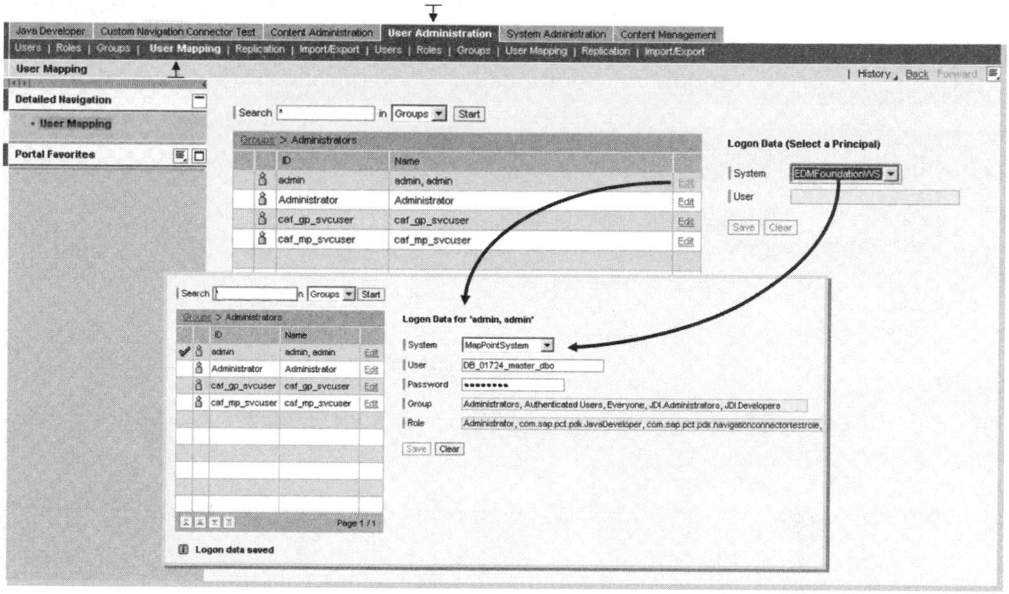

Figure 3.79 Adding the Database Account to the Portal Admin Account

Let's get back to the VS 2003 project. In the next steps, we have to add the portal components and the data sources SQL Server table and Mappoint web service to the project.

Adding data sources

Let's start with the *CustomerFind* portal component. It is used to display the customer data from the SQL Server table Customer, including a filter. The *CustomerFind* portal component is added by selecting the menu option **Add New Item**. In the dialog box, from the **SAP** area select the template **SAP Portal Component** and name it **Customer-Find.ascx**.

The following NetWeaver controls then need to be added to the interface of the *CustomerFind* portal component (see Table 3.1):

NetWeaver controls

Control	ID	Text	Default value
Label	customerLabel	Customer	
InputField	filterInput		A*
Button	searchBtn	Search	
Table	customersTable		

Table 3.1 Controls of the CustomerFind Portal Component

Figure 3.80 shows the selection of the portal component template in the dialog box as well as the finished design of the *CustomerFind* portal component. Additionally, the figure illustrates the database connection `SqlConnection1` and the corresponding database adapter `SqlDataAdapter1`.

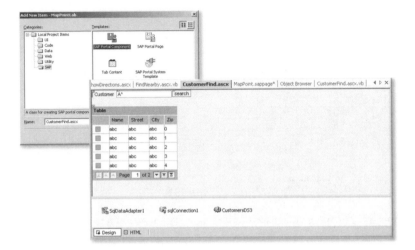

Figure 3.80 Adding and Designing CustomerFind

These can be obtained by selecting the **SqlDataAdapter** object from the VS Toolbox and following the **Data Adapter Configuration Wizard**. At the beginning, this wizard queries the database connection `SqlConnection`. If it has not been already created you can do so.

Creating the SQL statement

In the next step, specify the required SQL statement in the Data Adapter Configuration Wizard. In this example, we want to receive the customer data, so the SQL statement should read as follows:

```
SELECT    Name, Street, City, Zip
FROM      Customers
WHERE     (Name LIKE @fname)
```

In the **Advanced Options** area you have to specify that the `Insert`, `Update`, and `Delete` SQL statements need to be created in **SqlDataAdapter**.

The Data Adapter Configuration Wizard has now created a database connection to the first data source and stored the appropriate SQL statements in the adapter. They are now available to the project.

To be able to use a dataset, select the **Generate Dataset** option from the **Data** menu. In the dialog, specify the appropriate table as the source and select a name for the dataset. In this example, the name is **customersDS**.

Dataset

Figure 3.81 shows the creation of both the SqlDataAdapter and the customer dataset.

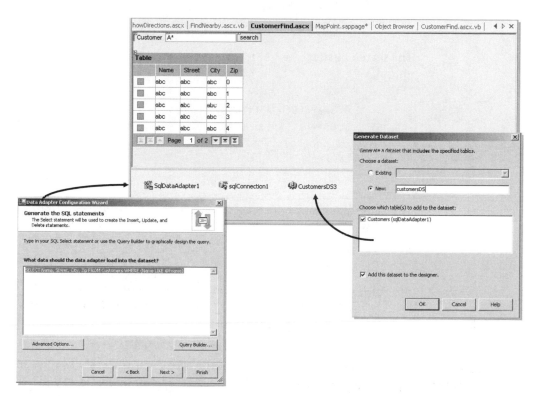

Figure 3.81 Creating the SqlDataAdapter and the Customer DataSet

Only the program code is still missing. To add the functionality of loading the customer data from the SQL Server Customer database table or the corresponding DataSet based on the filter in the filterInput input field to the *CustomerFind* portal component, the following functions must be implemented in the code area of the *CustomerFind* portal component.

Code

The actual data binding function BindData() is the core of this code:

```
Private Sub BindData()
Dim sys As MapPointSystem = _
```

```
  New MapPointSystem("MapPointSystem")
Dim conn As SqlConnection = _
  New SqlConnection(sys.ConnectionString)
SqlDataAdapter1.SelectCommand.Connection = conn
SqlDataAdapter1.SelectCommand.Parameters("@fname").Value = _
  filterInput.Value.Replace("*", "%")
SqlDataAdapter1.Fill(CustomersDS3.Customers)
customersTable.DataBind()
End Sub
```

The search button (`searchBtn`) triggers the `BindData` function shown above:

```
Private Sub searchBtn_Action(ByVal sender _
  As System.Object, ByVal e As _
  SAP.Web.UI.Controls.AbstractButton.ActionEventArgs)
    BindData()
End Sub
```

The same applies for loading (`Page_Load`) the *CustomerFind* portal component:

```
Private Sub Page_Load(ByVal sender As System.Object, _
  ByVal e As System.EventArgs) Handles MyBase.Load
    BindData()
End Sub
```

The project can then be updated in the SAP NetWeaver Portal using the **Deploy** function. If this has been carried out successfully you can right-click the file *CustomerFind.ascx* in the Solution Explorer and use the **View in Portal** function to preview the *CustomerFind* portal component. The result should then appear as shown in Figure 3.82.

Adding MapPoint functionalities
In the next steps, MapPoint functionalities are added to the project. Microsoft MapPoint is a product providing functions in the field of geographical data. It is provided for both a desktop and server versions. In this example, the MapPoint web service server will be addressed. This is achieved via a web service proxy previously mentioned. This web service proxy should be addressed via the next portal component.

The *FindNearby* portal component, for example, is used to display interesting objects like restaurants near a customer's address selected from a list. The *FindNearby* portal component is added to the project just like the *CustomerFind* portal component.

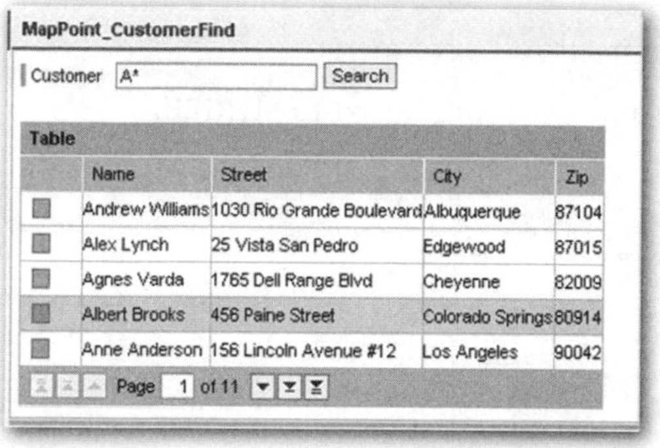

Figure 3.82 Preview of the CustomerFind Component as an iView

The following NetWeaver controls are added to the interface of the *FindNearby* portal component:

NetWeaver controls

Control	ID	Text	Default value
Label	searchLabel	Search for	
DropDownByKey	nearbyTypeDrop		
Table	resultsTable		

Table 3.2 Controls of the FindNearby Portal Component

Figure 3.83 shows how the *FindNearby* portal component is added and designed.

Figure 3.83 Adding and Designing FindNearby

The `resultsTable` table must be revised as follows (see Figure 3.84):

1. In every column, the field name and ID need to be set to **Name**, **Address**, and **Phone**.

2. The **Width** of the columns is to be set to **100**.

3. The **SelectionMode** property should be set to **SINGLE**.

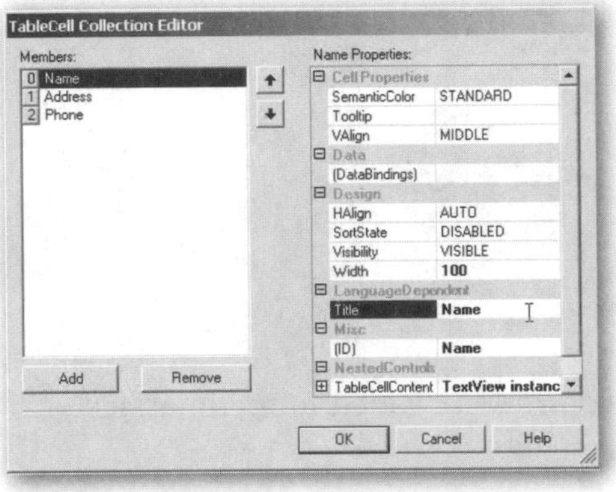

Figure 3.84 Settings of the resultsTable

Integrating the web service proxy

In the next step, the MapPoint web service proxy needs to be integrated. It is added to the project as a WebReference (see Figure 3.85).

As an address, the virtual directory initially created in the IIS is specified:

http://[host]/SAP.Demo.Webservice.Maps/MapServices.asmx

Methods of the MapPoint web service

The project can now use the relevant methods of the MapPoint web service. These are also addressed in the following program code of *FindNearby*. The following functions need to be implemented:

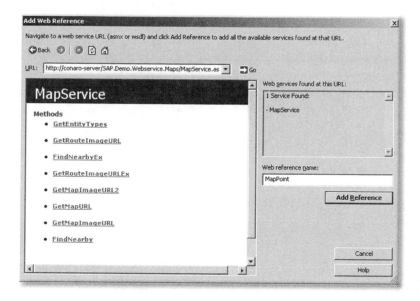

Figure 3.85 Adding the MapPoint Web Service

First, `Page_Load` the *FindNearby* portal component:

```
Private Sub Page_Load(ByVal sender As System.Object, _
  ByVal e As System.EventArgs) Handles MyBase.Load
Dim mapService As MapPoint.MapService = _
  New MapPoint.MapService
Dim entityTypes As String()()
If Cache("EntityTypes") Is Nothing Then
    entityTypes = mapService.GetEntityTypes
    Cache("EntityTypes") = entityTypes
Else
    entityTypes = CType(Cache("EntityTypes"), String())
End If
For Each type As String() In entityTypes
  Dim item As DropDownListItem = New DropDownListItem
  item.Key = type(0)
  item.Text = type(1)
  nearbyTypeDrop.Items.Add(item)
Next
If Not IsPostBack Then
    nearbyTypeDrop.SelectedKey = nearbyTypeDrop.Items(0).Key
End If
If IsPostBack AndAlso Not (Session("Address") Is Nothing) _
  Then
  Dim address As Address = CType(Session("Address"), _
```

```
      Address)
   Dim results As FindResult()
    Dim key As String = address.City.ToString + _
      address.Street + nearbyTypeDrop.SelectedKey
    results = CType(Session(key), FindResult())
    If Not (results Is Nothing) Then
        resultsTable.DataSource = results
          Me.DataBind()
    End If
End If
End Sub
```

Then the display of the results in the table:

```
Private Sub ShowResults(ByVal selectedAddress As Address)
Dim results As FindResult() = Nothing
Dim key As String = selectedAddress.City.ToString +
selectedAddress.Street + nearbyTypeDrop.SelectedKey
If Session(key) Is Nothing Then
    Dim mapService As MapPoint.MapService = _
    New MapPoint.MapService
    Try
       results = mapService.FindNearby(selectedAddress, _
         nearbyTypeDrop.SelectedKey.ToString, 10)
    Catch ex As Exception
       results = New FindResult(0)
    End Try
    Session(key) = results
Else
    results = CType(Session(key), FindResult())
End If
resultsTable.DataSource = results
resultsTable.DataBind()
Session("Address") = selectedAddress
End Sub
Private Sub resultsTable_ItemDatabound(ByVal sender _
  As Object, ByVal e As _
  SAP.Web.UI.Controls.Table.ItemEventArgs)
Dim findResult As FindResult = _
  CType(e.Item.DataSourceRow.DataItem, FindResult)
CType(e.Item.Cells(0).TableCellEditor, _
  SAP.Web.UI.Controls.TextView).Text = findResult.Name
CType(e.Item.Cells(1).TableCellEditor, _
  SAP.Web.UI.Controls.TextView).Text = _
  findResult.Address.Street
CType(e.Item.Cells(2).TableCellEditor, _
```

```
      SAP.Web.UI.Controls.TextView).Text = findResult.Phone
End Sub
Private Sub nearbyTypeDrop_Select(ByVal sender As Object, _
  ByVal e As _
  SAP.Web.UI.Controls.AbstractDropDownByKey.SelectEventArgs)
Dim address As Address = CType(Session("Address"), Address)
ShowResults(address)
End Sub
```

Additionally, the following needs to be added to the Namespace area in the *CustomerFind* portal component for the server-side communication between the two portal components (iViews):

```
Namespace MapPointLab
  <ProducerEvent("AddressSelected", _
  EventType.ServerSide)>
```

Moreover, the following program code needs to be implemented:

```
Private Sub customersTable_LeadSelect(ByVal sender As _
  System.Object, ByVal e As _
  SAP.Web.UI.Controls.Table.LeadSelectEventArgs)
Dim row As customersDS.CustomersRow = _
  CType(CustomersDS3.Customers.Rows(e.Row), _
  customersDS.CustomersRow)
Dim address As Address = New Address
address.City = row.City
address.Street = row.Street
address.ZipCode = row.Zip.ToString
Raise("AddressSelected", New Object() {address})
End Sub
```

In the Namespace area of the *FindNearby* portal component, the following must be added:

```
Namespace MapPointLab
<ConsumerEvent("OnAddressSelected", _
  EventType.ServerSide)>
```

Thus, the ProducerEvent (*CustomerFind*) and the ConsumerEvent (*FindNearby*) have been properly declared. Now the following functions must be added to the *FindNearby* portal component:

```
Public Overloads Overrides Sub _
  OnPortalComponentEvent(ByVal sender As Object, _
  ByVal eventName As String, ByVal args As Object())
MyBase.OnPortalComponentEvent(sender, eventName, args)
If eventName = "OnAddressSelected" Then
  onAddressSelected(CType(args(0), Address))
End If
End Sub
```

This is the function for the onAddressSelected event that, in turn, calls the ShowResults function:

```
Private Sub onAddressSelected(ByVal selectedAddress _
  As Address)
  ShowResults(selectedAddress)
End Sub
```

To complete this step, the project must be updated again using the **Deploy** function in the SAP NetWeaverPortal.

Portal Page Designer The next step uses an extension of the PDK for .NET, version 2.0: the Portal Page Designer. An *SAP Portal Page* named *MapPoint.sappage* is added to the project, as you can see in Figure 3.86.

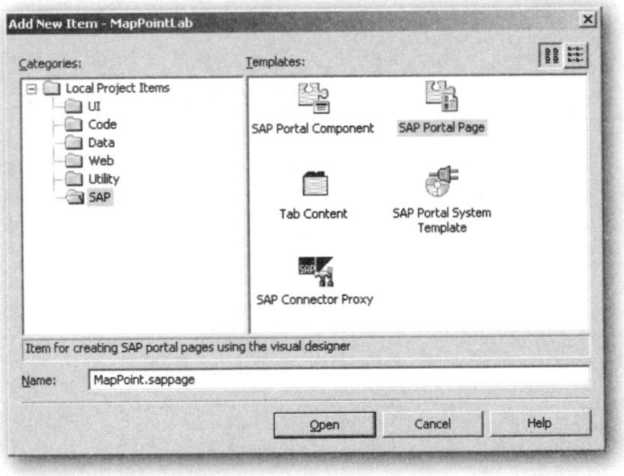

Figure 3.86 Adding the MapPoint SAP Page

Immediately after it has been created in the project, the project should be published in the SAP NetWeaver Portal. This is achieved via the **Publish Project** function. This not only updates the project in the SAP NetWeaver Portal but also creates subfolders for the iViews

184

and the SAP page in the area **Content Created with PDK for .NET** in the Portal Content Catalog.

If this has been completed successfully a double-click on the *MapPoint.sappage* file in the Solution Explorer opens the Portal Page Designer in VS.

To insert the portal components created so far in the SAP page, just drag the files from the Solution Explorer to the **Layout** tab of the Portal Page Designer.

The Portal Page Designer also supports you in linking the server events of the two portal components. The **Events** tab shows both portal components with their corresponding events, and you can select the events to be linked by using the mouse. In particular, the AdressSelected event of *CustomerFind* needs to be dragged and dropped on the OnAdressSelected event of *FindNearby*. Figure 3.87 shows both of the described procedures. Again, it is then recommended to update the project in the SAP Netweaver Portal.

Linking server events

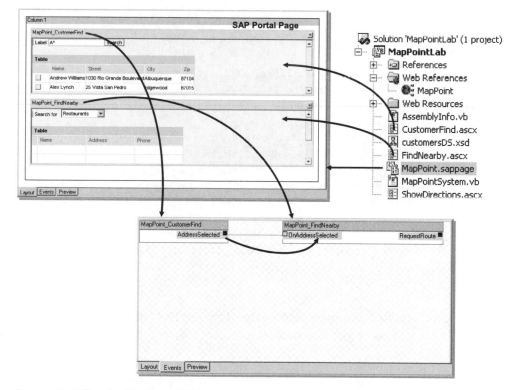

Figure 3.87 Filling the MapPoint SAP Page

As the last element, a portal component is added that, as a special feature, displays a MapPoint map suggesting a route between the selected customer address and the interesting object selected in *FindNearby*.

The *ShowDirections* portal component is added according to the procedure used for the two previous portal components. Its only control is the image control for the map to be displayed.

Server-side communication

Similar to the communication between *CustomerFind* and *FindNearby*, a server-side communication must be implemented between *FindNearby* and *ShowDirections* as well. For this purpose, the following must be added in the namespace area of the *FindNearby* portal component:

```
Namespace MapPointLab
<ConsumerEvent("OnAddressSelected", _
  EventType.ServerSide),
ProducerEvent("RequestRoute", EventType.ServerSide)>
```

Additionally, the following program code needs to be implemented in the *FindNearby* portal component:

```
Private Sub resultsTable_LeadSelect(ByVal sender _
  As Object, ByVal e As _
  SAP.Web.UI.Controls.Table.LeadSelectEventArgs)
Dim findResult As FindResult = _
  CType(resultsTable.DataSource, FindResult())(e.Row)
Dim fromAddress As Address = _
  CType(Session("Address"), Address)
Dim toAddress As Address = New Address
toAddress.City = findResult.Address.City
toAddress.Street = findResult.Address.Street
toAddress.ZipCode = findResult.Address.ZipCode.ToString
Raise("RequestRoute", New Object() {fromAddress, _
  toAddress})
End Sub
```

In the Namespace area of the *ShowDirections* portal component, the following must be added:

```
Namespace MapPointLab
 <ConsumerEvent("OnRequestRoute", _
   EventType.ServerSide)>
```

And as program code:

```
Public Overloads Overrides Sub
  OnPortalComponentEvent(ByVal sender As Object, _
  ByVal eventName As String, ByVal args As Object())
MyBase.OnPortalComponentEvent(sender, eventName, args)
If eventName = "OnRequestRoute" Then
  onRequestRoute(CType(args(0), MapPoint.Address), _
    CType(args(1), MapPoint.Address))
End If
End Sub
```

And the function for calling the map URL of the MapPoint web service must be added:

```
Private Sub onRequestRoute(ByVal fromAddress As _
  MapPoint.Address, ByVal toAddress As _
  MapPoint.Address)
Dim mapService As MapPoint.MapService = _
  New MapPoint.MapService
mapImage.Source = _
  mapService.GetRouteImageURL(fromAddress, toAddress, _
  Int32.Parse(mapImage.Height), _
  Int32.Parse(mapImage.Width), 100)
mapImage.Visible = True
End Sub
```

Now the *ShowDirections* portal component can be inserted in the SAP page via Drag&Drop from the Solution Explorer to the **Layout** tab of the Portal Page Designer. Afterward, on the **Events** tab of the Portal Page Designer, the events of *FindNearby*, attribute RequestRoute, and of *ShowDirections*, attribute OnRequestRoute, need to be linked.

After everything has been successfully updated and published in the SAP NetWeaver Portal, the result should look as shown in Figure 3.88.

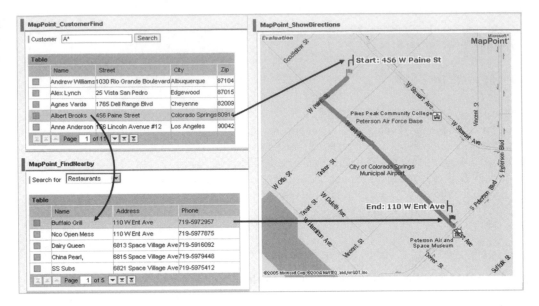

Figure 3.88 Result of the MapPointLab Portal Application

3.2.3 Collaboration

In addition to the individual development option using the PDK for .NET, the area of portal integration also includes the area of *Collaboration*. Collaboration refers to the cross-department or cross-enterprise cooperation of individual employees or virtual teams of any combination. Several users are involved in creating and editing documents and data.

In SAP NetWeaver, the Collaboration area is a part of the SAP NetWeaver Portal. In this context, we refer to *Collaboration Services*. Figure 3.89 shows an overview of the components of collaboration services in the SAP NetWeaver Portal. These services can be addressed both via the *Collaboration Launch Pad* (CLP) and in a *Collaboration Room*[17].

---

17 A Collaboration Room is a virtual room that can be used as a work platform. Depending on the user's authorization, there can be different variants of a public room or a private room.

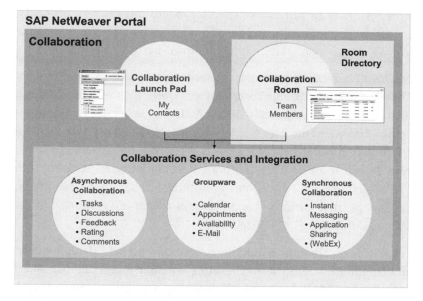

Figure 3.89 Overview of Collaboration Services in the Portal

The CLP is intended as a central point of entry for the user to collaborate. It is designed as a tool collection and provides functions like *instant messaging* or *application sharing*. Figure 3.90 shows how the CLP provides all functions as a package to the portal user in the form of a standalone menu.

Collaboration
Launch Pad

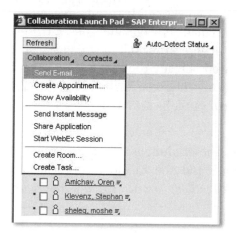

Figure 3.90 The Collaboration Launch Pad

189

However, the CLP can also be used for extensions of other products. In addition to the integration of real-time service providers like WebEx it is also possible to integrate third-party solutions.

Collaboration with SharePoint Microsoft now also provides collaboration functionalities with its SharePoint Products and Technologies. These include the Windows SharePoint Services (usually licensed already as a part of Windows Server 2003) and the superior SharePoint Portal Server, which virtually functions as a meta team site and contributes extended navigation, search and a number of other enterprise features. In contrast to SAP Collaboration, SharePoint is administered rather decentrally, can be operated intuitively and provides a tight integration with the various components of Office 2003.

It might seem obvious to link these collaboration modules. However, this should be examined to determine whether it makes sense and if it is required at all. Is there really a scenario where employees work together in both collaboration areas and therefore need the integration? In our opinion, probably not. Either you work together with your colleagues in the one collaboration room or in the other, but not in both; the effort necessary to make a bridge is usually not worth it.

Although a collaboration integration with the corresponding functionalities of Microsoft SharePoint makes sense only to a limited extent, an integration with the groupeware Microsoft Exchange is more worthwhile because the mail functionality of Microsoft Exchange is often a standard in an enterprise, and the calendar functions in Exchange or Outlook were already used by the employees even before a portal was introduced. The reconciliation of this data is therefore a realistic scenario. How can it be achieved?

Groupeware integration with MS Exchange SAP provides solutions for the groupware integration of IBM Lotus Notes and Microsoft Exchange. These solutions, however, primarily support the transport of e-mail and the calendar reconciliation (*scheduling*). This is achieved via the *Collaboration Groupware Framework* (see Figure 3.91).

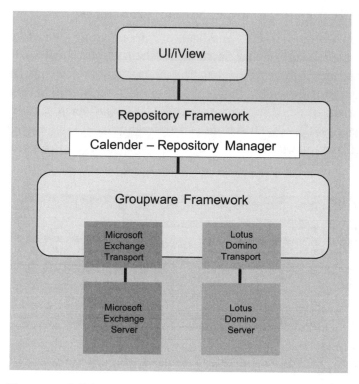

Figure 3.91 Collaboration Groupware Framework

This framework provides appropriate APIs for the integration with the Microsoft Exchange Server. For this purpose, an API set called *Transports* must be implemented. The configuration iView records the specifications for the e-mail transport (e.g., the SMTP server), then the e-mail service containing the activation mechanism for sending e-mails must be configured, and the user or the account in whose name the e-mails are to be sent is assigned.

However, please note that the access to more contents of the Microsoft Exchange Server, like *public folders*, cannot be implemented using this technology. But there are other possibilities that will be discussed in Chapter 4.

3.2.4 Exchange Integration: Outlook Web Access

Outlook Web Access integration

In addition to the described approach of implementing Microsoft Exchange e-mail and calendar functions via the transport functionality, there is another alternative that: The integration of the web variant of Microsoft Outlook, *Microsoft Outlook Web Access 2003*. This online variant of Outlook is based on ASP.NET, and version 2003 provides almost the same functions and a user interface that is nearly identical to the full version of Microsoft Outlook, as shown in Figure 3.92.

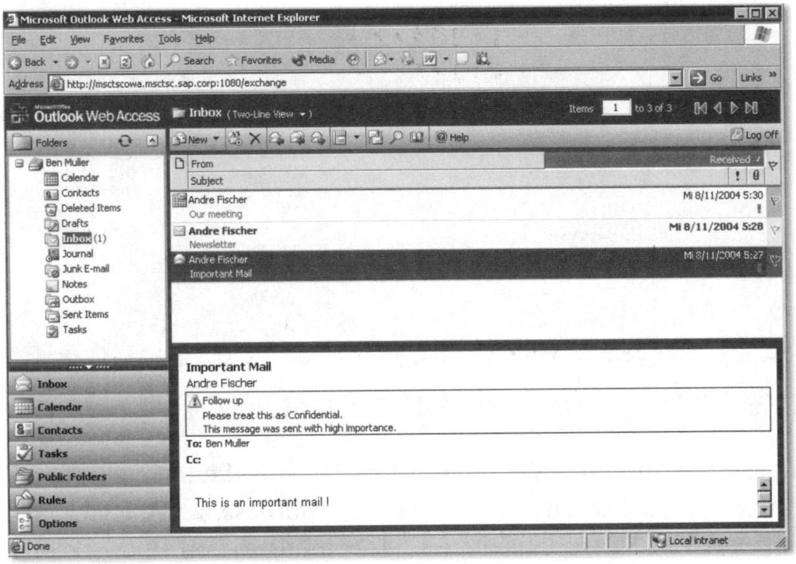

Figure 3.92 Microsoft Outlook Web Access 2003 (OWA)

OWA 2003 is integrated by manually configuring the SAP NetWeaver Portal Content Catalog via an iView template (see Figure 3.93)—in this example via the Application Integration iView template and, more specifically by using the URL capture, as shown in Figure 3.94.

User authorization, single sign-on

In addition to the frontend integration via the URL integration, user authorization and single sign-on must be considered. After all, the mail and calendar of the respective user are to be displayed continuously, and he should not have to log on several times.

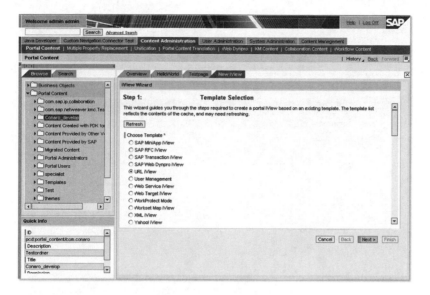

Figure 3.93 URL iView Template

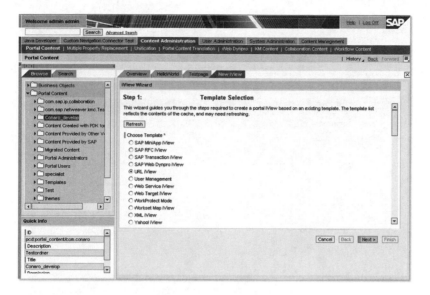

Figure 3.94 Specification of the URL in the iView Wizard

To access the OWA inbox, calendar, tasks and contact folder, the respective folder must be integrated. However, the problem of the *ExchangeAlias* first needs to be solved. What does that mean? For example, the URL for directly accessing the calendar folder of the OWA is:

http://<server>:<port>/Exchange/myExchangeAlias/Calendar/ ?cmd=contents.

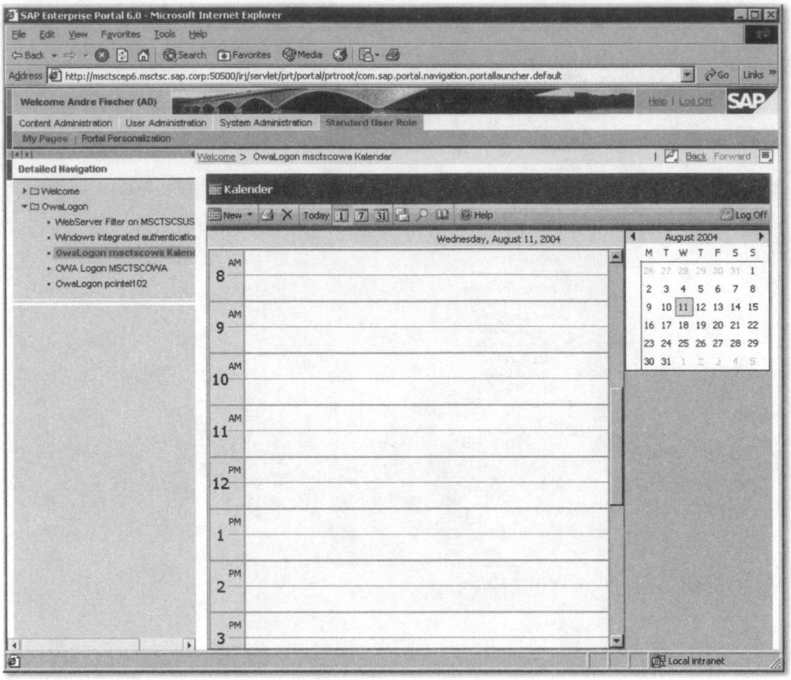

Figure 3.95 Integration of the OWA Calendar in the Portal

For the iView, this *myExchangeAlias* must be named depending on the respective portal user. Because the user is known in the SAP Portal, the user data of the SAP NetWeaver Portal can be mapped to the ExchangeAlias.

The following adaptation of the portal configuration file *dataSourceConfiguration.xml* enables a mapping between the SAP Portal user attribute and the ExchangeAlias:

```
<responsibleFor>
<principal type="user">
<nameSpaces>
  <nameSpace
    name="com.sap.security.core.usermanagement">
    <attributes>
      ...
      <attribute name="myexchangealias"/>
    </attributes>
    <attributeMapping>
      <principals>
```

```
        <principal type="user">
        <nameSpace
         name="com.sap.security.core.usermanagement">
        <attributes>
           <attribute name="myexchangealias">
               <physicalAttribute name="mailnickname">
           </attribute>
        </attributes>
     </nameSpace>
  </nameSpace>
```

For example, to integrate the OWA calendar of the respective user in the SAP NetWeaver Portal it is necessary to create a generic iView based on the SAP NetWeaver Portal application com.sap.portal.appintegrator.sap. Then the properties of the iView need to be edited. Particularly the **URL-Template** property needs to be configured using the following notation:

Setting up a URL template

http://<server_hostname>:<port>/Exchange/<User.UserID>/Calendar/?cmd=contents

or, as described above:

http://<server_hostname>:<port>/Exchange/<User.myexchangealias>/Calendar/?cmd=contents

Then the SAP NetWeaver Portal shows the Exchange/Outlook calendar will show the user logged on to the SAP NetWeaver Portal.

However, please note that this is a pure frontend integration. The SAP Collaboration calendar and the integrated Outlook calendar are not reconciled.

Information is an important commodity for companies. For this reason, providing information plays an important role from the perspective of interoperability and integration. This chapter discusses the options for integrating products with an emphasis on information management of Microsoft and SAP (BI and KM).

4 Information Integration

Microsoft and SAP offer products that can manage or process data and information in both unstructured and structured forms. For SAP, this involves SAP NetWeaver Business Intelligence and the SAP NetWeaver Portal (formerly SAP Enterprise Portal), including knowledge management (KM); for Microsoft, this means the SQL Server, Microsoft Exchange Server 2003, and the SharePoint products.

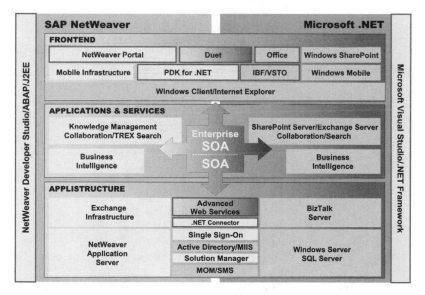

Figure 4.1 Information Interoperability between SAP and Microsoft

Figure 4.1 shows the many different combinations of interoperability scenarios between Microsoft and SAP products and systems; some will be reviewed in this chapter.

4.1 SAP Business Information Warehouse

The *SAP Business Information Warehouse* (BW) is the central component of *SAP NetWeaver Business Intelligence* (BI). This is SAP's *data warehouse* solution and its job is to provide company data, the so-called business content, in a processed and structured way. These solutions can include structured data from SAP ERP systems and data from third-party systems.

Components of SAP BW

Figure 4.2 shows the components of SAP BW. It consists of:

▸ SAP BW Server

▸ Open Hub Services

▸ Business Explorer (BEx) Suite

▸ Administrator Workbench

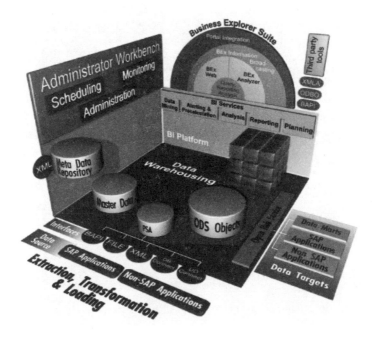

Figure 4.2 Overview of the Components of SAP BW

Within the SAP BW Server, the following components play a role in the movement of of structured data:

▶ Persistent Staging Area (PSA) with the Staging Engine

▶ Operational Data Store (ODS) with the ODS objects

▶ InfoCubes, that is, the OLAP Cubes of SAP BW

Two routes must be considered for integration scenarios, in addition to the display of data via the SAP BW frontend, for the Business Explorer (BEx) Suite: the route of the data into SAP BW, and the route of the data out of SAP BW; in other words, accessing SAP BW data from outside. This will be discussed in Sections 4.1.2 and 4.1.3 respectively.

But first, we will a look at an integrated Microsoft/SAP solution that has existed since the introduction of SAP BW: The SAP BW Business Explorer Suite (BEx Suite).

4.1.1 Business Explorer Suite (BEx Suite)

The Business Explorer Suite is the first point of contact for SAP BW users. It offers a range of tools for SAP BW data consumers to define and compile queries, reports, and analyses (see Figure 4.3).

Components of the BEx Suite

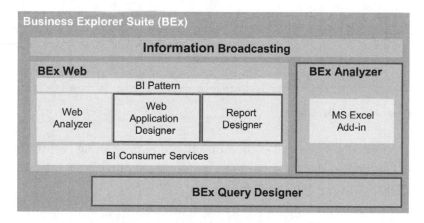

Figure 4.3 Elements of the Business Explorer Suite

The following BEx components will be discussed in further detail:

▶ BEx Analyzer

▶ BEx Query Designer

▸ BEx Report Designer

▸ BEx Web Application Designer

While the *BEx Analyzer* is an add-in for Microsoft Excel, the last three components mentioned are particularly interesting because they are applications that were recently developed for the current version of Visual Basic .NET and are based on the Microsoft .NET Framework.

BEx Query Designer

The *BEx Query Designer* (see Figure 4.4) is a stand-alone desktop application for defining multidimensional data queries from SAP BW. Here it provides functions for selecting the data basis (InfoCubes), defining the key figures and dimensions of the query and storing the defined query both in an Excel workbook and on the SAP BW system.

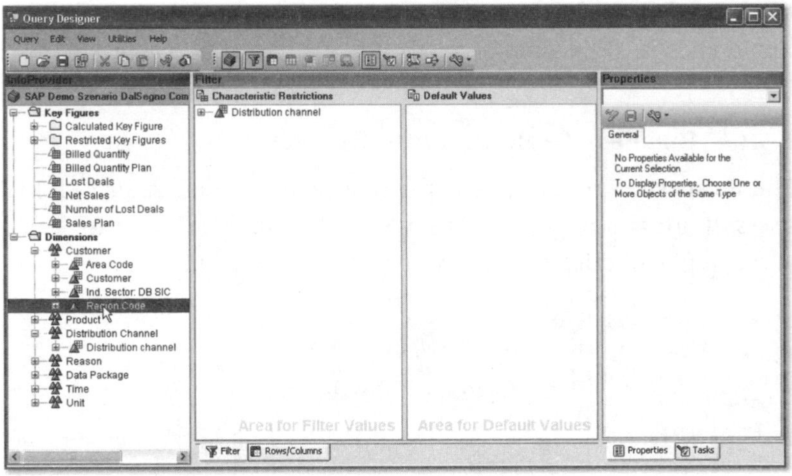

Figure 4.4 BEx Query Designer

BEx Report Designer

The *BEx Report Designer* is the BEx Suite tool for creating reports. It draws on the queries that were previously created with the BEx Query Designer (see Figure 4.5).

The reports created with the BEx Report Designer control the *drill-down* and *drill-up* functions, which navigate within multidimensional data structures, as well as the *slice and dice function*. These functions support the possibility of individual views. Here, *slice* describes the possibility of cutting individual slices from the OLAP Cube, while *dice* describes a view shift or a "tipping" of this view.

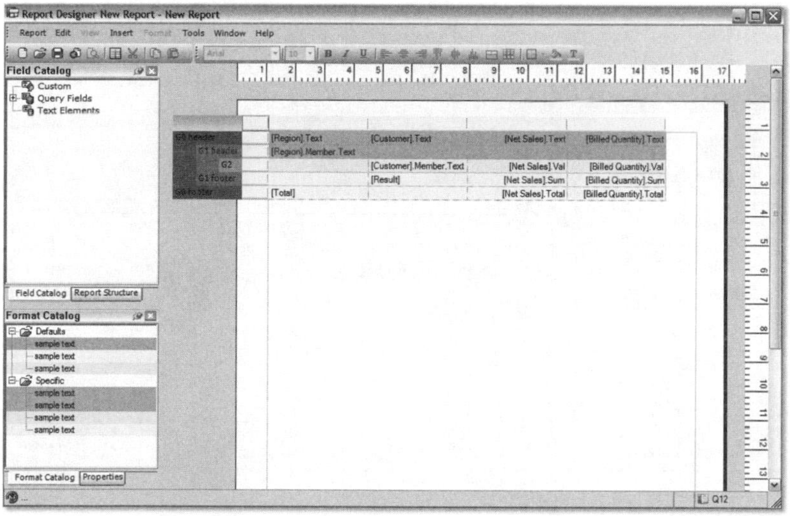

Figure 4.5 BEx Report Designer

The *BEx Web Application Designer* is a desktop application for creating Web applications that contain or show SAP BW-specific content. SAP describes the elements of such a Web application as *Web Items*, which may be tables, queries, diagrams, reports or cards, which create a HTML page with BW-specific content. Furthermore, the BEx Web Application Designer can also create these Web Items as iViews directly in the portal (Figure 4.6).

BEx Web Application Designer

The *BEx Analyzer* is different from the tools previously described because it is an add-in for Microsoft Excel. It both enhances Microsoft Excel with SAP BW functions and uses the full range of Excel functions. It offers a possible frontend next to Web applications created by the BEx Web Application Designer and the SAP NetWeaver Portal (see Figure 4.7). Like the other BEx components, the BEx Analyzer has been considerably reworked and is available in a new version for Microsoft Excel 2003 and SAP NetWeaver BI.

BEx Analyzer

The current version of Bex Analyzer differs from its predecessors in a number of ways.

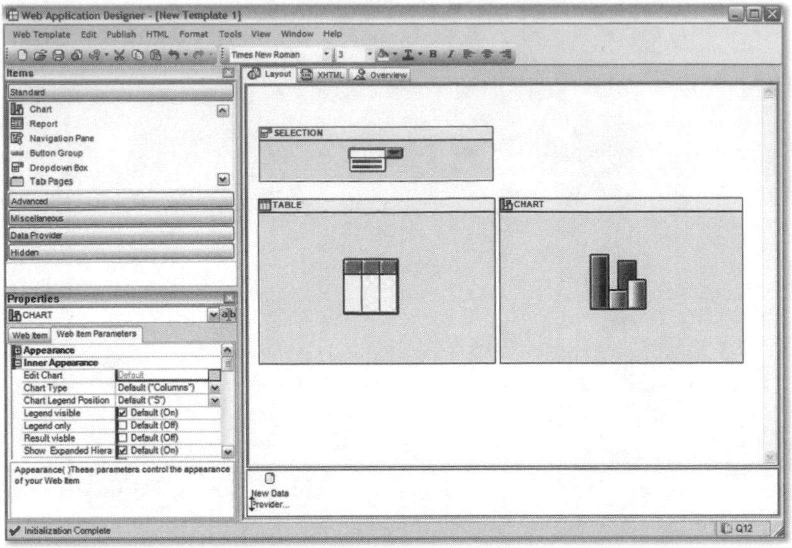

Figure 4.6 BEx Web Application Designer

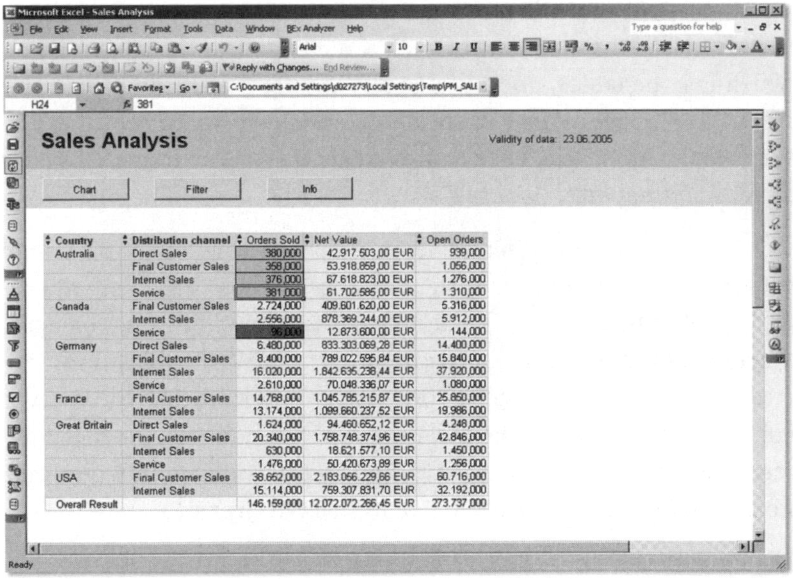

Figure 4.7 Excel and the New BEx Analyzer

Design mode   Design mode is the most outstanding new feature. It supports the creation of BI applications directly in Excel and its operation is similar to that of the BEx Web Application Designer. Figure 4.8 provides a primary insight into design mode. Each BI InfoProvider can be integrated into Microsoft Excel here. SAP delivers a range of design items for creating Excel-based applications, which are objects that call data from data providers. The two most important ones are the analysis table, which displays the results of a query, and the navigation area, which provides access to all the characteristics and structures in the query that can be used for navigation and analysis.

Additional design items include, among others, a dropdown box, a checkbox group and a radiobutton group, which allow you to set a filter through a dropdown box, a check box or a selection button.

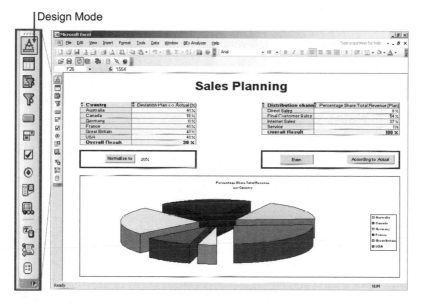

Figure 4.8 Design Mode of the New BEx Analyzer

The integration with Microsoft Excel has been further improved. In analysis mode you can run OLAP analyses on queries that have been created with the BEx Query Designer. The results of the query are shown in the design item *analysis table*. In this table, together with the design item *navigation area* and other design items, you can navigate through the context menu by a simple drag and drop or using symbols, such as sorting, opening or closing hierarchies.

User interaction (analysis mode)

Furthermore, it is now possible to activate each InfoProvider from Excel; in earlier versions it was only possible to access InfoCubes or the corresponding queries or query views.

Local calculations can easily be inserted by the user through the context menu into the Excel Workbook, which will present a subset of the options available in the Query Designer. The formulas are created using an intuitive dialog box with simple buttons. The calculations created in this way can be stored together with the Excel Workbook.

If a query has been defined as ready for input in BEx Query Designer, you can insert data into the cells that are ready for input. Planning functions are executed in this way.

Excel formatting and formulas

BEx Analyzer also offers a new function that allows the native formatting possibilities that Excel provides to be fully used for BEx Workbooks. This includes, among other things, the use of blank rows and different fonts. Each cell in the result set is described by the Excel function `BexGetData`. The combination of Excel formatting and formulas allows high-quality formatted workbooks to be created. These functions can be used for every query, and every query view or Info Provider (see Figure 4.9).

DalSegno *Your Source for Promotional Materials*

Income Statement September 2005

all financial figures in mio EUR

	Variance in Mio EUR			Variance in %		
	vs Last Cycle	vs Previous year	vs Budget	vs Last Cycle	vs Previous Year	vs Budget
Total Revenues	39.7	39.7	58.3	4.9 %	4.9 %	7.4 %
Total Net Sales	37.7	37.7	57.4	4.7 %	4.7 %	7.3 %
Indirect Sales	1.8	1.8	2.1	59.8 %	59.8 %	79.4 %
Sales to Other Division	0.5	0.5	-0.6	7.5 %	7.5 %	-8.0 %
Sales to Own Division	35.5	35.5	55.9	4.5 %	4.5 %	7.2 %
Total Other Revenues From Indirect Sales	2	2	0.9	59.7 %	59.7 %	19.0 %
Revenues From Indirect Sales Royalties	0.5	0.5	0.2	22.7 %	22.7 %	6.2 %
Revenues From Tele Sales	1.4	1.4	0.5	100.0 %	100.0 %	58.5 %
Other Revenues From Indirect Sales	0.1	0.1	0.2	10.9 %	10.9 %	18.2 %
Total Costs	-46.3	-46.3	-30.5	-11.4 %	-11.4 %	-7.3 %
% of Sales						
Total Costs for Production	-47.1	-47.1	-30.5	-12.1 %	-12.1 %	-7.5 %
Costs Own Division	-2.8	-2.8	-2.4	-44.7 %	-44.7 %	-36.6 %
Manufacturing Costs	0.8	0.8	2.5	19.5 %	19.5 %	44.4 %
Variances & Write-offs	2.3	2.3	-4.5	11.7 %	11.7 %	-35.3 %
Total Other Related Costs	0.8	0.8		5.3 %	5.3 %	-0.2 %
Amortization Related to Marketable Products			0.2	-1.1 %	-1.1 %	8.0 %
Royalties On Licensed Products	0.8	0.8	-0.2	6.3 %	6.3 %	-1.6 %
Other Product Related Costs						
Gross Profit	-6.6	-6.6	27.8	-1.6 %	-1.6 %	7.6 %

Figure 4.9 Formatted Excel Workbook with Additional Local Excel Authorizations (Created in Formula Mode)

4.1.2 Uploading Data in SAP BW

There is no point in having a data warehouse without data—it must be filled with data uploaded from different source systems. And you can't talk about the data warehouse area without discussing extraction, transformation and loading (ETL). With SAP BW, this is done in the first stage in the *Persistent Staging Area* (PSA). Here, the data is first stored unchanged using different tools. So, we are already in the SAP BW data loading process, which we will look at more closely.

Generally, the data loading process is always controlled from SAP BW. It is the active system. This means that the data loading process must be defined and saved in SAP BW but is also executed by SAP BW by using the "Pull" procedure.

Pull procedure

The data loading process is defined by:

▸ a source system

▸ an InfoSource as the target

▸ one or several DataSource(s) from the source system

▸ the assignment of the DataSource and InfoSource

▸ the update rules

▸ the transfer rules

Figure 4.10 shows an example of the source system selecting data. Figure 4.11 shows the application of the update and transfer rules.

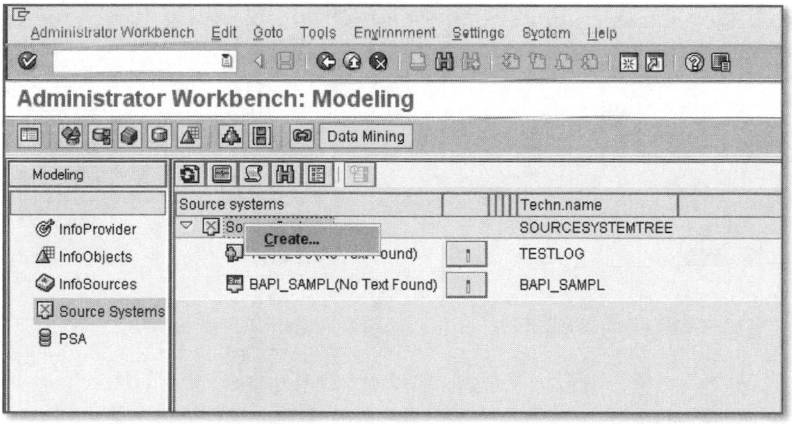

Figure 4.10 Selecting the Source System

InfoSource	BTCTAGGRST	Aggregation level	

Communication_Struct.

Transfer_Structure/Transfer_Rules

Source System			Transfer Method
DataSource			○ PSA
Status			○ IDoc

DataSource/Trans. Structure | Transfer Rules

Communication str./Transfer rules

InfoObject	Descript.		Tp	Rule	

Assign.InfObjct-field

InfoObject	Descript.	Field	

Figure 4.11 Fixing the Transfer Rules

Data that has been uploaded into the SAP BW staging area is consolidated in the next step and written in cleaned-up form either to Info-Cubes or the *Operational Data Store* (ODS) objects, as illustrated in Figure 4.12.

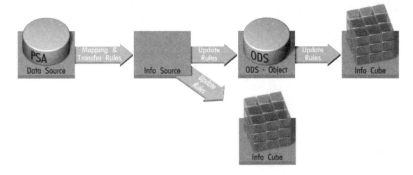

Figure 4.12 From the Staging Area to the InfoCubes

There are various ways to upload external data into the PSA of the
SAP BW Server. Often a flat-file import is used. However, the corresponding data can also be uploaded using the *Staging BAPIs* (BW-
STA) (see Figure 4.13). These business object methods play a decisive
role in the data loading process.

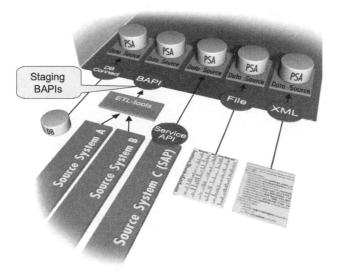

Figure 4.13 Staging BAPIs

Their methods are described as *Staging BAPIs*:

▶ **Business Object** InfoObject

▶ **Business Object** SourceSystem

▶ **Business Object** DataProvider

▶ **Business Object** InfoSourceTrans

▶ **Business Object** InfoSourceTransXfer

▶ **Business Object** InfoSourceMaster

▶ **Business Object** InfoSourceMasterXfer

▶ **Business Object** InfoSourceHirchyXfer

All of these objects can be accessed and used using the BAPI interface
previously discussed in Chapter 2 with Microsoft Visual Studio 2003
and the SAP Connector for Microsoft .NET 2.0. Figure 4.14 shows
the objects in the Visual Studio 2003 server explorer. By doing this,

an application based on the .NET Framework could externally define and manage the data loading process.

Figure 4.14 Staging BAPI in the Server Explorer

SOAP transfer   In the age of XML, SOAP and Web services there is yet another variant for uploading the data into SAP BW—SOAP-based transfer of data. Unlike the Pull method, which is the primary data loading function for SAP BW (in which the data loading process is controlled from SAP BW), in this variant the data is delivered from outside into an inbound queue in SAP BW. This inbound queue is the Delta queue of the Service API for SAP BW, which means that the data is loaded using the Delta process. This variant is only an addition to the actual uploading of (mass) data, which runs in the file transfer, for example. You must take this into account accordingly (see Figure 4.15).

The starting point in this variant is a DataSource file. When you define the transfer rules you have the option of specifying that it is a DataSource with a SOAP connection. An XML DataSource is then generated in the Workbench. This is required for the Delta queue and is intended for loading the Delta data records. For this XML DataSource, a function module (RFC) is also generated that posts the incoming data. This RFC is created in the function group /BIO/QI<xml-datasource> and has the name /BIO/QI <xml-data-source>_RFC, where <xml-Datasource> is the name of the XML DataSource. This DataSource is also the import parameter of the RFC.

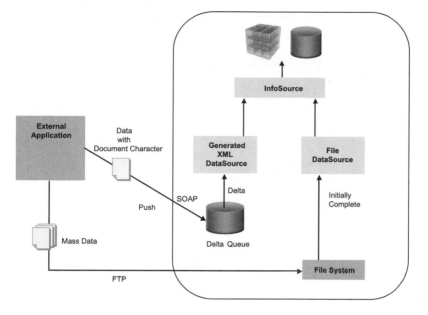

Figure 4.15 SOAP Transfer Process

This RFC can now be activated from outside after the activation of the data transfer, e. g., via a web service. From the Delta queue, the data is processed further with the staging methods already described.

However, you must be aware of the following restriction: only flat structures can be used during this SOAP-based transfer. In particular, hierarchy data cannot be transferred by this means.

Restriction during the SOAP transfer

4.1.3 Open Analysis Interfaces

Now, since SAP BW is an open architecture, there are a number of possibilities to access the SAP BW data for reporting purposes through an alternative frontend tool.

SAP BW Open Analysis Interfaces play the most important role here. They provide a group of interface technologies that allow external applications to address queries to the SAP BW system MDX processor. MDX stands for *MultiDimensional Expression* and is a query language for multidimensional data similar to the SQL syntax. An MDX query always returns a multidimensional result set (see Figure 4.16).

MDX

The SAP BW Open Analysis Interfaces include:

► OLAP-BAPI

► XML for Analysis (XMLA)

► OLE DB for OLAP (ODBO)

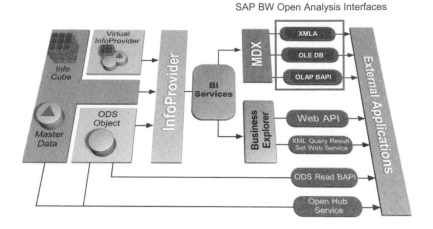

Figure 4.16 Overview of SAP BW Open Analysis Interfaces

OLAP-BAPI   Let's first look at the OLAP-BAPIs. As in the Staging area, SAP has also provided business objects and methods in the OLAP area. Specifically, there are two OLAP Business Objects:

► MDDataProviderBW
The Business Object MDDataProviderBW provides a multidimensional provider for BW metadata and master data.

► MDDataSetBW
The Business Object MDDataSetBW returns a result set for multidimensional queries.

Figure 4.17 shows the relevant methods of the two OLAP Business Objects. These objects and BAPIs, like the other BAPIs previously mentioned, can be accessed via Microsoft Visual Studio 2003 and the SAP Connector for Microsoft .NET 2.0.

Sample application   In a VB .NET sample application we want to use the Business Object MDDataProviderBW.Get_Cubes to list all SAP BW InfoCubes and their metadata. In the VS project, the Business Object MDDataProviderBW.Get_Cubes is added to the SAP proxy through the Server

Explorer. A WindowsForm must then be drafted. Figure 4.18 shows this sample form.

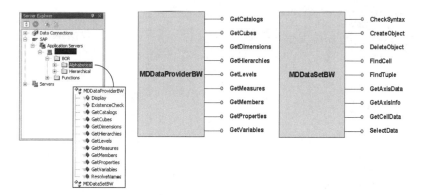

Figure 4.17 The OLAP-BAPI Methods

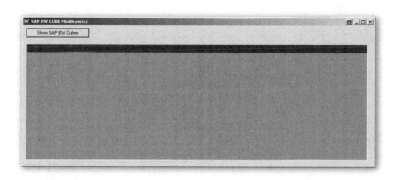

Figure 4.18 OLAP Sample Cube MiniBrowser

By clicking on the button **Show SAP BW Cubes** we execute the following VB .NET function:

```
Private Sub Button1_Click(ByVal sender _
As System.Object, ByVal e As System.EventArgs) _
Handles Button1.Click

'BAPI parameters
Dim ds_cubtab As BAPI6110CUBTable = New BAPI6110CUBTable
Dim ds_ret2 As BAPIRET2

'SAP BW connection data
Dim bw_system As New SAP.Connector.Destination
bw_system.AppServerHost = "sapwebas640"
```

```
bw_system.Username = "BCUSER"
bw_system.Password = "MINISAP"
bw_system.Client = 400
bw_system.SystemNumber = 0

'Establish connection to BW
Dim sap_bw_proxy As New SAPProxy1(bw_system.Connection-
String)

'BAPI call
sap_bw_proxy.Bapi_Mdprovider_Get_Cubes("", "", _
"", ds_ret2,_ ds_cubtab)

'Display result in DataGrid
DataGrid1.DataSource = ds_cubtab
DataGrid1.Refresh()
End Sub
```

The BAPI call `sap_bw_proxy.Bapi_Mdprovider_Get_Cubes` returns the SAP table `ds_cubtab` based on the `BAPI6110CUBTable` definition, which contains all the InfoCubes in the SAP BW system that are activated. The SAP table is assigned to the DataGrid as a data source, and after a refresh it displays the results in Figure 4.19.

XML for analysis

A further variant for small datasets is the specification *XML for Analysis* (XMLA), which also belongs to the group of SAP BW Open Analysis Interfaces and allows web-service-based access to SAP BW data.

XML for Analysis is a protocol specified by Microsoft and is now supported both by Microsoft and by SAP in version BW 3.0. It is automatically available as a web service after the SAP BW system is installed.

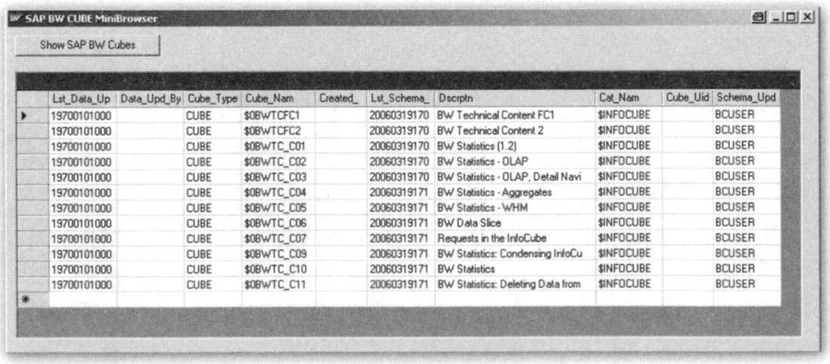

Lst_Data_Up	Data_Upd_By	Cube_Type	Cube_Nam	Created_	Lst_Schema_	Dscrptn	Cat_Nam	Cube_Uid	Schema_Upd
19700101000		CUBE	$0BWTCFC1		20060319170	BW Technical Content FC1	$INFOCUBE		BCUSER
19700101000		CUBE	$0BWTCFC2		20060319170	BW Technical Content 2	$INFOCUBE		BCUSER
19700101000		CUBE	$0BWTC_C01		20060319170	BW Statistics (1.2)	$INFOCUBE		BCUSER
19700101000		CUBE	$0BWTC_C02		20060319170	BW Statistics - OLAP	$INFOCUBE		BCUSER
19700101000		CUBE	$0BWTC_C03		20060319170	BW Statistics - OLAP, Detail Navi	$INFOCUBE		BCUSER
19700101000		CUBE	$0BWTC_C04		20060319171	BW Statistics - Aggregates	$INFOCUBE		BCUSER
19700101000		CUBE	$0BWTC_C05		20060319171	BW Statistics - WHM	$INFOCUBE		BCUSER
19700101000		CUBE	$0BWTC_C06		20060319171	BW Data Slice	$INFOCUBE		BCUSER
19700101000		CUBE	$0BWTC_C07		20060319171	Requests in the InfoCube	$INFOCUBE		BCUSER
19700101000		CUBE	$0BWTC_C09		20060319171	BW Statistics: Condensing InfoCu	$INFOCUBE		BCUSER
19700101000		CUBE	$0BWTC_C10		20060319171	BW Statistics	$INFOCUBE		BCUSER
19700101000		CUBE	$0BWTC_C11		20060319171	BW Statistics: Deleting Data from	$INFOCUBE		BCUSER

Figure 4.19 Result of the OLAP-BAPI Call

XMLA does not require any local client components. It allows platform-independent access to the SAP BW system using Internet technologies. Specifically, this means that a web service activates the XMLA interface, which transfers the query to the MDX processor (see Figure 4.20).

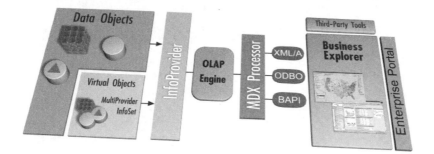

Figure 4.20 XMLA and the MDX Processor

The URL of the web service is formatted as follows:

http://[host]:8000/sap/bw/xml/soap/xmla

You can call up a description of the web service using the corresponding URL of the WSDL file:

http://[host]:8000/sap/bw/xml/soap/xmla?wsdl

The following SAP BW XMLA methods can be accessed, as shown in Figure 4.21:

XMLA methods

▶ Discover
This method is used to query metadata and master data. It corresponds to the BAPI MDDataProviderBW.

▶ Execute
This method is used to execute MDX commands and obtain the corresponding result set. It corresponds to the BAPI MDDataSetBW.

The third variant is a fat-client variant that is based on the COM protocol and can only be used on a Windows platform. It uses the SAP BW OLE DB Provider, which must first be installed on the Windows system. This can be done by installing the SAP BW frontend.

OLE DB for OLAP (ODBO)

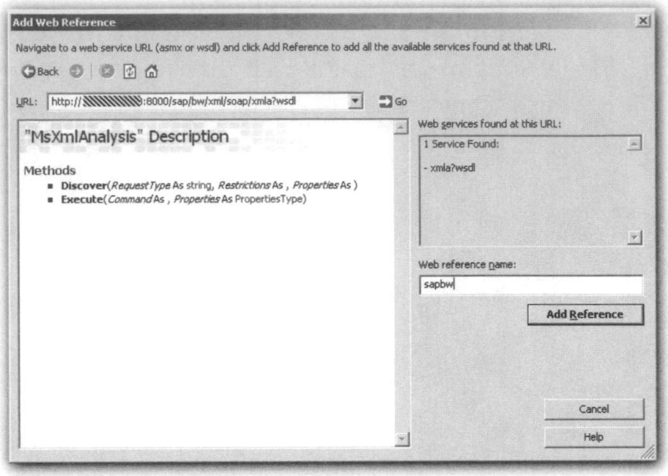

Figure 4.21 Methods of the XMLA Web Service

The corresponding setup[1] installs the following components of the SAP BW frontend, which are required by the SAP BW OLE DB Provider:

- *Mdrmsap.dll*: SAP BW OLE DB for OLAP Provider library
- *Mdrmdlg.dll*: Service library for establishing a link to the SAP server
- *Scerrlkp.dll*: Error processing library
- *Mdxpars.dll*: MDX parser library
- *Librfc32.dll*: SAP-RFC library
- *Wdtlog.ocx*: SAP-RFC logon dialog component
- *Saplogon.ini*: SAP connection parameter file

Mdrmsap.dll   The last three components should be familiar after reading Chapter 2, but the key role here is *Mdrmsap.dll* as the provider library. This provider library establishes a connection from the consumer client to the OLAP BAPIs (previously described) and their methods on the BW server, and allows online access to the desired InfoCubes.

For example, we can use the SAP BW OLE DB for OLAP Providers from the Office application Excel 2003, as shown in Figure 4.22.

---

1 The setup is located, among other places, on the SAP-GUI installation CD. It is installed with the SAP BW frontend.

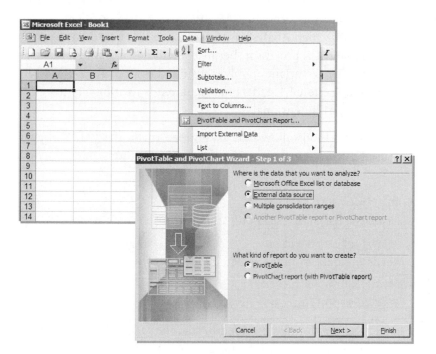

Figure 4.22 Excel and SAP OLE DB Providers

The result can then be evaluated in a pivot table, as you can see in Figure 4.23.

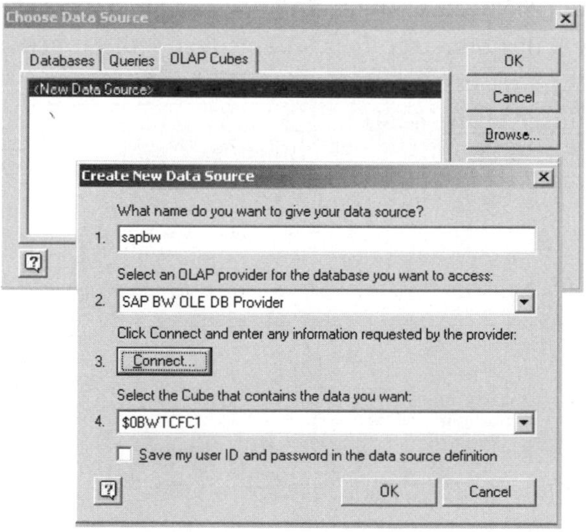

Figure 4.23 SAP OLE DB—Data in a Pivot Table

ODS-BAPI   Another variant for accessing SAP BW system data does not belong to the SAP BW Open Analysis Interfaces, nor is it based on the multidimensional MDX processor, because it will not access multidimensional data. This variant involves using the *ODS Read BAPI*. As described in Section 4.1.4, data management is relational in the ODS and is not multidimensional.

SAP's ODS methods allow data to be read from these ODS objects and used further, including the following methods and function modules:

▶ ODSObject.GetList
  Returns a list of the ODS objects

▶ ODSObject.ReadData
  Reads the data from the selected ODS object

▶ ODSObject.ReadDataUC
  The corresponding Unicode variant

Just like the previously described BAPIs, the ODS-BAPIs can also be accessed through Microsoft Visual Studio 2003 and the SAP Connector for Microsoft .NET 2.0 and integrated in a Windows application on a Microsoft .NET framework.

Example   In the following example we will create a simple ODS browser in the form of a Microsoft .NET-based Windows application. The application will show the ODS objects from the SAP BW system that are currently active. The SAP Connector for .NET activates the function BAPI_ODSO_GETLIST. This is the ABAP function of the ODSObject.GetList BAPI (see Figure 4.24).

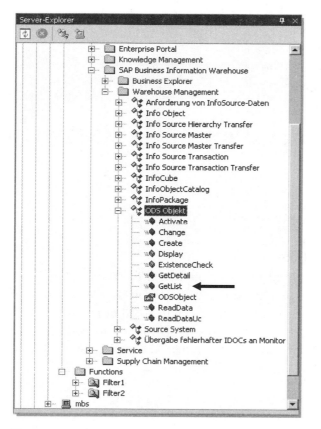

Figure 4.24 ODS-BAPI in the Server Explorer

Click on the button to call the ODS-BAPI to trigger the event.

```
Private Sub Button1_Click(ByVal sender _
As System.Object, ByVal e As System.EventArgs) _
Handles Button1.Click
'BAPI call parameters
Dim ods_ret2 As BAPIRET2
Dim ods_ltab As New BAPI6116LTable
Dim ods_sl16tab As New BAPI6116SLTable
Dim ods_sl00tab As New BAPI6100SLTable

'SAP BW connection data
Dim bw_system As New SAP.Connector.Destination
bw_system.AppServerHost = "sapwebas640"
bw_system.Username = "BCUSER"
bw_system.Password = "MINISAP"
bw_system.Client = 400
```

```
bw_system.SystemNumber = 0

'Establish connection to BW
Dim sap_bw_proxy As New SAPProxy1(bw_system.Connection-
String)

'BAPI call
sap_bw_proxy.Bapi_Odso_Getlist("A", ods_ret2, ods_ltab, _
  ods_sl16tab, ods_sl00tab)

'Display result in DataGrid
DataGrid1.DataSource = ods_ltab
DataGrid1.Refresh()

End Sub
```

The primary function of this example is that the BAPI call `sap_bw_proxy.Bapi_Odso_Getlist` returns the SAP table `ods_ltab` based on the `BAPI6116Ltable` definition, which contains all of the active ODS objects of the SAP BW system that is activated. The SAP table is assigned to the DataGrid as a data source, and after a refresh it displays the results in Figure 4.25.

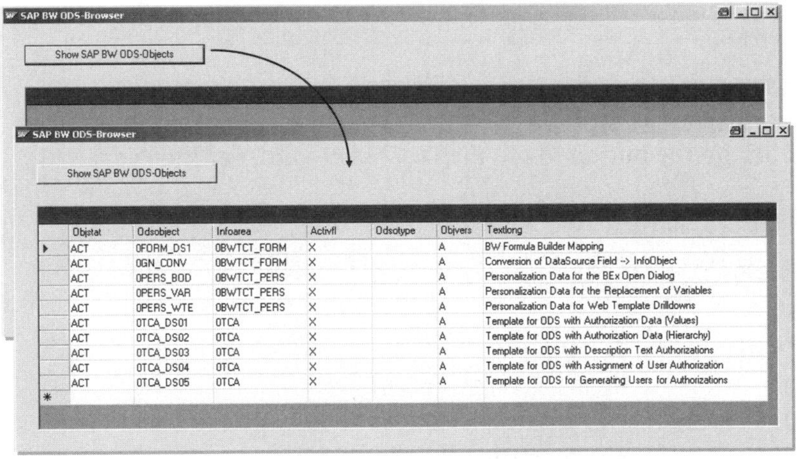

Figure 4.25 Result of the ODS-BAPI

4.1.4   Open Hub Service

While the previously discussed interfaces of the SAP BW Open Analysis Interfaces and the ODS-BAPI can be used to connect frontend tools for the reporting, SAP offers the interface *Open Hub Service* for exporting data from BW. The Open Hub Service allows data to be distributed from a SAP BW system into non-SAP data-marts, analytical applications and other applications (see Figure 4.26).

Open Hub Services are components that must be specially licensed by SAP customers.

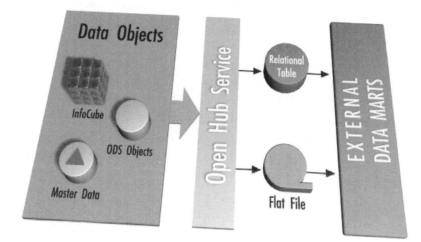

Figure 4.26 Classifying the Open Hub Service

The Open Hub Service can be called in the SAP BW Administrator Workbench (Transaction RSA1), as shown in Figure 4.27.

When you use the Open Hub Service, its primary task is to define an **InfoSpoke** *InfoSpoke* (see Figure 4.28). Within the InfoSpoke we define the:

▶ Open Hub datasource

▶ Extraction mode

▶ Objective—the Open Hub destination

As the Open Hub datasource we can use both ODS objects and Info-Cubes, but also BW metadata.

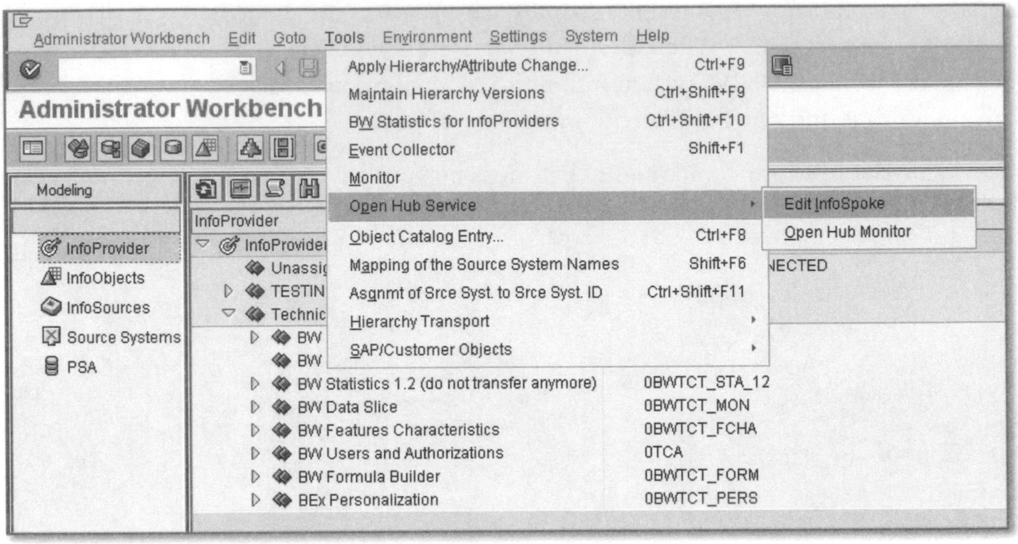

Figure 4.27 Calling the Open Hub Service

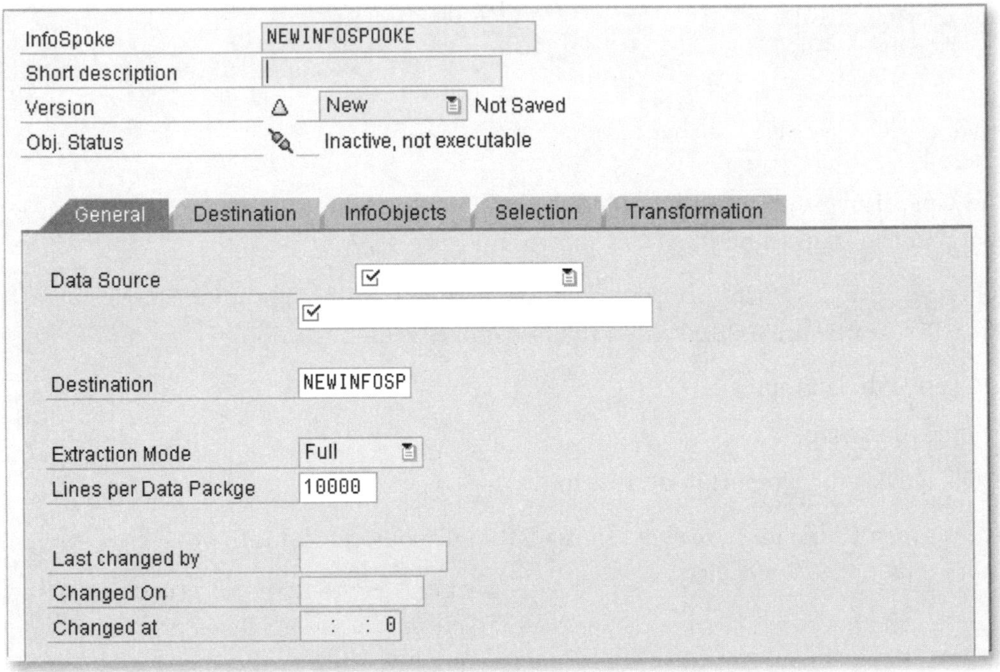

Figure 4.28 Defining the InfoSpoke

With extraction you have the option of either full mode or delta mode. In delta mode, the system only copies the data that has been newly added since the last extraction, while in full mode all data is copied from the defined data source.

As possible Open Hub destinations, an InfoSpoke can either use relational database tables with the prefix /BIC/OHxxx (xxx is the technical name of the destination) or flat CSV files.

If the data is unloaded into flat SQL server tables, they can be loaded with little effort into the corresponding Microsoft Analysis Services MOLAP Cube using the Microsoft OLE DB Provider for SQL Server for example.

Figures 4.29 and 4.30 show such an example for the Microsoft SQL Server 2000 Analysis Services.

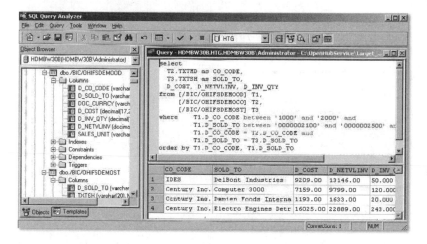

Figure 4.29 Accessing the Extracted BW Tables

Starting with version SAP BW 3.5, an API is offered for the Open Hub Service that helps automate the exchange of data with external programs.

Here, the data is first extracted into a database table in the BW system (destination type DB table). Once the extraction process has finished, the third-party tool (RFC destination and Open Hub destination) receives a notification. This extraction process can be started both by the SAP system and the external system.

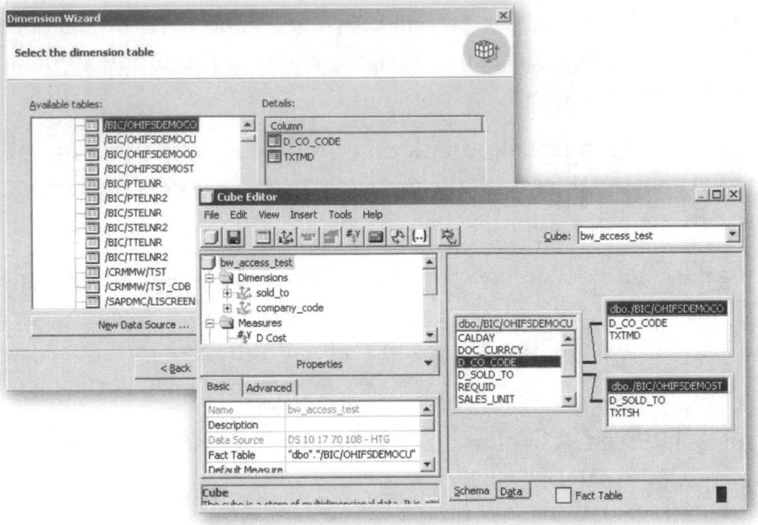

Figure 4.30 Generating MS-AS-OLAP Cubes

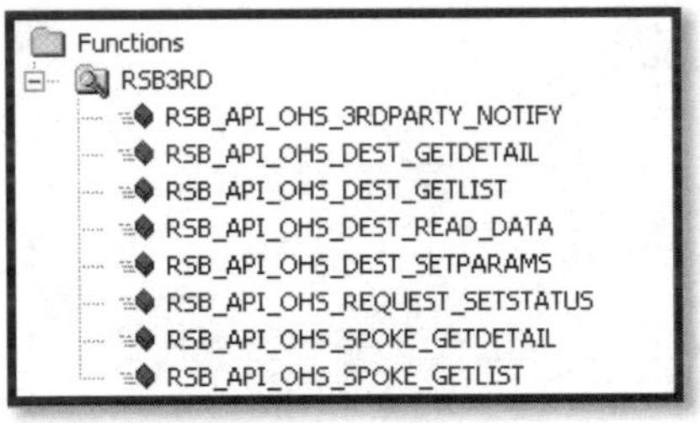

Figure 4.31 Open Hub Service APIs in Visual Studio 2003

The following Open Hub Service APIs are available in the form of RFCs and could be activated using the SAP Connector for .NET (see Chapter 2), as illustrated in Figure 4.31:

▶ **RSB_API_OHS_DEST_SETPARAMS**
This API copies the parameters of the third-party tool required for the extraction to the BW system. These parameters are saved in a parameter table in the BW system in the metadata of the Open Hub destination.

▶ **RSB_API_OHS_3RDPARTY_NOTIFY**
This API sends a notification after the extraction to the third-party tool. It transfers the Open Hub destination, Request ID, name of

the database table, number of extracted data records and time stamp. Furthermore, a parameter table can also be provided containing parameters that are only relevant for the third-party tool.

▶ RSB_API_OHS_REQUEST_SETSTATUS
This API sets the status of the extraction into the third-party tool in the Open Hub Monitor. If the status is red, it means that the existing table was not overwritten; if the status is green, the request was processed.

▶ RSB_API_OHS_DEST_GETLIST
This API returns a list of all Open Hub destinations.

▶ RSB_API_OHS_DEST_GETDETAIL
This API determines the details of an Open Hub destination.

▶ RSB_API_OHS_DEST_READ_DATA
This API reads the data from the database table in the BW system.

Optionally:

▶ RSB_API_OHS_SPOKE_GETLIST
This API returns a list of all InfoSpokes.[2]

▶ RSB_API_OHS_SPOKE_GETDETAIL
This API determines the details of an InfoSpoke.

The data extraction process can also be started from the third-party tool using the process chain API RSPC_API_CHAIN_START. The notification to the external system is sent via RSB_API_OHS_3RDPARTY_NOTIFY.

The external system now reads the data from the BW table and finally copies the status of the extraction with the API RSB_API_OHS_DEST_SETSTATUS to the monitor.

4.1.5 Microsoft SQL Server 2000 and 2005

Another option is to use Microsoft SQL Server as a database for the SAP system and also for an SAP BW system. For *Information Integration,* the additional SQL Server components of *Microsoft SQL Server Analysis Services* and, more recently, the *Microsoft SQL Server Reporting Services* are also important.

Additional components

---

2 In the forthcoming BW version, the architecture will be changed in such a way that it will no longer be possible to use InfoSpokes. However, the option of the Open Hub Destination will remain.

Analysis Services, which have been available since SQL Server 2000, are data warehouse enhancements that can be installed if required. Analysis Services for OLAP and data mining functions offer an intermediate layer between the relational database and report applications, such as Microsoft Excel. Reporting Services complement the SQL Server with sophisticated (Web) reporting functions based on ASP.NET and have been offered for download by Microsoft only to SQL Server customers since 2004 as an addition to Microsoft SQL Server 2000.

Outlook Microsoft SQL Server 2005 At the time of publication, Microsoft SQL Server 2005 is available. In general terms, this version offers improved functions compared with its previous version; however, it would go beyond the scope of this chapter to attempt to list all of these improvements. Nevertheless, a number of new developments are interesting in the are of SAP Information Integration.

First, the *SQL Server Enterprise Manager* was replaced with the *SQL Server Management Studio, which* will be the primary tool for SQL Server 2005 administration. Furthermore, SQL Server Management Studio also replaces the functions of the previous *SQL Query Analyzer*. Figure 4.32 shows the user interface of the new SQL Server Management Studio.

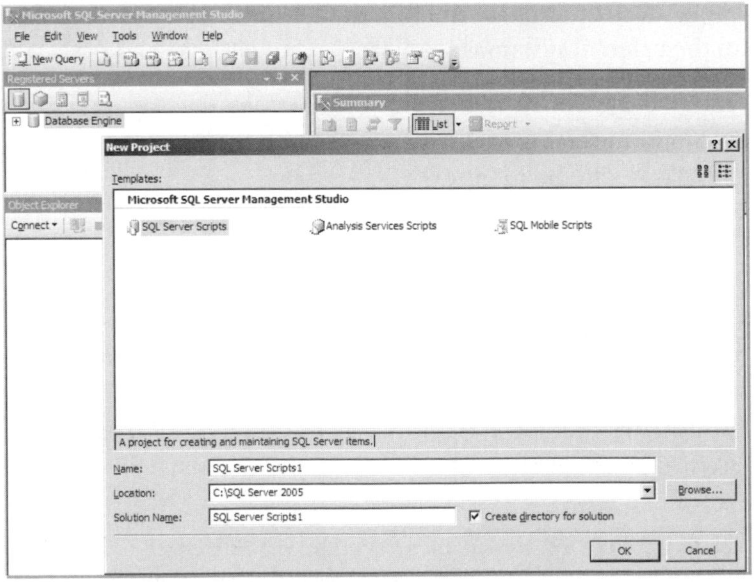

Figure 4.32 User Interface of the SQL Server Management Studio

Even more important for our topic of SAP integration is the fact that application development has been strengthened with Microsoft SQL Server 2005. It is separate from the database administration and has a separate development environment with the *Business Intelligence Development Studio*. This studio is in Visual Studio 2005 with SQL Server-specific add-ins and corresponding project templates.

SQL Server Integration Services are also newly added and they replace the previous DTS jobs. Integration Services provide data procurement and are developed in the Business Intelligence Development Studio. These services offer developers of ETL solutions additional controls and new functions. What DTS developers will like is the fact that the days of Visual Basic ActiveX-Script are over, as it is now possible to work with VB .NET. Figure 4.33 shows the user interface of Business Intelligence Development Studio for creating an Integration Services solution.

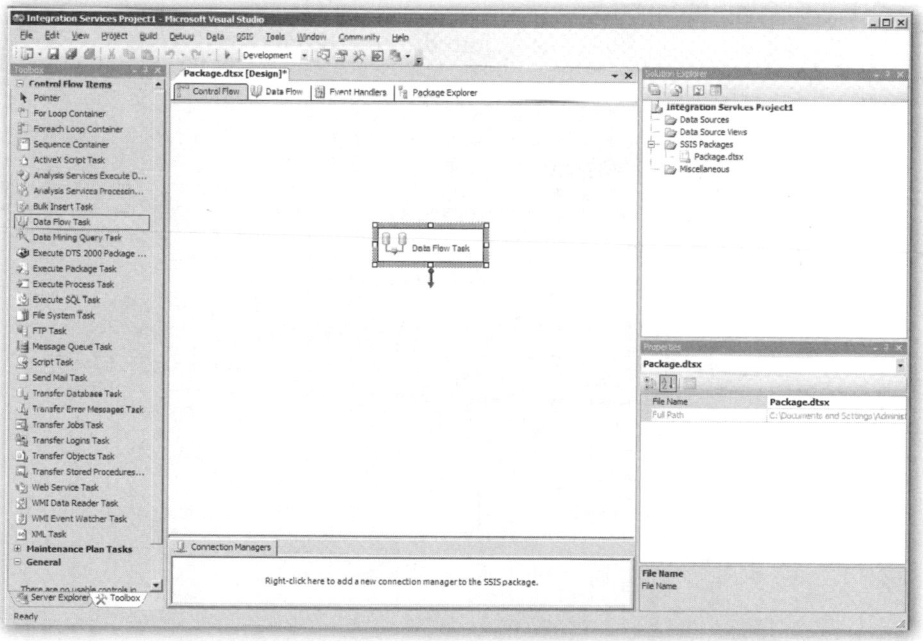

SQL Server
Integration
Services

Figure 4.33 Integration Services Project in the BI Development Studio

The Microsoft SQL Server Integration Services can also be used as an ETL tool for SAP BI if the data from the external sources is first imported into an SQL Server database through the standard interface

SAP BW DB Connect. However, customers must have a suitable SQL Server license to do this. If the SAP BW system is based on the SQL Server and the SQL Server Runtime license has been obtained by SAP, this SQL Server license may *not* be used, because it does not allow any access to data outside the SAP system.

SAP integration

There is a new version of SAP integration in addition to the SQL Server 2000 possibilities. Microsoft has made a Data Provider available, that you can use to locally access the data of the relevant system. It is roughly comparable to a driver for an ODBC data source.

In March 2006, an SAP-related Data Provider was delivered by Microsoft together with the *SQL Server 2005 SP1 CTP*. The full name is *Microsoft .NET Data Provider 1.0 for SAP NetWeaver Business Intelligence*, the shortened form is *Microsoft .NET Data Provider 1.0*.

This Data Provider was certified by SAP in June 2006.[3] It uses the XMLA interface to access SAP BI data. So, it is possible to use the reporting services as a client for SAP BI. Figures 4.34 and 4.35 show examples of the steps required in the report assistant of SQL Server 2005.

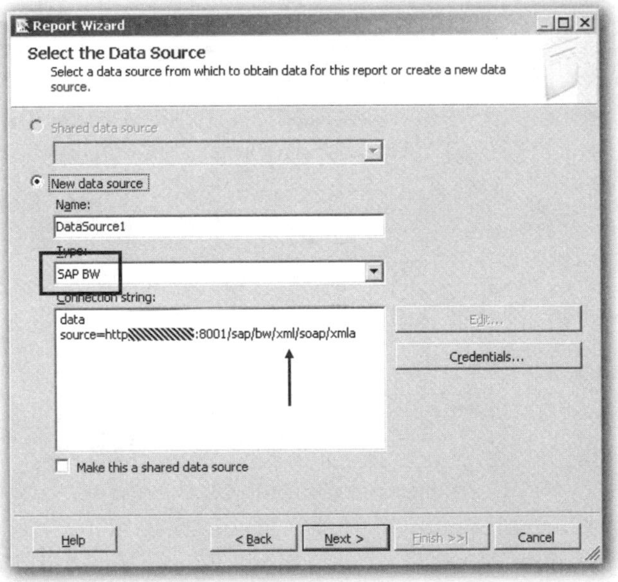

Figure 4.34 Creating an SAP NetWeaver BI Data Source (1)

---

3   See *http:\\www.sap.com\partners\directories\searchsolution.eps*.

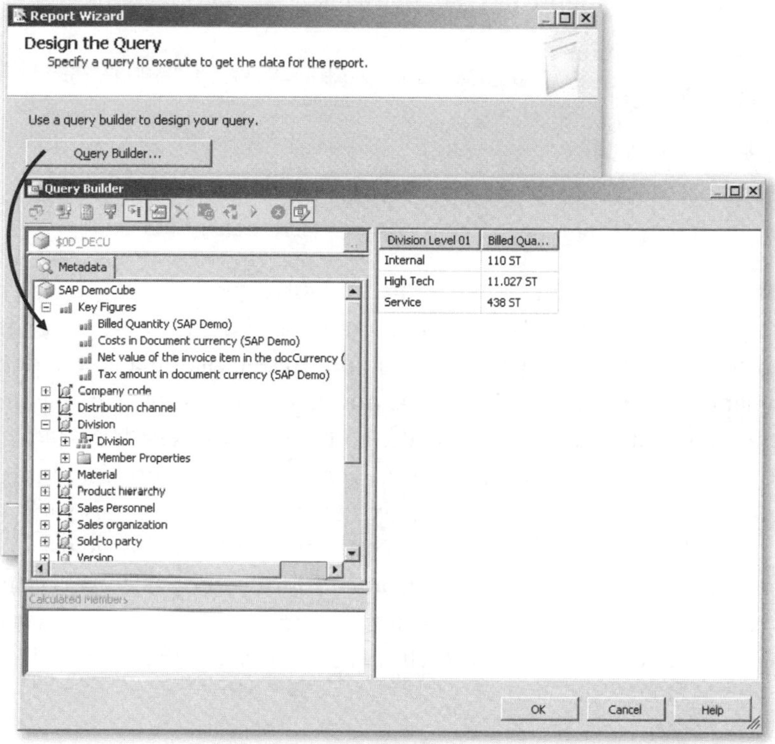

Figure 4.35 Creating an SAP NetWeaver BI Data Source (2)

4.2 SAP Knowledge Management

While structured data is handled with a Data Warehouse solution such as SAP BW, other tools are used for unstructured data and documents.

Within SAP NetWeaver, SAP Knowledge Management (KM) as a component of the SAP NetWeaver Portal, supports the user in managing unstructured data, by finding it and incorporating it into the company's work processes. These unstructured data stocks, such as Office and PDF documents contain corporate knowledge that must be organized transparently and in an easy to access way. Retrievability and re-usage are very important here, regardless of whether the documents are stored in the KM itself or in another document management system, since this will determine whether you achieve a goal-oriented handling of this knowledge.

Handling
unstructured data

The SAP KM therefore has the following tasks and functions:

▶ Data integration

▶ Data processing

▶ Data access

First, we must clarify in general terms how the data integration of external data runs into the SAP KM.

Repository
Manager As is illustrated in Figure 4.36, the *SAP KM Repository Framework* is responsible for the data integration of SAP KM. This forms an abstraction layer between the KM and different manufacturers' document storage systems. As well as offering functions for storing and editing documents, it provides the so called *Repository Managers*. A Repository Manager is used to access relevant data sources and integrate the data in the Portal—ideally through open protocols such as the WebDAV protocol,[4] the most common open standard for exchanging documents. These protocols look after basic operations such as reading, copying or deleting files or data. A Repository Manager must be configured for each data source being incorporated.

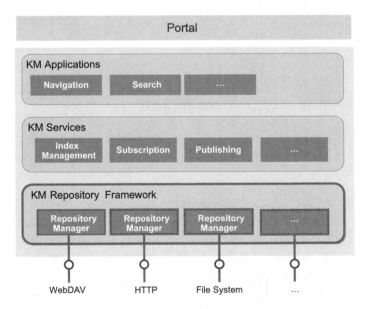

Figure 4.36 Classification of the KM Repository Framework

---

4 WebDAV stands for *Web-based Distributed Authoring and Versioning* and is an enhancement of HTTP-1.1. As an open standard, it supports the provision of files on the Internet or intranet.

In the standard version, SAP delivers the following Repository Managers for accessing Microsoft-based repositories:

1. **File system Repository Manager**
   The file system Repository Manager allows you to access Windows-based file servers. Here, the file system Repository Manager allows both read and write access to Windows file systems.

2. **WebDAV Repository Manager**
   The WebDAV Repository Manager allows read and write access to repositories that support the WebDAV protocol. You can add the following repositories using the WebDAV Repository Manager:

   ▶ Microsoft Exchange Server (public folders)

   ▶ Microsoft Internet Information Server (Windows file systems published via WebDAV)

   ▶ Microsoft Windows SharePoint Services 2.0 with Microsoft's **Windows SharePoint Services (WSS) Connector for WebDAV**

3. **Web Repository Manager**
   The Web Repository Manager allows read access to documents that are saved on a Web server such as an Internet Information Server (IIS).

When you access the documents through the Portal, the same authorizations should apply for users as those in the Windows operating system whose documents you want to integrate into the KM (e. g., read, write or delete authorizations). If the SAP NetWeaver Portal is being run on a Unix platform, note the functional restrictions for the file system Repository Manager listed in Table 4.1.

Figure 4.37 shows examples of the parameters that must be entered for a Repository Manager. Required parameters are the name of the Repository Manager and the prefix used to identify the Repository Manager responsible for a data source. Requirements to use additional parameters will depend on the type of relevant Repository Manager. For example, for a Repository Manager for a WebDAV access, an HTTP system must first be created in the Portal System Landscape with the corresponding system ID and cache. These details must then be given to the WebDAV Repository Manager as parameters.

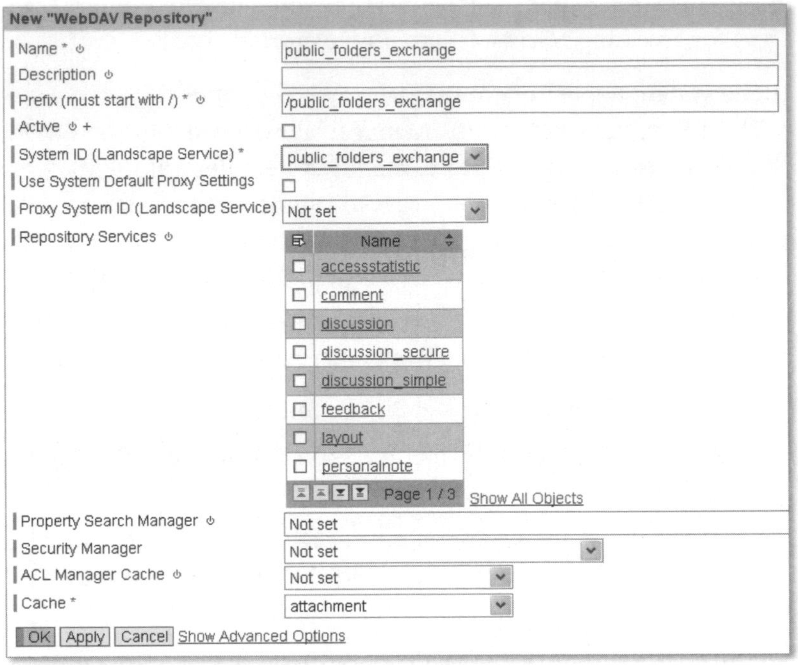

Figure 4.37 Parameters of a Repository Manager

The user accesses the data that has been integrated with the KM Repository Framework through the SAP NetWeaver Portal's interface. Here, users can access the folders of the KM Repository according to their user authorizations (see Figure 4.38).

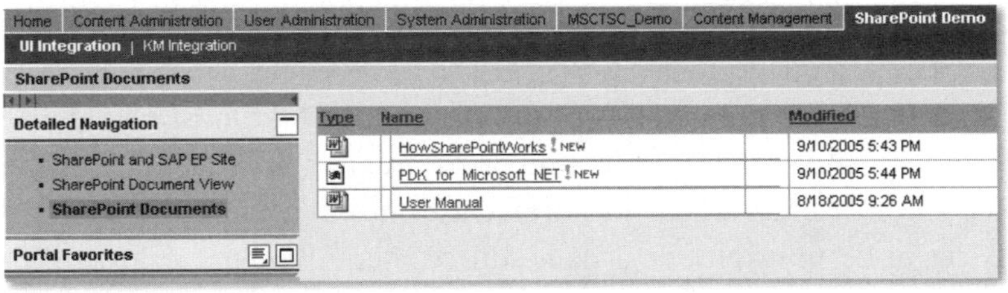

Figure 4.38 SAP KM User Interface

SAP KM provides a flexible user interface for navigating in the system. While a standard layout is stored in the profile, the Explorer for end users is flexible in that it changes the layout within the iView from folder to folder when the user navigates in the repositories being used.

4.2.1 File System Repository Manager

To integrate documents into a NetWeaver Portal on the Unix operating system platform with the File System Repository Manager, Active Directory must be running in the function level *Windows 2000 Mixed Mode*. If you are using Windows as the operating system platform for your NetWeaver Portal, as well as the function level Windows 2000 Mixed Mode, you can use the function modes *Windows 2000 native* and *Windows Server 2003*. The last two modes mentioned are also referred to as *Windows Server 2000* and *2003 Native Mode*.

Function modes of the Active Directory

If the File System Repository Manager is used in the Portal, a Windows system must be configured to allow the Portal users to maintain the user mapping. Table 4.1 shows an overview of the availability of the File System Repository Manager, depending on the function mode of the Active Directory.

SAP NetWeaver Portal operating system	Windows		Unix	
Active Directory function level	Windows 2000 Mixed Mode	Windows 2000 Native Mode and Windows Server 2003	Windows 2000 Mixed Mode	Windows 2000 Native Mode and Windows Server 2003
File system mount service with Windows 2000 security manager	X	X	X (except for HP/UX)[5]	Not supported
Microsoft IIS through the WebDAV Repository Manager	X	X	X	X

Table 4.1 Accessing Windows File Systems Taking Windows Access Authorizations into Account

For SAP Portals running on a Unix-based operating system that integrate the Windows file systems, instead of the File System Repository Manager you can connect the file systems through the IIS and the WebDAV Repository Manager, if the file systems are published through the IIS with WebDAV.

---

5 The current release restrictions for NetWeaver 2004 and NetWeaver 2004s can be found in SAP Notes 709354 and 853509.

4.2.2 WebDAV Repository Manager

The configuration of the WebDAV Repository Manager is identical for all repositories, except for the URL included. All repositories are based on IIS, but have different WebDAV implementations. Since all repositories are technically based on the IIS, a user assignment can be used for authenticating the access. If the Active Directory has been upgraded to the Windows Server 2003 function level, you can use single sign-on (SSO) with the SSO22KerbMap module. Once the authentication is successful, it uses a SAP Logon Ticket to create corresponding Kerberos tickets based on the mechanism specified by *Kerberos Constrained Delegation using Protocol Transition*.

Configuring the HTTP System and the WebDAV Repository Manager

Configuring the HTTP system

First, we must define an HTTP system in the portal system landscape before configuring the WebDAV Repository Manager, as shown in Figure 4.39. The system landscape is edited with the *System Landscape Editor*. Go to **System Administration • System Configuration • System Landscape** to reach the area for administering the portal's system landscape. In the detailed navigation, select **Knowledge Management • Content Management** and in the subareas **Global Services • System Landscape Definitions • Systems • HTTP System**.

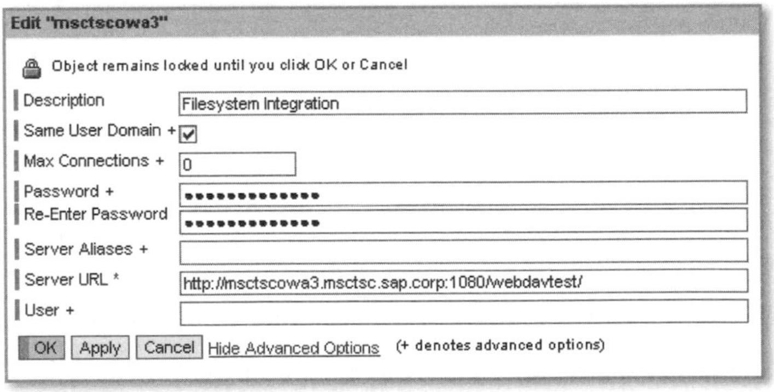

Edit "msctscowa3"

🔒 Object remains locked until you click OK or Cancel

Description	Filesystem Integration
Same User Domain +	☑
Max Connections +	0
Password +	••••••••••••••
Re-Enter Password	••••••••••••••
Server Aliases +	
Server URL *	http://msctscowa3.msctsc.sap.corp:1080/webdavtest/
User +	

[OK] [Apply] [Cancel] Hide Advanced Options   (+ denotes advanced options)

Figure 4.39 Editing an HTTP System

Ensure that the option **Same User Domain** is activated for the single sign-on with SAP Logon Tickets. The various options for authenticating against the WebDAV repositories will be outlined next.

Three options are available for specifying the authentication information (credentials) for the WebDAV Repository Manager and Web Repository Manager:

1. The authentication information is given statically in the underlying HTTP system with the parameters **User** and **Password**.

2. The credentials stored in the user mapping used.

3. Single sign-on is used, based on SAP Logon Tickets.

If a central user is maintained in the HTTP system, you can access the system with the credentials of this central user; that is, all portal users will access the repository with the same access rights. If a user name and password are maintained in the HTTP system, these details will have the highest priority and any other user assignments will be disregarded.

If the user assignment is used, each user must maintain his or her own authentication information (user name and password) for this system. For service users, such as the user index_service, the user assignment must be performed by the system administrator.

To use a user assignment, a *WebDAV Repository Manager System Template* must be created and a WebDAV system must be set up in the portal's system landscape based on this template.

If you use the single sign-on option **Same User Domain**, with each WebDAV request, a SAP Logon Ticket will be sent to the WebDAV repository. Systems that accept SAP Logon Tickets can be integrated for the authentication of users, such as other SAP portals. With the SSO22KerbMap Module, we also can use SAP Logon Tickets for SSO to an IIS.

Since all three of Microsoft's WebDAV repositories are based on IIS, we can use SAP Logon Tickets for SSO when accessing them, and users don't have to maintain any user assignments (see Figure 4.40).

If the SSO option was chosen using SAP Logon Tickets, service users must be created in Active Directory, for example the index_service user. Note that the attribute used for identifying the user in Active Directory and specified in the configuration file *SSO22KerbMap.ini* of the SSO22KerbMap module is maintained for Active Directory users. If such a user does not yet exist, it must be created.

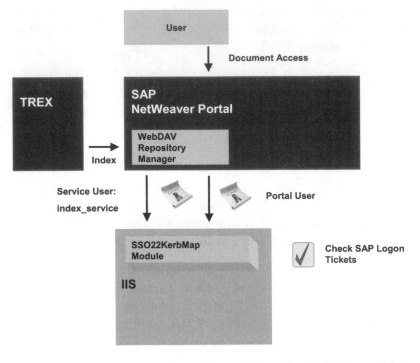

Figure 4.40 WebDAV Repository Manager—Single Sign-On with SAP Logon Tickets

For example, if the attribute userprincipalname is used as the user name for the SAP Portal, a user must be created in Active Directory whose userprincipalname has the value index_service, or the userprincipalname of an existing user must be changed in the Active Directory to the value index_service.

Configuring the WebDAV Repository Manager

The configuration of the WebDAV Repository Manager then takes place. In the portal's *System Landscape Editor*, choose **Knowledge Management • Content Management** in the detailed navigation. In the subareas, choose the option **Repository Managers** and under **Topics** choose **WebDAV Repository**. Figure 4.41 shows the parameters of a WebDAV Repository Manager to access a Windows file system published by an IIS.

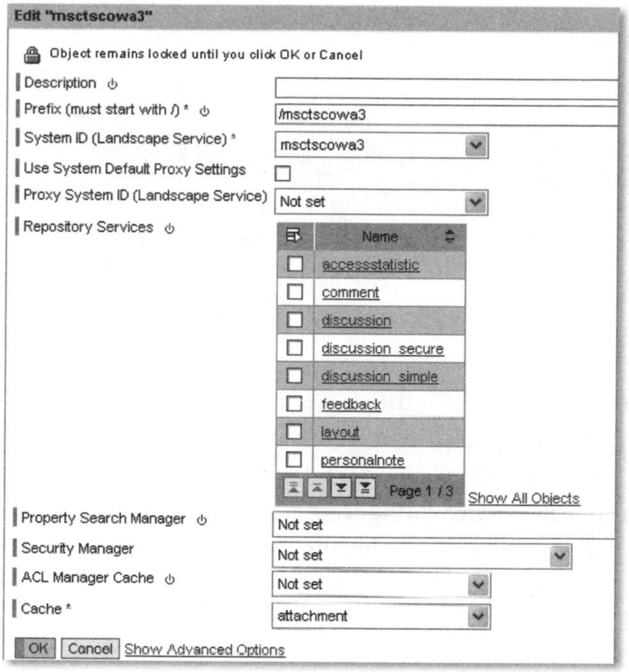

Figure 4.41 WebDAV Repository Manager

KM Integration of Windows File Systems Through IIS and WebDAV

WebDAV is an optional component that is not automatically installed with IIS 6.0. If WebDAV was not installed during the installation of IIS 6.0, it must be added after the IIS installation.[6] Finally, we must create a virtual directory on an IIS website. Through this virtual directory we can either publish a local directory or share on another server through the UNC name. Let's look at accessing the directory *C:\inetpub\WebDAVTest* (see Figure 4.42).

WebDAV

The directory *C:\inetpub\WebDAVTest* is published through IIS on the server *msctscowa3.msctsc.sap.corp* by the virtual directory *WebDAVTest*. The directory can be accessed through the following URL via WebDAV:

http://msctscowa3.msctsc.sap.corp/WebDAVTest

---

6 WebDAV Publishing Directories (IIS 6.0), *http://www.microsoft.com/technet/ prodtechnol/WindowsServer2003/Library/IIS/002a6134–27a4–42e5-ba0b-27d9 a4440c0b.mspx?mfr=true.*

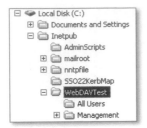

Figure 4.42 Windows File System

The *WebDAVTest* directory contains two subdirectories—*All Users* and *Management*. The security settings are chosen so that only members of the Management group have access to the *Management* directory, while all users can access the *All Users* subdirectory. *Windows Integrated Authentication* was configured for virtual directory *WebDAVTest* in the IIS. Figure 4.43 shows the result for a user who is a member of the Management group, and for a normal user. As you can see, the *Management* directory is not shown to the normal user.

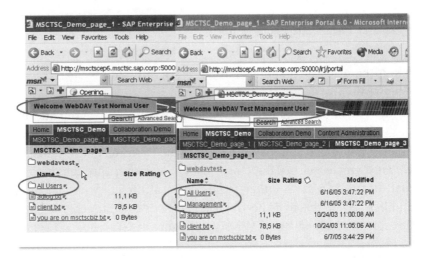

Figure 4.43 Accessing the Windows Repository with Windows Authorizations

KM Integration of Microsoft Windows SharePoint Services

SharePoint Services — KM SharePoint integration is becoming more popular. This is due to the increasing prevalence of Microsoft Windows SharePoint Services in real or virtual teams, as well as the installation of a company-wide portal based on the SAP NetWeaver Portal. Often, SharePoint Services have replaced the previous departmental directories (file shares) and contain, among other things, the corresponding Office documents that were previously stored on Windows file servers. To allow this unstructured data to also be available as content in the portal, you can incorporate it into the SAP NetWeaver Portal using the SAP-KM functionality.

To now access the content of the SharePoint Services, it is important to know how the data is stored in SharePoint Services and how "external" access is possible. SharePoint Services work with the WebDAV protocol; this standard was implemented by Microsoft for SharePoint Services, however not completely.

To offer WebDAV in the same scope as SAP KM, Microsoft announced the *Windows SharePoint Services Connector for WebDAV*. We had access to a beta version of this connector while writing this book. Using the Windows SharePoint Services Connector for WebDAV by Microsoft, it is possible to integrate Windows SharePoint Services by setting up a WebDAV Repository Manager in the SAP KM Repository Framework (as shown in Figure 4.36 above).

Windows SharePoint Services Connector for WebDAV

Figure 4.44 shows the result of this integration.

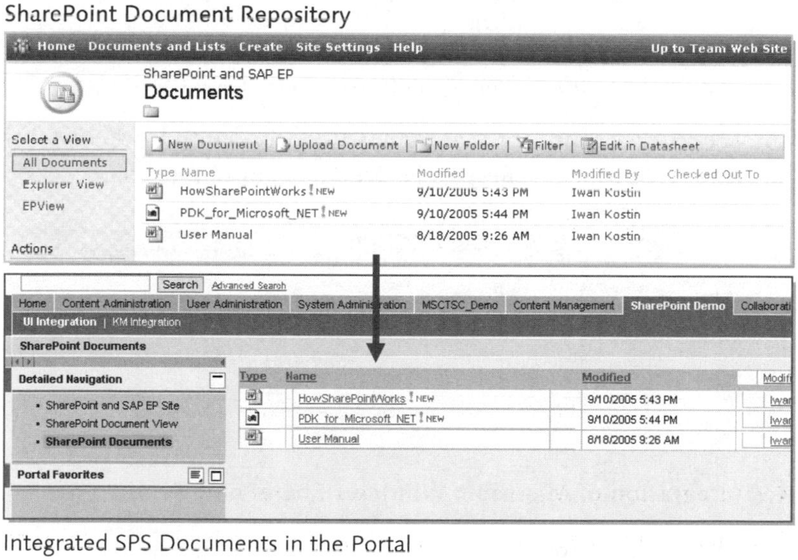

SharePoint Document Repository

Integrated SPS Documents in the Portal

Figure 4.44 Displaying SPS Documents in the SAP NetWeaver Portal

Here you can see two views of the data stored in SharePoint, which illustrate how Microsoft SharePoint Services documents are shown within the KM user interface and how they are available to the user when accessed through Windows SharePoint Services.

KM Integration of Microsoft Exchange

In Chapter 3 we discussed the integration possibilities of Microsoft Exchange Server 2003 elements in relation to *Portal Integration*, *Collaboration* and the Exchange Server's email and calendar functions.

Integrating public folders

However, if we now want to integrate additional elements, such as public folders as content, it is also possible to set up a WebDAV Repository Manager here because Microsoft Exchange Server 2003 already fully supports WebDAV technology in the standard system. This option is particularly interesting for companies that distribute information internally through public folders. It must be stressed that the idea is not to integrate individual mailboxes using SAP KM.

The procedure to incorporate this is similar to the previously described SharePoint variant. First, we must set up a new HTTP system; specify the Exchange Server URL here. To use the public folders, the following notation must be used for Microsoft Exchange Server 2003:

http://[Exchange Server]:[Port]/public/

The WebDAV Repository Manager is then configured for accessing the Microsoft Exchange Server. Figure 4.45 shows the result.

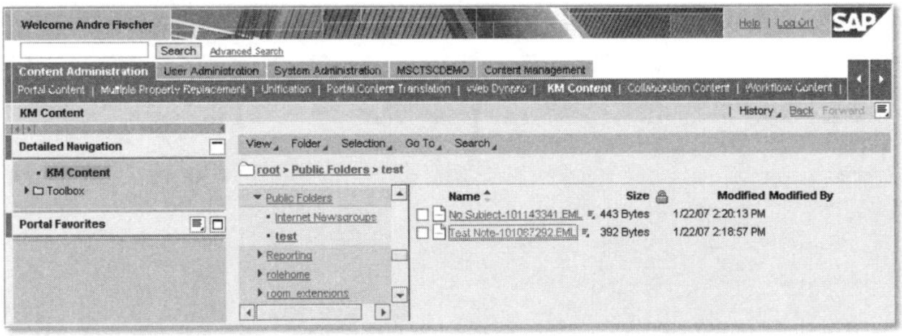

Figure 4.45 Displaying the Public Folders of Exchange in the Portal

4.2.3 Portal Drive—Simple Inclusion of KM in the Windows File Explorer

With SAP NetWeaver 2004 SP14 or SAP NetWeaver 2004s, an additional tool is provided by SAP for the KM integration called the *Portal Drive*.

While in the previous examples, the KM acted as a WebDAV client and used a WebDAV Repository Manager, this time the KM is a WebDAV server and the Portal Drive is the local client for accessing this WebDAV server. Through this Portal Drive, the portal content is displayed in Windows Explorer like a local drive. The Portal Drive is a local desktop application that must be installed on every machine on which it is to be used. Installation of the Portal Drive is straightforward with the standard SAP installation tools.

Instead of the Portal Drive, KM content can also be accessed using the *Webfolder* technology with Windows File Explorer. Until NetWeaver 2004 SP13, the only way to access KM content was by standard methods from the Windows File Explorer. Unlike the Webfolder technology of Windows File Explorer, the Portal Drive offers significant advantages when accessing KM content (see Figure 4.46).

Webfolder vs. Portal Drive

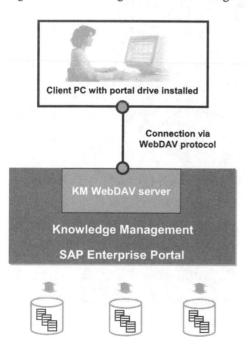

Figure 4.46 Portal Drive and the KM

239

In Windows Explorer, the Portal Drive with the portal content appears as a network drive under a separate drive letter. Therefore, with the Portal Drive it is also possible for batch jobs to access portal content. Furthermore, portal content can be accessed with all Windows applications (including Notepad). Webfolders only allow access to WebDAV-enabled applications, such as the Office products. However, you cannot access with Notepad on Webfolders.

Advantages of the Portal Drive

Key advantages of the Portal Drive are the offline and synchronization functions of the network drive. With Webfolders, these features are not available in conjunction with KM. The Portal Drive also allows access to the KM-specific attributes[7] of the documents stored in the KM. Webfolders only allow access to Windows-specific file attributes.

When the local installation has been performed, you can create a new *Portal Drive Service* by calling the Portal Drive application, as you can see in Figure 4.47 and Figure 4.48.

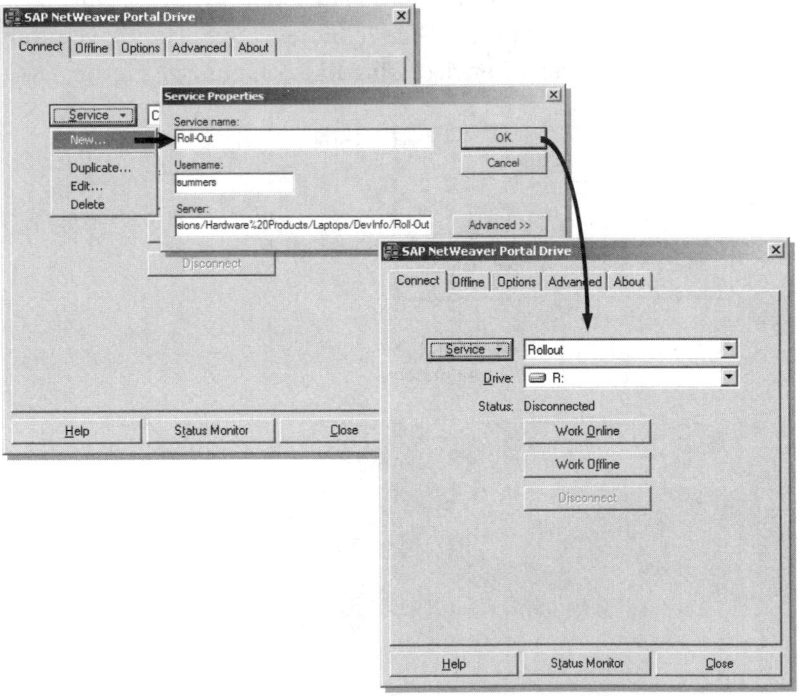

Figure 4.47 Creating a Portal Drive Service

---

7 Without checking for allowed values.

In these figures a network drive (R:) is now available to the user.

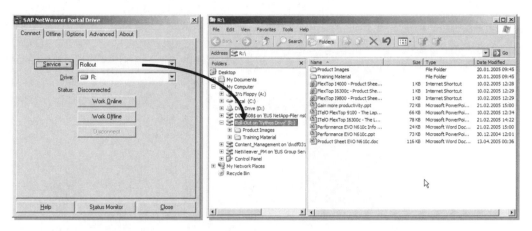

Figure 4.48 View of the Created Directory as a Network Drive (R:)

Figure 4.49 shows both the network drive (R:) created with the Portal Drive and the view of the KM directory in the portal.

Figure 4.49 Views of the SAP-KM Document Directory

The SAP NetWeaver Exchange Infrastructure creates new interoperability possibilities at the process level. SAP XI minimizes the number of point-to-point connections and centralizes integration knowledge in a single location, thus facilitating a seamless flow of business processes in heterogeneous IT landscapes and across companies. By supporting open Internet and industry standards, SAP XI also enables interoperability with third-party EAI[1] products, such as BizTalk Server from Microsoft.

5 Process Integration

With the SAP NetWeaver Exchange Infrastructure (SAP XI), SAP NetWeaver provides open integration technologies that support process-oriented collaboration between SAP and non-SAP components, both within and across companies. SAP XI is based on industry-standard technologies, such as web services and XML messaging. SAP XI also equips customers with predefined SAP integration knowledge and business processes. Increasing numbers of SAP applications use SAP XI, including xApps (xRPM, Resource and Program Management), MDM (SAP NetWeaver Master Data Management), mySAP SRM (Supplier Relationship Management), mySAP SCM (Supply Chain Management), BI (SAP NetWeaver Business Intelligence, for global spending reporting), R/3 Enterprise (to support industry standards), and mySAP CRM (Customer Relationship Management, for Extended Order Management). Since SAP XI also supports the integration of non-SAP systems, it is also used by many customers as a strategic integration platform.

SAP XI

In some cases, customers are already using EAI solutions from other manufacturers, such as BEA, IBM, Microsoft, SeeBeyond, TIBCO, Vitria, and so on, when they implement SAP XI. This is in part due to

---

1 *Enterprise application integration* (EAI) refers to the companywide integration of business functions along the value chain, comprising various applications on various different platforms.

the partially decentralized IT structure of many companies, whereby individual departments or subsidiaries use different integration solutions. Some customers have been using other integration solutions for many years, or have taken over a company that uses products from other manufacturers.

Interoperability In each of these scenarios, interoperability of the various products is essential if they are to interact seamlessly with one another. The crucial question is what form this interaction should take. By supporting open Internet and industry standards, SAP XI enables interoperability with third-party EAI products, such as BizTalk Server from Microsoft (see Figure 5.1).

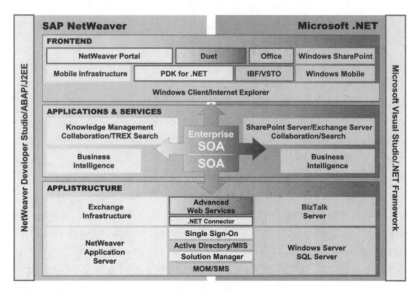

Figure 5.1 Integration with Microsoft BizTalk Server

5.1   Integration with Standard Adapters

Out-of-the-box integration SAP provides three adapters for integration at message level, which are ideally suited to out-of-the-box integration with third-party EAI products because they implement the following Internet standard protocols:

▶ JMS—Java Messaging Service

▶ SOAP—Simple Object Access Protocol

▶ HTTP(S)—Hypertext Transfer Protocol (over Secure Sockets Layer)

Both HTTP and SOAP can be used for integration with Microsoft Biz-Talk Server because BizTalk Server also has an HTTP adapter and a SOAP adapter.

5.1.1 HTTP Adapter

SAP XI's plain HTTP adapter allows application systems to communicate with the Integration Engine and exchange business data via a plain HTTP connection. The HTTP body is used as a payload for the XI message.

The HTTP adapter can be configured as both a sender and receiver, thus enabling bidirectional communication. Best Effort (BE)[2] is supported as the default Quality of Service level (QoS, see Section 5.1.3). The QoS Exactly Once (EO)[3] can be implemented using special parameters, which can be transferred with the message.

BizTalk Server also has an HTTP adapter with similar properties. The QoS Exactly Once can be implemented in the BizTalk Server HTTP adapter using the BizTalk Server Framework.

5.1.2 SOAP Adapter

The SOAP adapter enables the exchange of SOAP messages between a web service consumer or web service provider and the Integration Server.

Like the HTTP adapter, the SOAP adapter facilitates two-way communication with the connected systems as a sender and receiver. SAP XI's SOAP adapter also supports the QoS Best Effort and Exactly Once. In contrast to the HTTP adapter, you can specify modules to equip the SOAP receiver adapter with additional functions.

BizTalk Server similarly has a SOAP adapter for web service integration. However, unlike the XI SOAP adapter, BizTalk Server only supports communication with the QoS Best Effort.

5.1.3 Reliable Messaging

Reliable messaging refers to an exchange of messages, whereby the sender can be sure that the sent message has reached the receiver. We can distinguish between different QoS levels with regard to reli-

What is reliable messaging?

---

2 BE: Best Effort, at least once.
3 EO: Exactly Once.

able messaging. The QoS defines whether a message is to reach the receiver at least once (BE), EO, or, in the case of several messages, exactly once and in a certain sequence (EOIO)[4]. The sender can use defined message elements to determine a certain QoS.

Why use reliable messaging? With the integration of various applications via the Internet and thus via communication channels that may not always be available, reliable messaging is crucial when using Web services. In many business processes, the systems and users involved rely on the successful exchange of messages.

One way to ensure this is to call Web services synchronously. However, this is only a feasible option in a very small number of cases because synchronous communication requires the availability of both communication partners. In addition, synchronous calls may result in performance bottlenecks because the calling web service client can only continue processing data after it has received an answer from the system called. Reliable messaging is therefore essential to the asynchronous communication of Web services.

A shared standard supported by all manufacturers would be required to implement reliable messaging out of the box. In an effort to meet this obvious requirement, a number of software companies tried to establish a shared standard for *Enhanced Web Services*. In 2004, Microsoft and SAP agreed to collaborate more closely on the interoperability of web services and to implement the results of this collaboration in their products.[5] The specifications for the implementation of web service reliable messaging were sent to the newly established working group *OASIS Web Services Reliable Exchange (WS-RX) TC*. The next major Microsoft and SAP NetWeaver releases will thus enable an adapterless communication between SAP XI and Microsoft BizTalk Server, based on Enhanced Web Services.

Reliable messaging with SAP XI 3.0 and Microsoft BizTalk Server 2004 In the past, there were no consistent standards for implementing reliable messaging based on SOAP. Manufacturers were therefore forced to address the issue of reliable messaging with proprietary implementations. Proprietary SOAP 1.1 header extensions are used in both SAP

---

4 EOIO: Exactly Once in Order.
5 Press release, May 2004, *Microsoft and SAP Raise the Stakes for Web Services for the Enterprise.*

XI and Microsoft BizTalk Server. While SAP developed the XI protocol, Microsoft developed the BizTalk Server Framework 2.0.

If customers want to implement SOAP-based reliable messaging with the standard tools that are currently available, rather than waiting for Enhanced Web Services, they can follow the approach described below.

Out-of-the-box reliable messaging can be implemented if the sending system creates a message with SOAP header extensions that are compatible with those of the receiving system. Both products support the receipt of XML-based documents from an external system with a certain QoS, provided that the external system sends the documents in a compatible format.

Therefore, to implement reliable messaging between SAP XI 3.0 and Microsoft BizTalk Server 2004 based on SOAP protocol with the existing parameters, you can use the:

▶ BizTalk Server Framework 2.0 protocol to achieve reliable messaging from SAP XI to Microsoft BizTalk Server

▶ SAP XI protocol to achieve reliable messaging from Microsoft BizTalk Server to SAP XI

The SAP XI protocol is based on the SOAP message format. A SOAP message that is compatible with the XI message format complies with the SOAP standard, Version 1.1, and contains XI-specific entries in the SOAP header (for example, the message GUID). The SAP XI components involved in processing an XML message are shown in Figure 5.2.

XI protocol

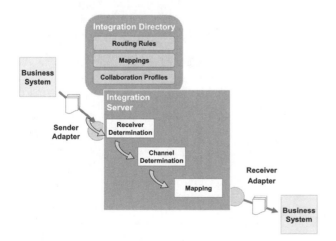

Figure 5.2 Message Processing in XI

247

There are two alternative ways in which a SOAP client can transfer the XI-specific parameters, such as the GUID, to the SOAP sender adapter:

▶ The calling client can transfer the entire SAP XI SOAP header.

▶ The relevant values can be transferred to the SOAP send adapter as URL parameters.

If you want to use the second alternative, you must activate the **Use Query String** option in the **Conversion Parameters** of the communication channel. If the SOAP adapter in XI is configured in this way, you can transfer the data contained in the XI SOAP header to the SOAP adapter via the parameters of a URL, which has the following syntax:

http://host:port/XISOAPAdapter/MessageServlet?channel=party:service:channel&MessageId=<GUID>&version=3.0

Example:
XI-specific entries

A simplified example of the SOAP header of an XML message containing the XI-specific entries is provided below:

```
<SOAP:Header>
. . .
<sap:Main versionMajor="3" versionMinor="0"
SOAP:mustUnderstand="1">
 <sap:MessageClass>ApplicationMessage</sap:MessageClass>
 <sap:ProcessingMode>asynchronous</sap:ProcessingMode>
 <sap:MessageId>
   db29a811-b331-11d9-b3dc-cc3b0a126058
 </sap:MessageId>
 <sap:TimeSent>2005-04-22T13:24:29Z</sap:TimeSent>
 <sap:Sender>
  <sap:Party agency="http://sap.com/xi/XI"
            scheme="XIParty">myBizParty
  </sap:Party>
  <sap:Service>myBizService</sap:Service>
 </sap:Sender>
 <sap:Interface namespace="http://sap.com/example/biztalk">
   BizInterface
 </sap:Interface>
</sap:Main>
. . .
<sap:ReliableMessaging SOAP:mustUnderstand="1">
 <sap:QualityOfService>ExactlyOnce</sap:QualityOfService>
</sap:ReliableMessaging>
```

```
. . .
</SOAP:Header>
```

BizTalk Server supports reliable messaging with Microsoft BizTalk Server Framework 2.0 (BTF2). A document that is compatible with the BizTalk Framework 2.0 complies with the SOAP standard, Version 1.1, and contains BizTalk-specific entries in the SOAP header (for example, the message GUID). The BizTalk Framework Disassembler functions as an XML parser in the receiver pipeline, and checks whether the XML message contains BizTalk Framework-specific information. The BizTalk Server components involved in processing an XML message are shown in Figure 5.3.

BizTalk Server Framework

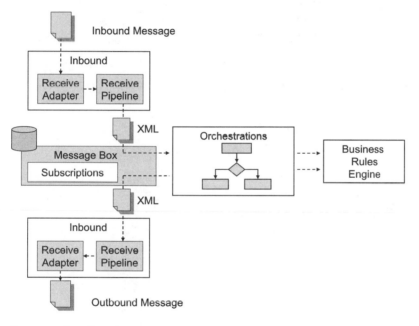

Figure 5.3 BizTalk Architecture

The information that uniquely identifies a BTF2 document is contained in the SOAP header entry indicated by the <identity> tag. The <identity> tag contains a GUID, which is used as the message ID of the message generated in the BizTalk Server after the BTF2 document was successfully processed.

If the sender of the message used the deliverReceiptRequest header to request confirmation that the message has been successfully generated, this confirmation is generated by the BizTalk Framework Disassembler component and sent to the address defined in the header information.

The `<sentAt>` tag contains the time stamp indicating the time when the document was sent to the BizTalk Server. Finally, the `<expiresAt>` tag contains a time stamp indicating the validity period of the XML message. After the time specified in this tag, the message is classified as invalid by the BizTalk Server and therefore can no longer be processed.

Example: BizTalk Server Framework-specific entries

A simplified example of the SOAP header of an XML message containing the BizTalk-specific entries is provided below:

```
<endpoints SOAP-ENV:mustUnderstand="1"
xmlns:ta="http://schemas.trading-agreements.com/"
xmlns="http://schemas.biztalk.org/btf-2-0/endpoints">
 <to>
  <address xsi:type="ta:httpURL">
   http://www.we-love-books.org/receipts
  </address>
 </to>
 <from>
  <address xsi:type="ta:department">Book Orders</address>
 </from>
</endpoints>

<properties SOAP-ENV:mustUnderstand="1"
xmlns="http://schemas.biztalk.org/btf-2-0/properties">
<identity>
  uuid:24d304a0-b6e1-493a-b457-4b86c684d6f3
</identity>
<sentAt>2000-05-13T10:34:00-08:00</sentAt>
<expiresAt>2000-05-14T08:00:00+08:00</expiresAt>
<topic>http://electrocommerce.org/delivery_receipt/</topic>
</properties>

<deliveryReceipt xmlns=
"http://schemas.biztalk.org/btf-2-0/receipts"
SOAP-ENV:mustUnderstand="1">
  <receivedAt>2000-05-13T10:04:00-08:00</receivedAt>
  <identity>
    uuid:74b9f5d0-33fb-4a81-b02b-5b760641c1d6
  </identity>
</deliveryReceipt>
```

The SOAP adapter is used to send messages from SAP XI to Microsoft BizTalk Server. In this case, the SOAP adapter is configured in such a way that messages are sent without an SAP-specific XI SOAP header. An adapter module can be developed instead, which generates a BTF2-compatible SOAP header.[6] When a message is received by BizTalk Server, a duplicate check is performed in the BTF2 receiver pipeline. If necessary, confirmation messages can be requested to confirm that a message has been successfully sent to the BizTalk Server. With the Business Process Engine (BPE), you can implement a resend mechanism in XI (see Figure 5.4)

Architecture: reliable messaging from XI to BizTalk

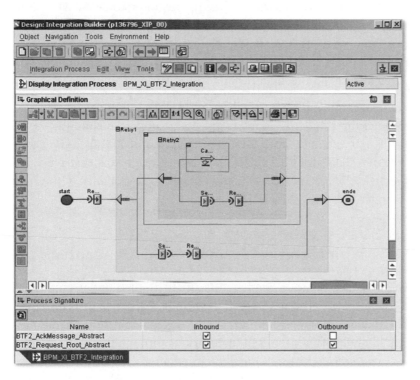

Figure 5.4 Resend Mechanism Based on the BPE

The XI SOAP adapter supports the QoS Exactly Once (EO). In this case, the call involves the transfer of a GUID as part of the URL parameter in the calling URL. In this scenario, the web service published by SAP XI is called with a URL that transfers the BizTalk mes-

Architecture: reliable messaging from BizTalk to XI

---

6   Collaboration brief on the SAP Developer Network (*http://www.sdn.sap.com*), *Reliable Messaging Between SAP XI 3.0 and Microsoft BizTalk Server 2004 Using SOAP-Compliant Communication*.

sage ID to SAP XI as a unique identifier. The URL is generated with C# code in the BizTalk orchestration and called by a dynamic HTTP port, which enables calls with URLs generated at runtime.

5.2 Industry Standards

In addition to the open Internet standards already discussed, generally accepted industry standards also exist for various industries, which facilitate communication across companies. Support for a range of industry standards is already integrated into SAP XI. Specifically, SAP XI contains preconfigured, industry-specific business content, and supports XML-based standards for the exchange of data. For example, SAP XI supports the *RosettaNet* and *CIDX* industry standards for the high-tech and chemical industries, respectively.

Therefore, integration with Microsoft BizTalk Server can be achieved through the standards adapters and joint support for industry standards. For example, both SAP XI and Microsoft BizTalk Server support the CIDX and RosettaNet standards. This means that messages can be exchanged between XI and BizTalk in compliance with Chem eStandards for the chemical industry.

5.3 XI Integration Examples—SOAP Adapter

Demo examples   SAP provides demo examples to facilitate a quick understanding of the concepts of process integration with the Exchange Infrastructure. These demo examples involve a travel agency that sells airline tickets, and two airlines that sell flight tickets through the travel agency. In the *CheckFlightSeatAvailability* integration scenario, the travel agency can check seat availability for a flight with an airline. The practical examples provided in this chapter supplement the standard *CheckFlightSeatAvailability* integration scenario provided by SAP in its demo examples. Two variants are introduced, whereby SAP XI functions as a web service provider in the first case, and as a web service consumer in the second.

Our discussion is based on the assumption that the demo examples have been configured with the two variants *Proxy-to-Proxy Communication* and *Proxy-to-RFC Communication* in accordance with the instructions provided in the SAP online help.[7] The business systems of the travel agency (client 105) and the airlines LH (client 106) and AA (client 107) are configured in both variants. In the standard scenario, the travel agency uses a BSP application to check seat availability with the LH and AA airlines. Depending on the airline specified in the query, the XI Integration Server forwards the query to one of two business systems configured in SAP XI.

In the scenario discussed here, the same business systems implemented in a configuration of an IDES XI system are used as the reference business systems in the demo example. The systems referred to here therefore differ from those referred to in the online help. To reproduce the following steps in a system configured in accordance with the standard documentation, you must substitute the systems named below for those named in the online help:

	Online help	This book (IDES XI system)
Business system of travel agency	<SID>_105	Travel_Agency_Summer
Business system of airline LH	<SID>_106	Airline_Group_One
Business system of airline AA	<SID>_107	Airline_Group_Two

5.3.1 XI as a Web Service Provider

In our first variant, the standard scenario is enhanced so that SAP XI provides a web service that returns the available flight seats for the airlines. A .NET-based web service client assumes the role of the travel agency in this case. The .NET-based client uses the SOAP adapter to call the web service provided by the XI Integration Server, which then checks flight availability in the connected business systems of the two airlines (see Figure 5.5).

We start by creating a new configuration scenario called **XI_FlightCheckSeatAvailability_dotNET**. Log on to the Integration Directory and open the **Scenarios** tab. Select the menu option **Object · New** to create a new configuration scenario. Save your changes (see Figure 5.6).

Creating a configuration scenario

---

7 For more information, refer to the online documentation at *http://help.sap.com* · *SAP NetWeaver 04* · *Process Integration* · *SAP Exchange Infrastructure* · *Overview* · *Demo Examples*.

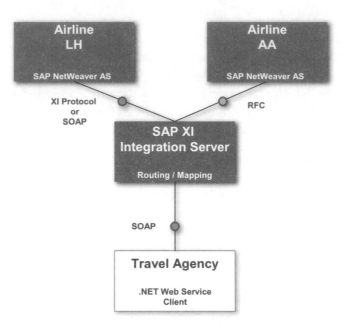

Figure 5.5 XI as a Web Service Provider

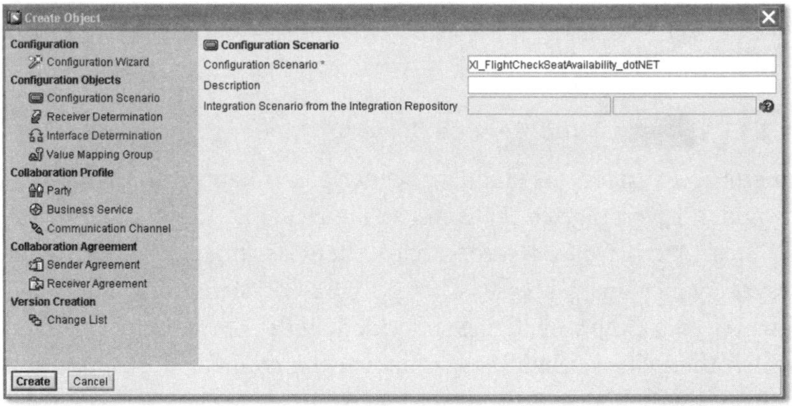

Figure 5.6 Creating a Configuration Scenario

Adding business
systems to the
scenario

Next, we assign the existing business systems of airlines LH and AA to our new configuration scenario. To do this, open the **Objects** tab and expand the tree structure containing the business systems and the communication channels of the business systems (see Figure 5.7).

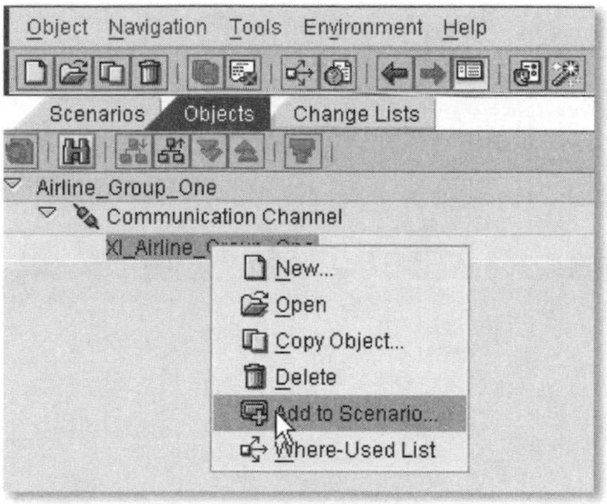

Figure 5.7 Adding Business Systems and Communication Channels to the Scenario

Add the business systems **Airline_Group_One** and then **Airline_Group_Two**, together with the corresponding communication channels (**XI_Airline_Group_One** and **RFC_Airline_Group_Two**) to your integration scenario. To do this, right-click the relevant communication channel of your business system and select the ☒ **Add to scenario** option in the context menu. When you select a communication channel, its higher-level business system is automatically assigned to the new scenario.

In addition to the existing business systems, we must create a business service for the .NET client, which will assume the role of the travel agency. To do this, right-click to select the **Business Service** entry under **Service Without Party** in the integration scenario, and select the **New** option in the context menu. Create a new business service called **dotNET_Travel_Agency** and save your changes.

Creating a service for the .NET client

Create a communication channel for the incoming web service request. Expand your new business service and select the **New** option in the context menu of the communication channel, as shown in Figure 5.8. Create a new communication channel called **SOAP_dotNET_Travel_Agency_Sender**.

Creating a communication channel

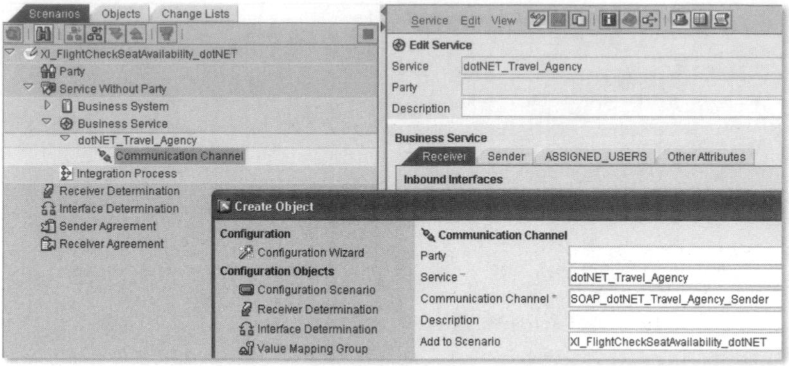

Figure 5.8 Creating a Communication Channel

On the **Parameters** tab, use the input help to enter the value **SOAP** in the **Adapter Type** field.

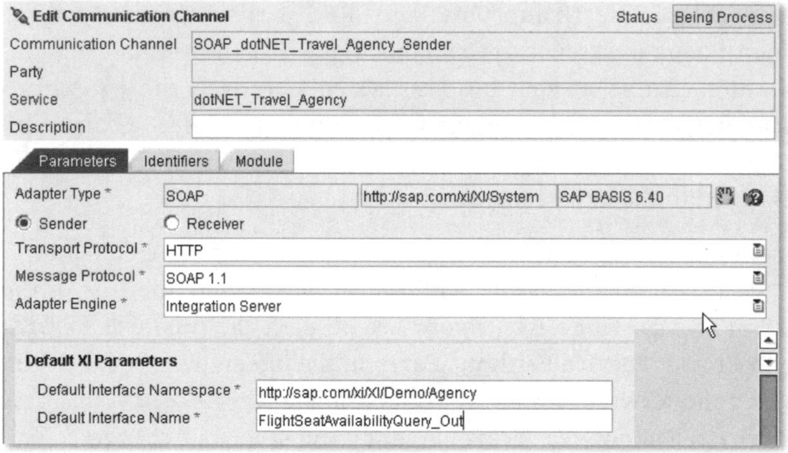

Figure 5.9 Editing a Communication Channel

Select the **Sender** option and enter the value *http://sap.com/xi/XI/Demo/Agency* for the **Default Interface Namespace** and the value **FlightSeatAvailabilityQuery_Out** for the **Default Interface Name** under **Standard XI Parameters**. Finally, save your entries (see Figure 5.9).

Receiver and interface determination

With the receiver determination, you define the receiver of the message. You can specify that the receiver depends on certain conditions, which you formulate using the XPATH standard. Alternatively, you can use context objects. These refer to a specific element of the message payload that meets the conditions in the receiver determination. With the interface determination, the inbound interface(s) are defined as receiver interfaces for the message.

Open the **Objects** tab and expand the receiver determinations. Right-click to select from the list the receiver determination of the **Travel_Agency_Summer/FlightSeatAvailabilityQuery_Out** demo example from the **http://sap.com/xi/XI/Demo/Agency** namespace, and select the **Copy Object** option in the context menu (see Figure 5.10).

Figure 5.10 Copying a Receiver Determination (1)

In the **Copy Receiver Determination** window, enter **dotNET_Travel_Agency** as the service (see Figure 5.11).

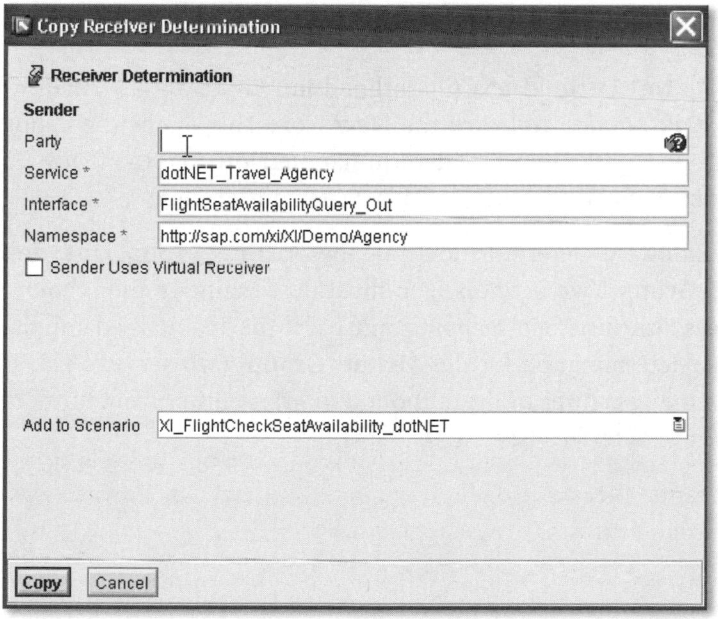

Copy Receiver Determination ✖

  🔲 **Receiver Determination**

Sender

Party	
Service *	dotNET_Travel_Agency
Interface *	FlightSeatAvailabilityQuery_Out
Namespace *	http://sap.com/xi/XI/Demo/Agency

☐ Sender Uses Virtual Receiver

Add to Scenario	XI_FlightCheckSeatAvailability_dotNET

[Copy] [Cancel]

Figure 5.11 Copying a Receiver Determination (2)

You now have to edit the new receiver determination. In Figure 5.12, you can see that the conditions for the receiver determination have also been copied. However, the configuration overview shows that the interface determinations are not yet configured.

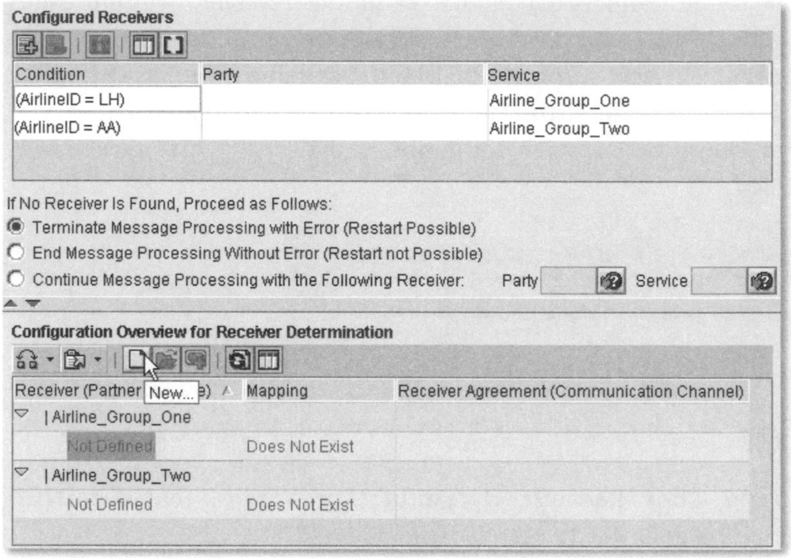

Figure 5.12 Creating a Receiver Determination

Select the **Not Defined** text (underlined in red) below the **Airline_ Group_One** service and click the **New** icon. This opens the dialog box for creating the interface determination. Note that the fields are already predefined (see Figure 5.13). Save your entries.

In the interface determination for the **Airline_Group_One** and **Airline_Group_Two** services, you must now maintain the inbound interfaces. An interface mapping must also be maintained for the interface determination for the **Airline_Group_Two** service. This is because the structures of the outbound interface differ from those of the inbound interface (see Figure 5.14).

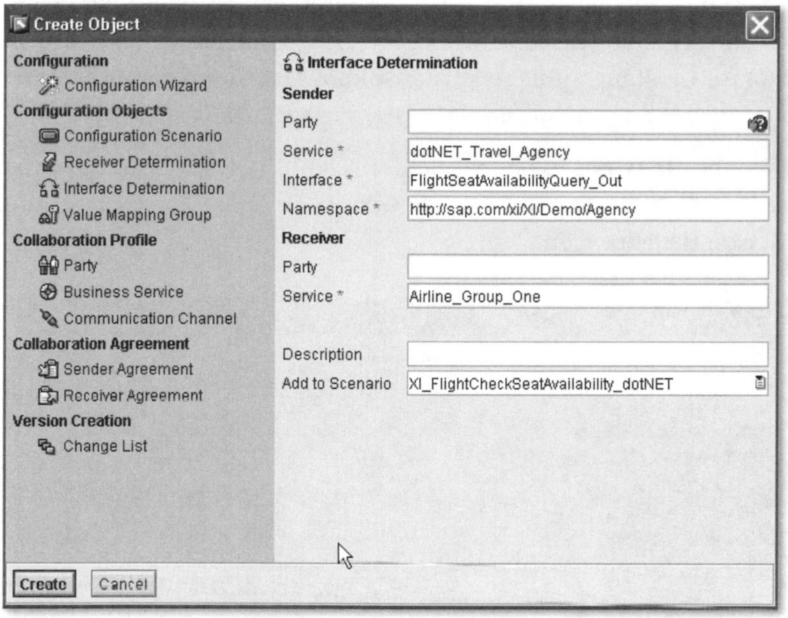

Figure 5.13 Creating an Interface Determination

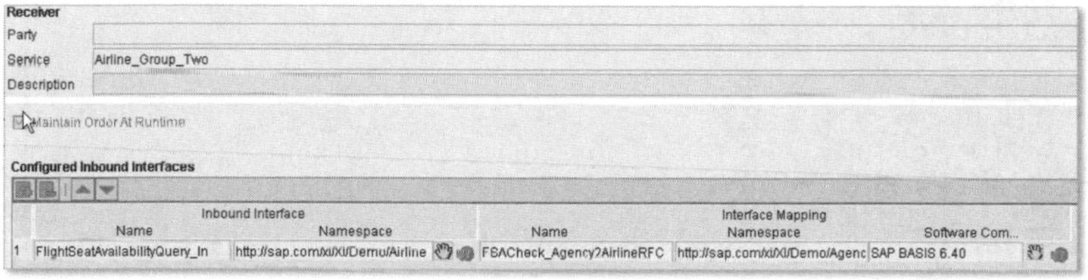

Figure 5.14 Configuration of the Inbound Interfaces and Interface Mapping

Enter the following values to configure the inbound interfaces for both services:

Configuring inbound interfaces

▶ For **Airline_Group_One**, enter an inbound interface called FlightSeatAvailabilityQuery_In with the namespace **http://sap. com/xi/XI/Demo/AirlineFlightSeatAvailabilityQuery**.

▶ For **Airline_Group_Two**, enter an inbound interface called **FlightSeatAvailabilityQuery_In**, with the namespace **http://sap .com/xi/XI/Demo/AirlineFlightSeatAvailabilityQuery**, as well as an interface mapping called **FSACheck_Agency2AirlineRFC**, with the namespace **http://sap.com/xi/XI/Demo/Agency** and the component SAP Basis 6.40. Save your entries.

After you have maintained the inbound interfaces, you must maintain the receiver agreements. Receiver agreements are mandatory
because the Integration Server must know the adapter to which the
message is to be sent.

Click the **Does not exist** text (underlined in red) for both receivers
Airline_Group_One and **Airline_Group_Two** (see Figure 5.12) and
click on the **New** icon.

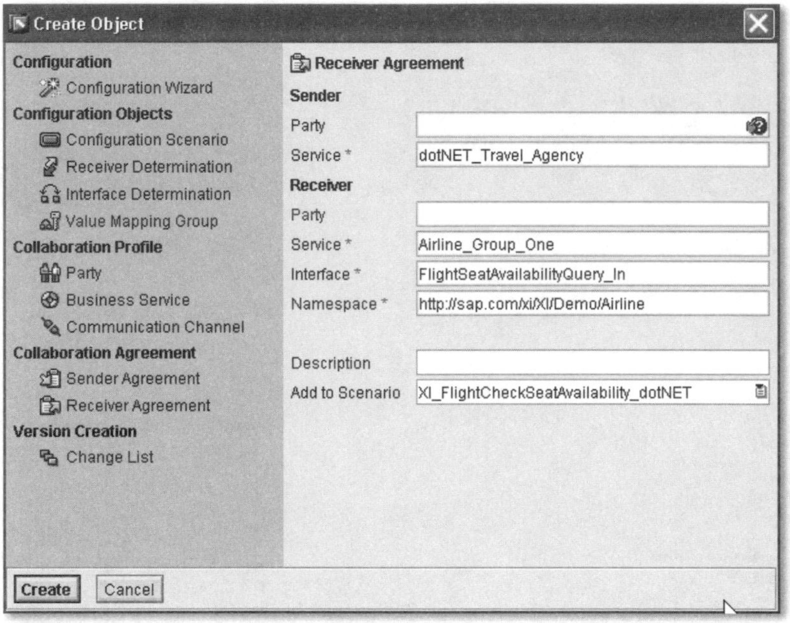

Figure 5.15 Creating a Receiver Agreement

This opens the dialog box shown in Figure 5.15. From the **Add to
scenario** selection list, select the **XI_FlightCheckSeatAvailability_
dotNET** scenario and click **Create.**

In the dialog box shown in Figure 5.16, you must then use the input
help to select the **communication channel of the XI_Airline_
Group_One receiver** for **Airline_Group_One** and **XI_Airline_
Group_Two** for **Airline_Group_Two**.

Then switch to the **Change lists** tab and activate the new configuration objects.

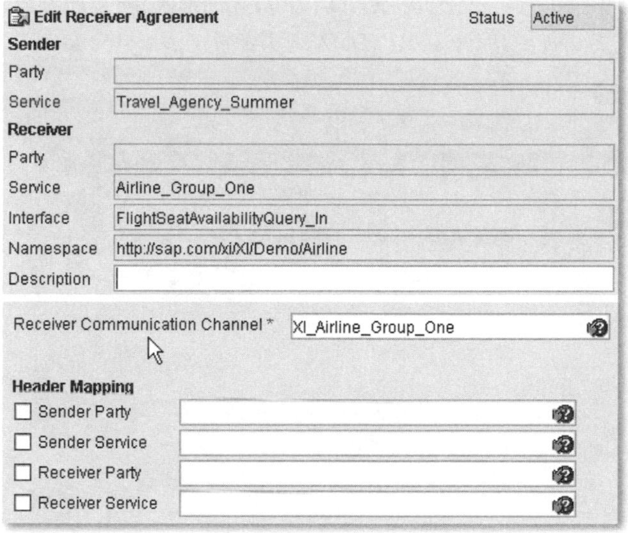

Figure 5.16 Editing a Receiver Agreement

We have now completed all configuration steps required to set up our configuration scenario. Next, we can use a wizard to create a web service in XI and export the relevant WSDL file. This WSDL file can be used to create a web service proxy with any standard development tool. This is how you create an application that can consume the web service.

Creating a web service in SAP XI

In the Integration Builder, select the menu option **Tools · Define Web service ...** for the configuration. This starts the wizard for generating a WSDL description, which guides you through the remaining steps.

Step 1: Introduction

Choose **Continue**.

Step 2: Specify the URL of the Web Service

After you choose **Continue** enter the URL of the web server that is to receive the web service. The URL specified must have the following form:

http://host:port/XISOAPAdater/MessageServlet?channel=
party:service:channel

In our example, the following URL is used:

http://iwdf9606.wdf.sap.corp:50000/XISOAPAdapter/MessageServlet?
channel=:dotNet_Travel_Agency:SOAP_DotNet_Travel_Agency_Sender

Choose **Continue**.

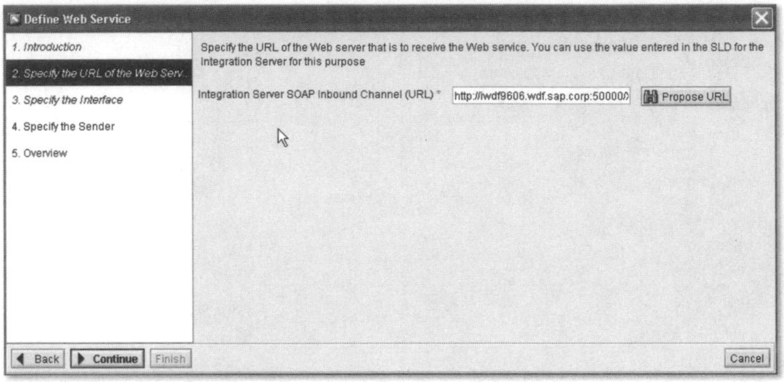

Figure 5.17 Entering the Web Server URL

Step 3: Specify the interface

Enter the synchronous message interface from the Integration Repository for which the web service document is to be created. Use the input help to enter the name of the interface (see Figure 5.18):

- Name: **FlightSeatAvailabilityQuery_Out**
- Namespace: **http://sap.com/xi/XI/Demo/Agency**
- Software component version: **SAP Basis 6.40**

Choose **Continue**.

Step 4: Specify the sender

Enter the message sender (partner, service and outbound interface; see Figure 5.19). The details of the message sender (partner, service, and outbound interface) are required by the Integration Server to format the header of the message and to clearly identify the sending service:

- Service: **dotNET_Travel_Agency**
- Name of interface: **http://sap.com/xi/XI/Demo/Agency**
- Interface namespace: **FlightSeatAvailabilityQuery_Out**

Choose **Continue**.

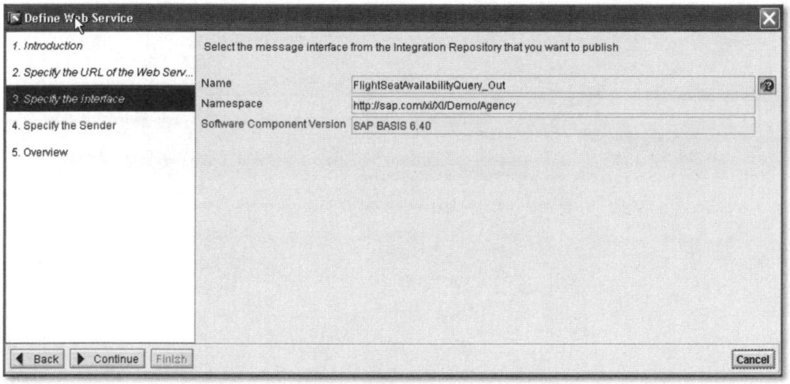

Figure 5.18 Specifying an Interface

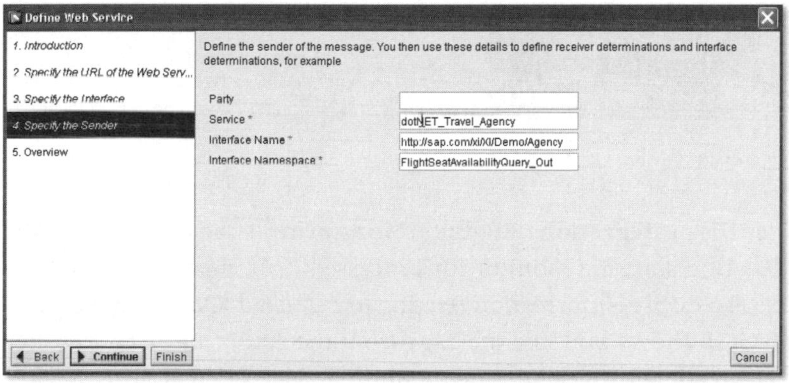

Figure 5.19 Specifying the Sender

Step 5: Overview

In the final step, all information that is to be used as a basis for generating the web service document is displayed in an overview. Choose **Finish** and then **Save** to save the WSDL file (see Figure 5.20).

To call a web service application, you must create a .NET-based console application, which assumes the role of the travel agency (as described in Section 2.3.5). The result of a successful call is shown in Figure 5.21.

Calling a web service

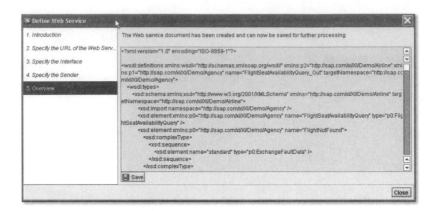

Figure 5.20 Saving the WSDL File

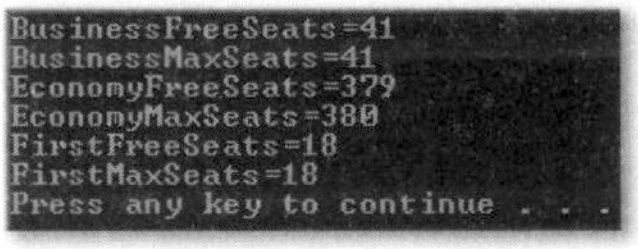

```
BusinessFreeSeats=41
BusinessMaxSeats=41
EconomyFreeSeats=379
EconomyMaxSeats=380
FirstFreeSeats=18
FirstMaxSeats=18
Press any key to continue . . .
```

Figure 5.21 Output of the .NET-Based Client Application

Use the **Integration Engine—Monitoring** transaction (SXMB_MONI) to start the monitor for processed XML messages. Here you can also display information relating to persisted XML messages. Figure 5.22 shows how the message from the call of the travel agency (shown above) appears in the monitor.

Figure 5.22 XI Integration Engine: Monitoring

5.3.2 Example: XI as a Web Service Consumer

In our second variant, web services are used to integrate a backend system. In addition to the SAP-based business systems, the external business system of a partner airline is also integrated into the scenario. The external business system, which simulates airline UA, is a Microsoft BizTalk Server, which makes flight data available via a web service. Communication between SAP XI and Microsoft BizTalk Server is based on the SOAP adapters of both products (see Figure 5.23).

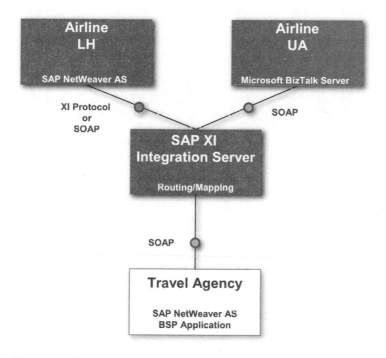

Figure 5.23 XI as a Web Service Consumer

XI Setup

Each design object in the Integration Repository is assigned to a software component version. The design objects delivered by SAP with the demo examples cannot be changed because they are in the SAP namespace. However, some new objects must be created in order to integrate an external system. For example, the WSDL file of the BizTalk Server must be created as an external definition. To configure our scenario variant, certain configuration steps are therefore

265

required in the System Landscape Directory, in the Integration Repository, and in the Integration Directory.

Step 1: Create objects in the System Landscape Directory

As a first step, create the product **XI BizTalk Demo** from the manufacturer **xi.com** and software component version **XI_BIZTALK_ DEMO** in the System Landscape Directory for our demo example. Next, create a technical **third-party** system for the BizTalk Server and assign the **XI BizTalk Demo, 1.0 of xi.com** product to this system (see Figure 5.24).

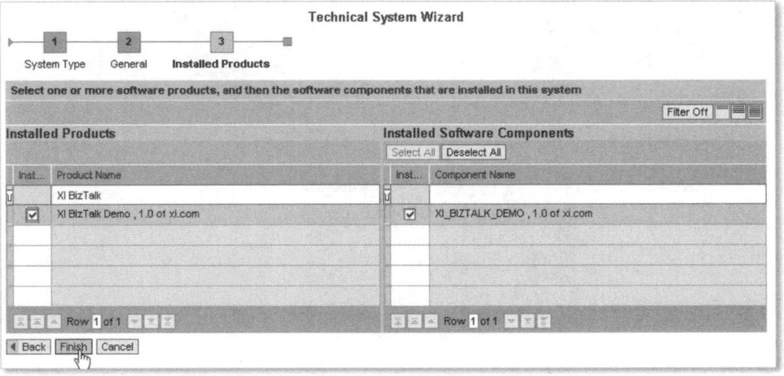

Figure 5.24 Technical System—Software Components

Then create the business system **XIDemoBizTalk** in the SLD for the BizTalk Server and assign the newly created **BIZTALK on msctscbiz** technical system to this business system.

Step 2: Create the design objects in the Integration Repository

Importing the software component version

After you have created a new product and software component version in the System Landscape Directory, you must import these into the Integration Repository and then create a new namespace. To do this, select **Tools · Transfer from System Landscape Directory · Import Software Component Versions** and import the software component version **XI_BIZTALK_DEMO, 1.0 of xi.com.**

Creating a namespace

Next, create a new namespace *http://xi.com/demo/biztalk*. To do this, select the **Namespace** option in the context menu of your imported software version component (**XI_BIZTALK_DEMO, 1.0 of xi.com**) in the navigation tree.

266

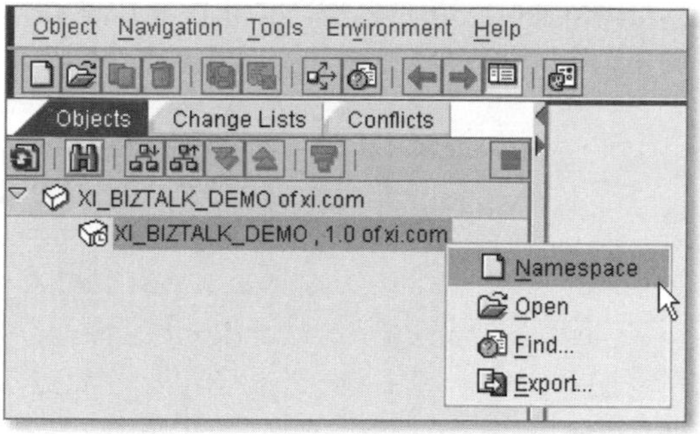

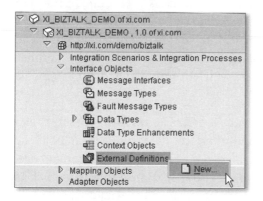

Figure 5.25 Creating a Namespace

The uniqueness of namespaces in customer scenarios can be ensured by extending company-specific URLs (for example, *http://www.mycompany.com/XI/scenario<nn>*). As shown in Figure 5.25, XI creates containers for the various repository object types within the newly created namespace.

As shown in Figure 5.26, an external definition called **CheckFlight-SeatAvailability** is created for the import of the WSDL files. Right-click to select the **External Definitions** container and select **New** in the context menu.

Importing a WSDL file as an external definition

Figure 5.26 Creating an External Definition

The WSDL file of the BizTalk Server can then be imported in the **Edit External Definition** dialog box. This procedure is shown in Figure 5.27. When you select the **From All Available Message Definitions** option from the **Messages** selection list, the two external messages

Operation_1SoapIn and Operation_1SoapOut are imported and can be used in subsequent configuration steps.

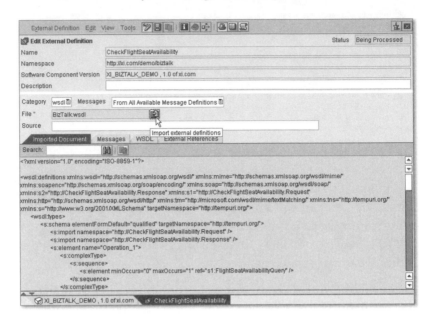

Figure 5.27 Importing a WSDL File as an External Definition

Outbound and inbound interfaces

Next, the outbound and inbound interfaces are defined. The outbound interface is the interface called by the travel agency. This has already been configured as part of the demo examples. The inbound interface is used by XI to call the BizTalk Server in the backend. Interfaces comprise message types, which are in turn defined using data types.

Each interface has its own request message, response message, and fault message. For an inbound interface, the request message is the input message for the receiving system (see Figure 5.28). In our scenario, this is the external message **Operation_1SoapIn**, which is used by SAP XI to transfer the flight availability data to the BizTalk Server. The response message of an inbound interface is the output message. This message contains the data of the called application. In our scenario, this is the external message **Operation_1SoapOut**, which contains the response data from the BizTalk Server.

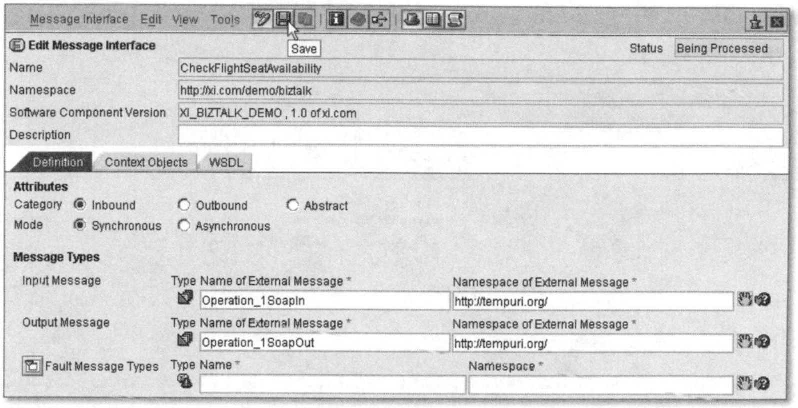

Figure 5.28 Creating a Message Interface

The next step involves generating the message mapping. First, create the two message mappings **CheckFlightSeatAvailabilty_Request** and **CheckFlightSeatAvailabilty_Response**. The interface mapping can then be created based on your new message mappings.

Message mapping

With the first message mapping, the output message of the outbound interface (the query sent by the travel agency) is mapped to the input message of the inbound interface (the query sent to the airline). Figure 5.29 shows how the output message of the outbound interface can be selected with the input help 🛈. At runtime, when the travel agency sends a flight availability query to XI, this data is transferred as an output message from the outbound interface to the XI Runtime. The XI Runtime receives the data contained in the output message and uses the message mapping to fill the input message for the inbound interface (that is, the query to the BizTalk Server).

With the second message mapping, the output message of the inbound interface is mapped to the input message of the outbound interface. If the result of the query sent to the airline (that is, to the BizTalk Server) is returned with a response message, XI uses this message mapping to fill the data for the input message that is sent to the travel agency.

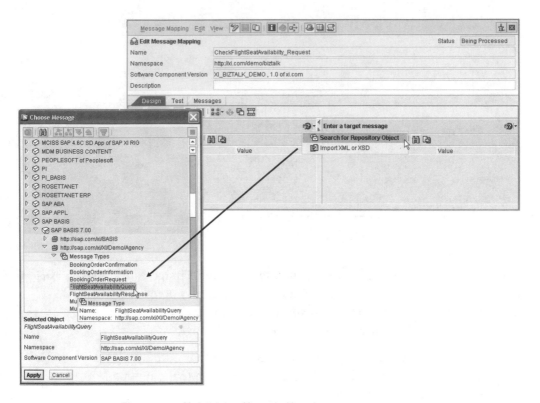

Figure 5.29 Maintaining Message Mapping

To complete message mapping, you must finally copy a source field into the corresponding target field using the Drag&Drop function. The Data-Flow-Editor (at the bottom of the mapping editor) then displays the simple assignment shown in Figure 5.30. The assignment is so simple in our scenario because the messages we created in the Biz-Talk Server have the same structure as those in the XI demo example. However, the Data-Flow-Editor can also be used to create more complex mapping procedures, without any need for additional programming.

Note, if you want to display all field assignment relationships, press the **Dependencies** button and select **Show All**,.

Creating interface mapping

Before you configure the interface determination in the Integration Directory, you must first create two interface mappings in the Integration Repository (design time). With interface mapping, you select the mapping programs that are to be executed during processing of the request and response messages (see Figure 5.31).

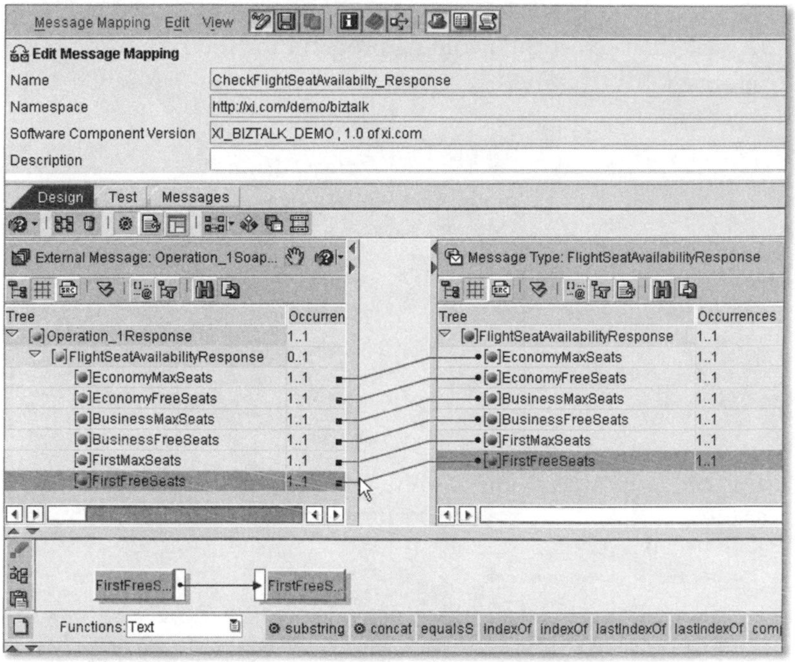

Figure 5.30 Message Mapping—Response—Data-Flow-Editor

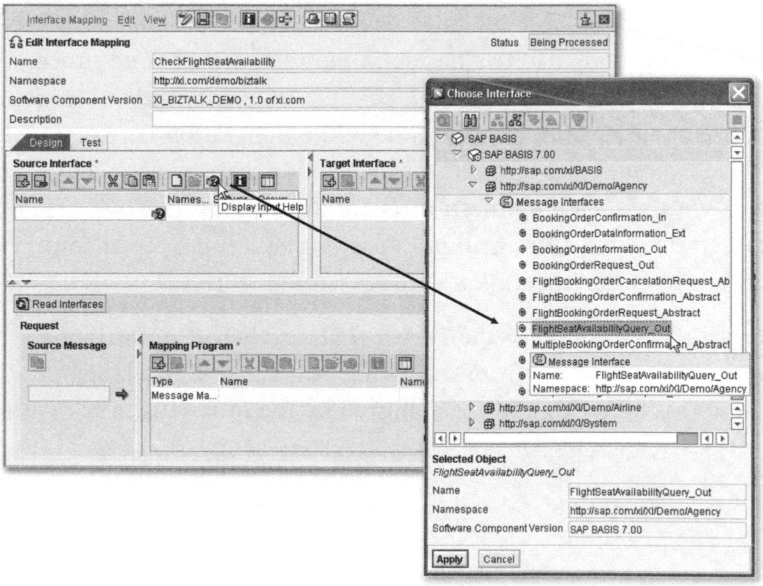

Figure 5.31 Interface Mapping—Request—Outbound Interface

First, select the mapping program for the request as shown in Figure 5.32, and then select the mapping program for the response on the **Response** tab.

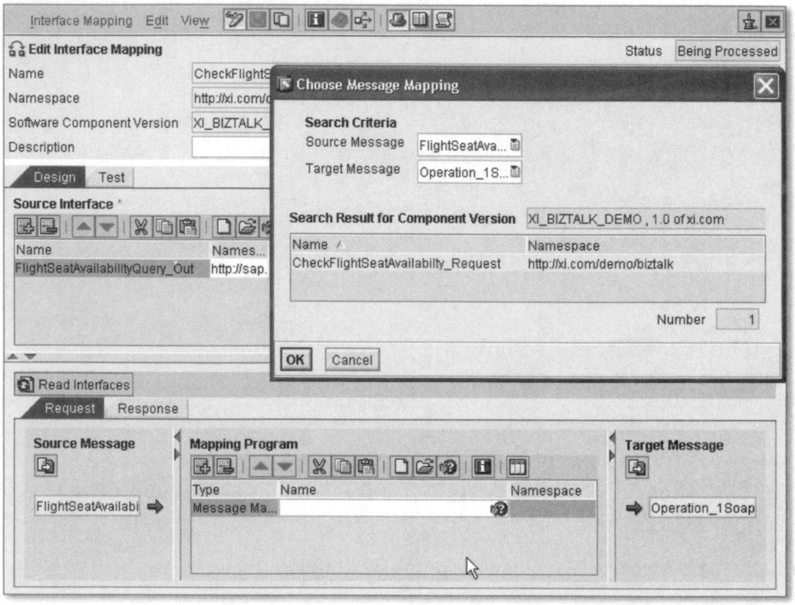

Figure 5.32 Interface Mapping—Request—Mapping Program

Creating a communication channel template

Communication channels define inbound and outbound processing for the Integration Server. The channel used for communication is defined during configuration time in the Integration Directory using the collaboration agreement for the sender or receiver. In our example, we use a communication channel template that we create at design time in the Integration Repository and use again at configuration time in the Integration Directory (see Figure 5.33).

To select the values for the **Target URL** and **SOAP Action**, press [icon] and copy the values from the WSDL file of the BizTalk Server. The values in the WSDL file are indicated by the following tags:

```
<soap:address location="http://..."/>
<soap:operation soapAction="http://..." />
```

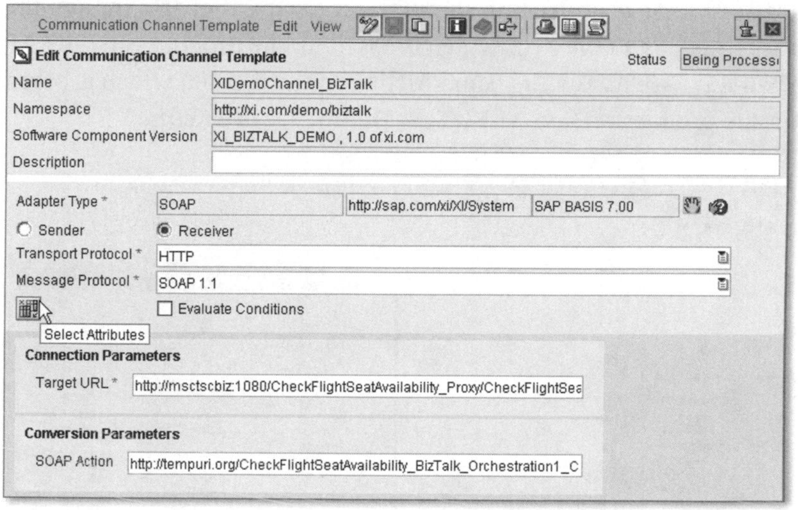

Figure 5.33 Creating a Communication Channel Template

In the next step, an *integration scenario* is created in the Integration Repository. An integration scenario is a design object used as a template for creating a *configuration scenario* in the Integration Directory.

Creating an integration scenario and action

Applications form part of an integration scenario. An application is a piece of software that you can install in a system and execute. An installed product can also send and receive messages. To visualize this, integration scenarios use *application components,* which are represented by colored rows called *swimlanes* in the integration scenario editor. *Actions* represent the exchange of messages between application components. Communication between the actions of different application components is represented by arrows referred to as *connections*.

First, a new action called **DetermineFlightSeatAvailability_BizTalk** must be created for the integration scenario. The second action, **Check_Flight_Seat_Availability**, can be taken from the SAP demo example (see Figure 5.34).

Creating an action

Now you must create an integration scenario with the Integration Scenario Editor. To do this, right-click in the interactive graphical work area entitled **Component View** to insert a new application component.

Creating an integration scenario

Create two new application components for this scenario. Assign the name **Agency** to the first, which is based on the product version **SAP Web AS 6.40**. Assign the name **Airline** to the second, which is based on the product version **XI BizTalk Demo, 1.0 of xi.com**.

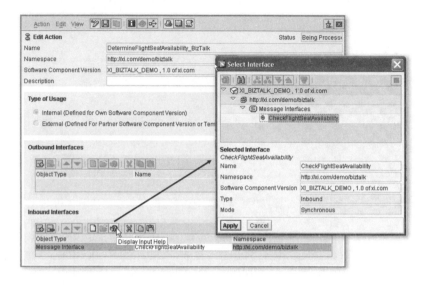

Figure 5.34 Creating an Action

Connecting actions

Hold down the Shift key on your keyboard and click the two actions **Check_Flight_Seat_Availability** and **DetermineFlightSeatAvailability_BizTalk** in the two rows. Both actions are then underlined in red and you can right-click to open the context menu. In the context menu, select the **Create Connection Between Selected Actions** option (see Figure 5.35). Then assign the interface mapping and a communication channel template to the connection.

Step 3: Configuration in the Integration Directory

Configuration scenarios group together configuration objects. This allows you to arrange the contents of the Integration Directory in a clear structure. Here we will use the integration scenario from the Integration Repository created in Step 2 as a template for our configuration scenario using the *Integration Scenario Configurator* function.

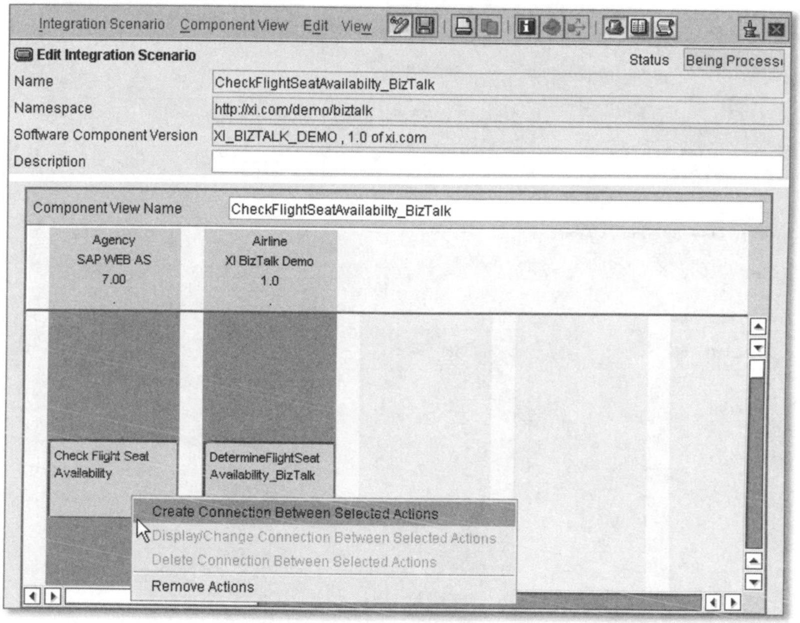

Figure 5.35 Connecting Actions

First, create a new configuration scenario called **CheckFlightSeat-Availability_BizTalk**. Then assign the **XIDemoBizTalk** business system imported from the SLD to the configuration scenario as a service without partners. Deactivate the **Create Communication Channels Automatically** check box because the communication channel template you created earlier is to be used instead.

Select the **XIDemoBizTalk** business system you assigned to the configuration scenario, and use the context menu to create a new communication channel called **XIDemo_BizTalk_Receiver**. Select the menu option **Communication channel · Import Template** and select the **XIDemoChannel_BizTalk** template with the namespace **http://xi.com/demo/biztalk** from the list of component versions.

Creating a communication channel

To start the Integration Scenario Configurator, select the **CheckFlightSeatAvailability_BizTalk** scenario in the navigation tree and click the Integration Scenario Configurator button ⊕. Make sure that you are in change mode because the configuration steps described below are only possible in change mode.

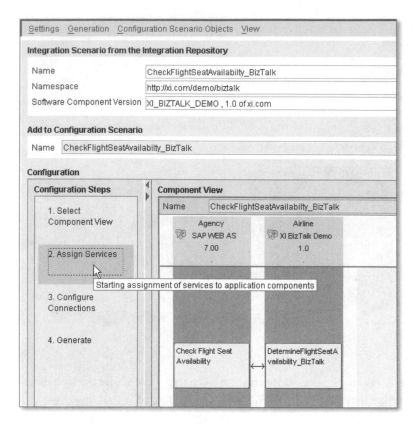

Figure 5.36 Assigning Services to Application Components

In the configuration steps, select Step 2: **Assign services**. Assign the **Travel Agency Summer** service to the **Agency** role. Then switch to the **Airline** role and assign the **XIDemoBizTalk** service (see Figure 5.36).

In the configuration steps, select Step 3: **Configure connections**. In this step, you assign communication channels to the services. This step is necessary for the generation of the collaboration agreement. Use the input help to assign the **XIDemo_BizTalk_Receiver** communication channel to the **Business-System-Service** receiver (see Figure 5.37).

Receiver determination Add another condition for queries with **AirlineID=UA** to the existing **|Travel_Agency_Summer|FlightSeatAvailabilityQuery_Out** receiver determination configured with the demo example, so that this can be forwarded to the BizTalk Server (see Figure 5.38).

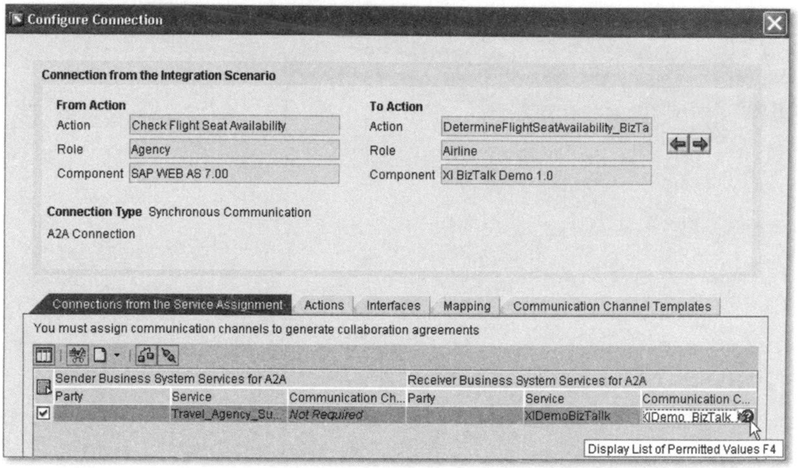

Figure 5.37 Configuring Connections

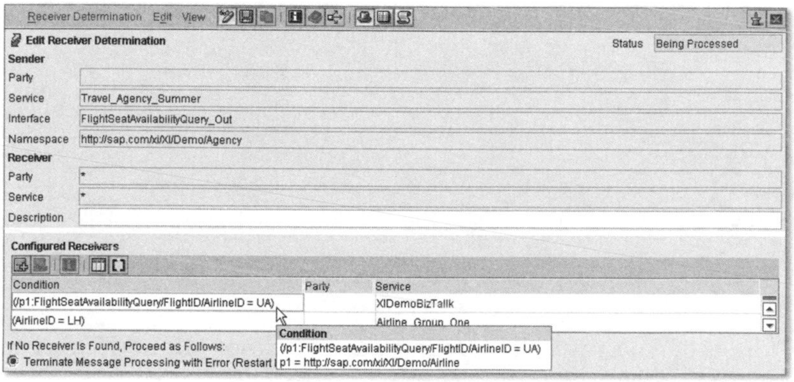

Figure 5.38 Specifying an Additional Condition in the Receiver Determination

Start the demo examples in transaction SXIDEMO in the Exchange Infrastructure system. Select the **Check Flight Seat Availability** option and click **Start**.

Testing the scenario

Select **United Airlines** as the **Airline** and assign any flight number. The query returns the default value 1 (preconfigured in the BizTalk orchestration) for all parameters (see Figure 5.39).

277

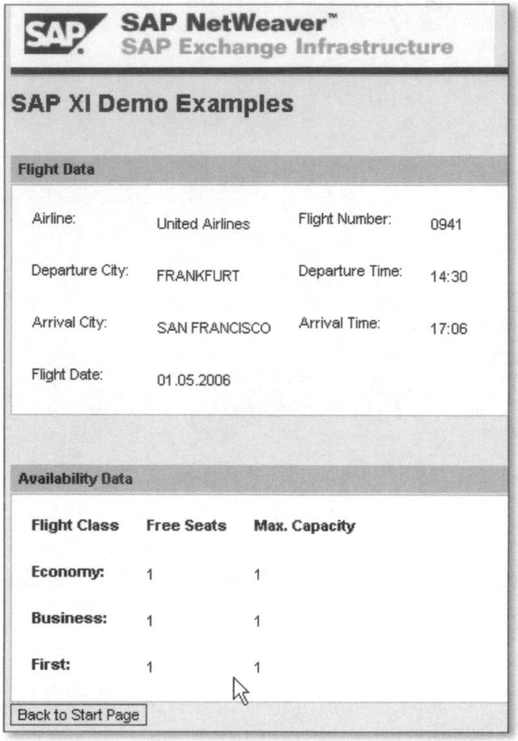

Figure 5.39 Result of the Availability Query Sent to United Airlines (BizTalk)

BizTalk Setup

Publishing a web service

This section describes how you can use Microsoft BizTalk Server to publish a simple web service like the one required to integrate a backend system with the SOAP adapter in the scenario described above.

Configuration comprises two steps:

1. Create a BizTalk orchestration.
2. Publish the orchestration as a web service.

In the first step, you create a BizTalk orchestration. The orchestration used in our example is a very simple one. It receives a message from SAP XI, which contains the flight data for which an availability check is to be performed. The incoming message undergoes a simple transformation, which simulates the availability check in a backend system. In the final step, the transformation generates a message containing the number of seats available on the flight. This message is sent to SAP XI.

This example was developed with BizTalk Server 2004, which uses Microsoft Visual Studio .NET 2003 as a development environment. However, it can also be implemented with BizTalk Server 2006, which uses Microsoft Visual Studio 2005 as a development environment. Therefore, the term Microsoft Visual Studio is used below.

Step 1: Create a BizTalk orchestration

The following steps are required to create a BizTalk orchestration:

Creating an orchestration

1. Create a new BizTalk project.
2. Create a Request schema.
3. Create a Response schema.
4. Create an empty BizTalk orchestration.
5. Add workflow items to the BizTalk orchestration.
6. Configure the workflow items.
7. Map the schemas.
8. Create a Request/Response port.
9. Connect your schemas to the port.
10. Create a strong key name.
11. Assign the strong name to the current BizTalk project.
12. Build and deploy your solution.

In the first step, you create a BizTalk project in Microsoft Visual Studio in order to generate the orchestration.

Schemas are created for the request and response messages for the sample application. These schemas have the same data structure as the inbound and outbound messages of the availability query in the XI demo example. Figure 5.40 shows the maintenance dialog in which the Request schema was created. Like the message that is to be sent to the travel agency, the schema contains the elements **AirlineID** and **ConnectionID** of the type string, and the element **FlightDate** of the type date.

Request and Response schemas

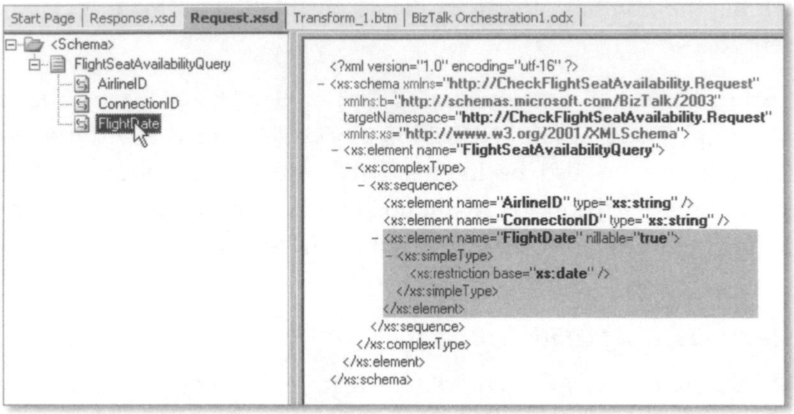

Figure 5.40 BizTalk—Request Schema

The orchestration maps the process of receiving, transforming, and sending the message in BizTalk. After the empty BizTalk orchestration is created, the workflow items for the mapping process can be added in the *BizTalk Orchestration Designer*. The following workflow items are added in sequence to the orchestration: A Receive Shape, a Construct Message Shape, a Send Shape, and a Transform Shape, which is dragged into the Construct Message Shape. After you have added the workflow items to the orchestration, connect them to the schemas you created earlier (see Figure 5.41).

Mapping the schemas After you configure the workflow items, the Request and Response schemas can be mapped to each another. To do this, start the BizTalk Mapper. Since no call to a backend system is incorporated into the BizTalk orchestration, we use mapping functions to ensure that the response message from BizTalk is filled with demo data (see Figure 5.42).

Both the source schema and the destination schema must be expanded in the BizTalk Mapper for this purpose. Next, drag a *Scripting Functoid* from the Toolbox into the mapping area and connect the attributes of the source and destination schemas to this.

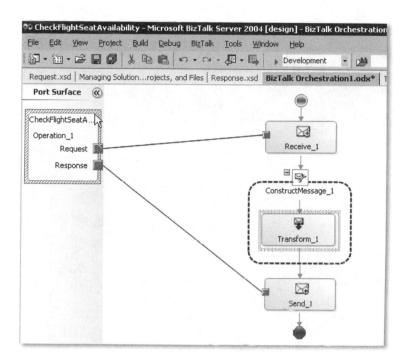

Figure 5.41 BizTalk Orchestration

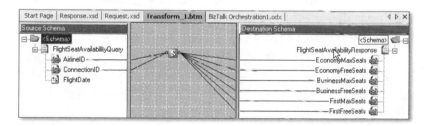

Figure 5.42 BizTalk Mapper

The following Inline C# script is created for the scripting functoid. It checks the airline ID transferred in the inbound message and returns a value for the number of seats in each case.

```
public int MyConcat(string airlineID, string _
connectionID)
{
    int seat = 0;
        if (airlineID == "UA")
        {
            switch (connectionID)
```

```
                        {
                            case ("0007"):
                                seat = 20;
                                break;
                            case ("1234"):
                                seat=40;
                                break;
                            default:
                                seat=1;
                                break;
                        }
                    }
                    else
                    {
                        seat=99;
                    }
        return seat;
        }
        }
```

Finally, create a Request/Response port and connect it to the orchestration.

Creating a strong name

A *strong name* must be generated before the BizTalk orchestration can be deployed. This ensures that the name of the assembly is unique. To generate a strong name, call the sn tool with the following options: sn -k CheckFlightSeatAvailabilityKey.snk. Then assign this strong name to the BizTalk project. After a strong name has been assigned to the orchestration, the build and deploy process can begin.

Step 2: Publish the orchestration as a web service

Publishing the orchestration

After the build and deploy process has been successfully completed, you can publish the orchestration as a web service. The process consists of three steps:

1. Publish the web service with the BizTalk Web Services Publishing Wizard.

2. Verify the publication with the IIS Manager.

3. Execute the Bind method for the ports and the Enlist method for the orchestration.

To start the BizTalk Web Services Publishing Wizard (see Figure 5.43) from the Visual Studio, select the menu option **Tools · BizTalk Web Services Publishing Wizard**. The wizard guides you through the different steps involved in publishing a BizTalk orchestration as a Web service.

On the **BizTalk Assembly** screen, select the DLL created in Step 1.

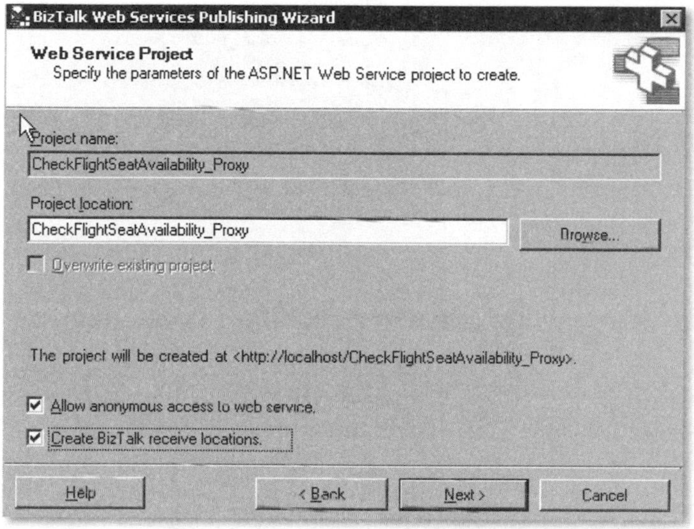

Figure 5.43 BizTalk Web Services Publishing Wizard

If you are calling the wizard for the second time, you must select the **Overwrite existing project** check box.

In the Internet Information Services (IIS) Manager, you can now check whether the orchestration has been successfully published as a web service. To do this, start the IIS Manager (see Figure 5.44) and select the virtual directory that contains the sample data.

ISS Manager

If you right-click the **CheckFlightSeatAvailabity_BizTalk_ Orchestration1_CheckFlightSeatAvailability_InPort.asmx** file and select **Browse**, the start page of the web service appears. From here, you can download the WSDL file (see Figure 5.45).

Next, execute the **Bind** and **Enlist** steps. Once these steps are completed, you have successfully published the BizTalk Server orchestration as a web service. If the BizTalk Server was configured as a business system in SAP XI, the web service can be called from SAP XI at runtime and is thus integrated into the XI demo example.

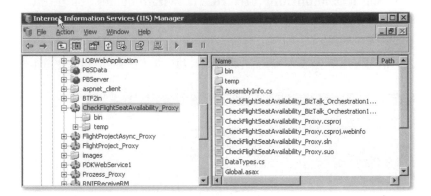

Figure 5.44 IIS Manager

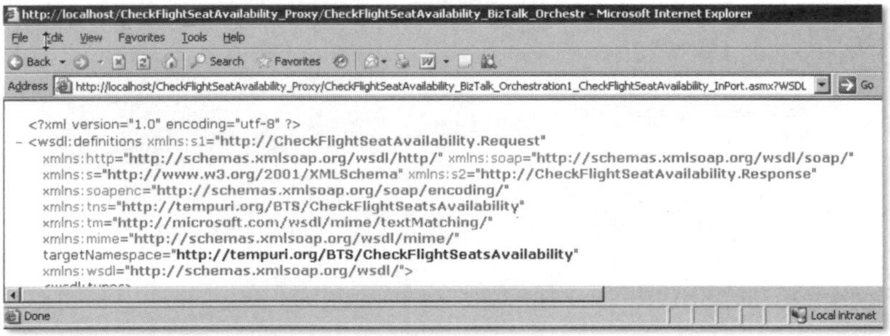

Figure 5.45 WSDL File of the BizTalk Web Service

5.4 BizTalk Adapter for mySAP Business Suite

With the SAP-certified *Microsoft BizTalk Adapter for mySAP Business Suite v2.0*, Microsoft offers an application-specific adapter that enables the integration of individual SAP systems into a BizTalk scenario.

This adapter facilitates both synchronous access to released SAP functions via BAPI or RFC and asynchronous access via IDoc. This access is largely "codefree." In other words, access is enabled first and foremost by configuring the adapter, rather than programming it.

What does this configuration consist of, and what is an adapter from a BizTalk perspective? A BizTalk adapter normally allows the BizTalk server to communicate with a third-party system by transforming the information to be communicated into a format that can be understood by that third-party system. In the case of technical adapters, this mostly involves protocol adjustments. However, there are also application-specific adapters that support the special features of the relevant business application. The Microsoft BizTalk Adapter for mySAP Business Suite v2.0 is one such application adapter.

The BizTalk Server normally comprises receiver and sender adapters, receiver and sender pipelines, orchestrations, the BizTalk message store, and a business rule module. The adapters play the role of "interpreters" in the BizTalk Server. As shown earlier in Figure 5.3, they "translate" external message formats into the internal XML-based message format of the BizTalk Server. Unlike the protocol-based adapters, which "understand" SOAP, HTML, or FTP, for example, the Microsoft BizTalk Adapter for mySAP Business Suite v2.0 can handle SAP-specific concepts such as IDocs, BAPIs, or RFC. To do so, it requires the SAP Connector for Microsoft .NET 1.0.x in the runtime environment.[8]

The BizTalk Adapter for mySAP Business Suite is currently available in the following two versions:

1. **Microsoft BizTalk Adapter for mySAP Business Suite v2.0**
   Version 2.0 only works with BizTalk 2004 Server and Visual Studio 2003. It does not form part of the BizTalk license, and must be purchased as an additional product. It supports SAP R/3 systems as of Release 4.x, and the SAP Web Application Server as of Version 6.20.

2. **Microsoft BizTalk Adapter for mySAP Business Suite v2.0 SP1**
   The new SP1 version supports not only BizTalk Server 2004[9], but also BizTalk Server 2006, Visual Studio 2005, and Microsoft.NET Framework 2.0, Furthermore, this adapter is part of BizTalk Server 2006 and therefore incurs no extra charge.

If we examine how the *BizTalk SAP Adapter* works, we can distinguish between the two distinct areas of development (design time) and runtime.

---

8   Important: The SAP Connector for Microsoft .NET Version 2.0 cannot be used for this purpose!

9   The previous 2.0 version is also required to support BizTalk Server 2004.

Development
(design time)

During development (design time), developers can use the BizTalk Explorer in a BizTalk project in Visual Studio. Here they can quickly and easily make various settings for the BizTalk Server. These settings are then stored in the BizTalk Config Database. In relation to the Microsoft BizTalk Adapter for mySAP Business Suite v2.0, the receive and send ports for communication with SAP can be configured in the BizTalk Explorer, as shown in Figure 5.46.

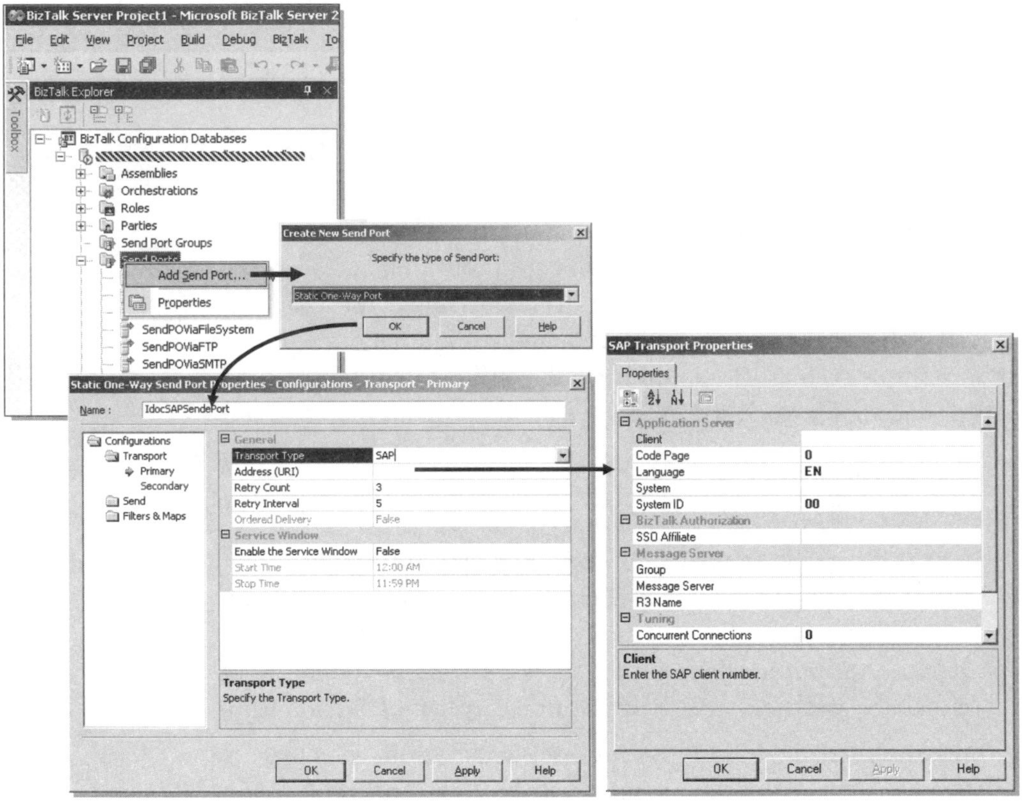

Figure 5.46 Configuring a Port in BizTalk Explorer

Alternatively, the BizTalk Administration Console and the *Adapter Configuration Page* can be used to make the basic settings for the Adapter. This is shown in Figure 5.47.

The logon entries of the relevant SAP system must be entered in the send and receive properties of the SAP adapter.

Schema Generation
Wizard

Another tool for development (design time) is the *Schema Generation Wizard*. This allows you to generate Request and Response schemas by accessing the SAP metadata. As mentioned above, the schema specifies, in XML, the format of the incoming or outgoing message.

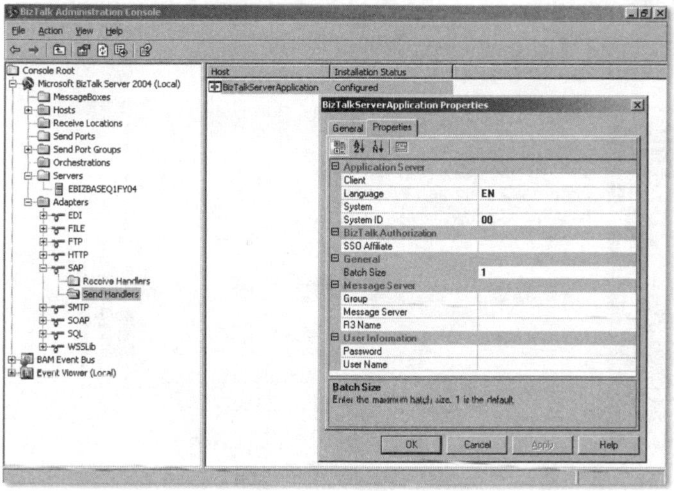

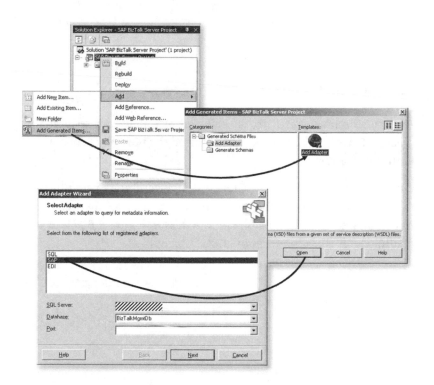

Figure 5.47 Adapter Configuration Page

Figure 5.48 Adding an SAP Adapter to the BizTalk Project

Figures 5.48 and 5.49 show examples of how the Schema Generation Wizard of the BizTalk Adapter for mySAP Business Suite can be used.

In Figure 5.48, an adapter of the type SAP is added to a previously empty BizTalk Server project in Visual Studio.

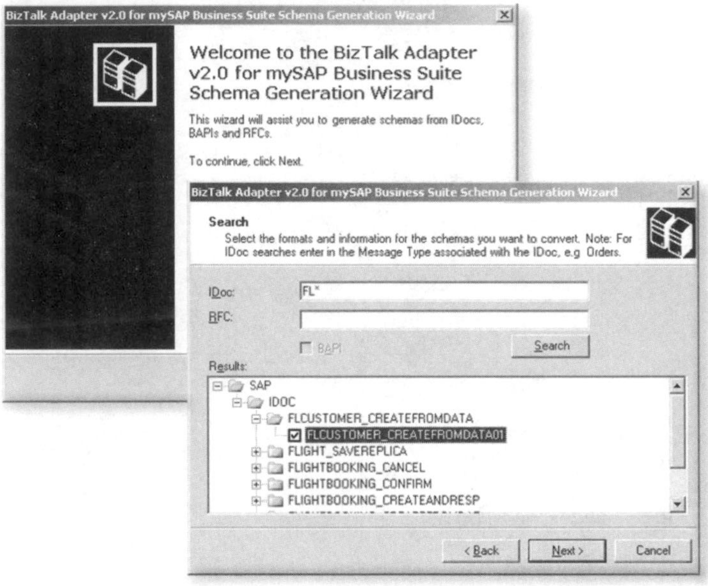

Figure 5.49 Starting the Schema Generation Wizard

An available port must then be selected or a new SAP-specific port created. Once you have selected or created the port, the Schema Generation Wizard starts.

One of the steps the Schema Generation Wizard guides you through is specifying the IDoc or RFC/BAPI for which the relevant metadata is to be accessed in order to generate the (*.xsd). Figure 5.50 shows the result, which takes the form of an XSD schema file.

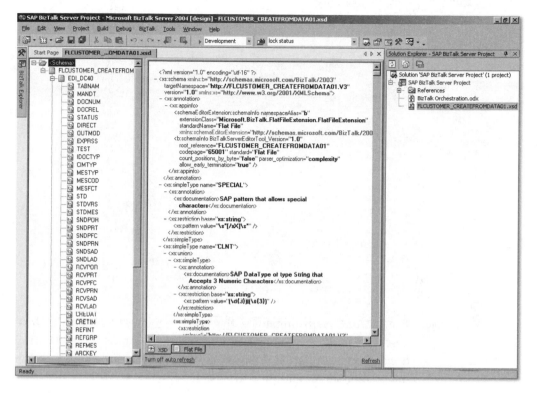

Figure 5.50 SAP Schema File in BizTalk Project

This schema can then be used in the process definition and in the orchestration of the BizTalk Server. A simple example of an orchestration is shown in Figure 5.51.

The orchestration represents the runtime environment for business process in the BizTalk Server, and is developed with the Visual Studio Designer.

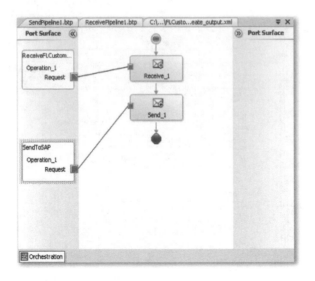

Figure 5.51 Orchestration in the BizTalk Server

Runtime

The runtime environment of the BizTalk Adapter for mySAP Business Suite in BizTalk Server uses the following components to ensure transactional support for communication in both directions between the BizTalk Server and the SAP system:

- **Transmitter**
  The transmitter sends IDocs, BAPIs, and RFCs to the SAP target system, using the SAP Connector for Microsoft .NET (see above). The transmitter is configured with the send port.

- **Receiver**
  The receiver can receive IDocs, BAPIs, and RFCs from SAP systems, and is similarly based on the SAP Connector for Microsoft .NET. The receiver is configured with the receive port.

- **Exception Handler**
  The Exception Handler provides full transactional support between the BizTalk Server and the SAP system. A full rollback is possible should an error occurs.

Centralized user management and single sign-on can significantly reduce the operating costs of an IT system landscape, while simultaneously increasing the productivity of end users. The SAP NetWeaver platform provides the technical basis for central identity management and single sign-on in an existing Microsoft infrastructure.

6   Identity Management and Single Sign-On

Although centralized user management and single sign-on (SSO) offer a wide range of benefits, the reality is that many companies are not currently availing of these. In today's complex system landscapes, employees often have to log on separately to various SAP systems, using different passwords in each case. These are in addition to the user names and passwords required to log on to their PCs, which are usually members of a Windows domain. And yet more user IDs and passwords are often needed to access other, non-SAP applications.

The situation is usually compounded by the fact that security guidelines within the company require users to change their passwords for the various applications on a regular basis. This naturally makes it difficult for many users to remember the details of their various user accounts and passwords. At the very least, many users are unable to remember which passwords to use to log on to the various systems when they return to work after a vacation. It is therefore unsurprising that a large percentage of requests sent to internal support organizations are from users who have forgotten their passwords.

Security guidelines as a security risk

These problems also pose a security risk for the company. This is because users tend to choose passwords that are either easy to remember and therefore also easy to guess, or so complex that they cannot be remembered and have to be written down. In this case, the passwords are jotted down on a piece of paper and left on desks or in other obvious locations (on keyboards, monitors, and so on).

User management for all these applications is decentralized in many cases. Whenever a new employee joins the company or whenever an employee transfers to a different area within the company, the relevant user accounts must be manually created or changed. This task often has to be carried out by different administrators in different systems.

Example of a user management process Take the example of a new employee whose HR master data is entered in mySAP ERP Human Capital Management (mySAP ERP HCM) as soon as he/she joins the company. Various administrators then generate an e-mail address in the groupware system, user accounts in the Microsoft Active Directory and in the SAP NetWeaver Portal, mySAP ERP, mySAP CRM, and other systems for the new user. Groups and roles are assigned to the employee's user accounts, which enable access to the data and services he/she requires.

In most cases, the employee will have to wait a certain time for the required system accesses and authorizations to be made available. Another problem occurs when an employee leaves the company. Administrators must be able to lock business-critical data and applications so that they can no longer be accessed by that employee. This is not easily accomplished without centralized user management.

6.1 Identity Management and Single Sign-On as a Solution Approach

What is identity management? *Identity management* comprises business processes, guidelines, and technologies that allow a company to control user access to applications and resources and to prevent unauthorized access to confidential information.

The objective of implementing identity management is to automate processes. For example, after HR master data is entered, the user accounts for the relevant employee are generated almost automatically, together with the required access rights. Similarly, if an employee changes their role in the company, his/her user accounts are automatically adjusted. And, if an employee leaves the company, user administration can deactivate all relevant user accounts simultaneously with one keystroke.

Single sign-on (SSO) means that, after a single authentication, users can access all systems within a system landscape, without having to authenticate themselves again for each individual system. If you implement the scenarios described in this chapter, users are initially authenticated in the SAP NetWeaver Portal with the Kerberos ticket that is issued when they log on to their Windows PC. The SAP NetWeaver Portal can use Active Directory as a data source for the portal users. After authentication, the portal assigns users a logon ticket, which they can use to log on to various SAP or non-SAP systems in the backend.

What is single sign-on?

A company will quickly reap the rewards of implementing this scenario. With single sign-on and central user management, the costs involved in user administration and resetting of passwords are dramatically reduced. The total cost of ownership (TCO) can be reduced because existing SAP and Microsoft licenses can be used and no third-party software is required to implement the interfaces.

Reducing the total cost of ownership

An SAP customer's Help Desk was able, for example, to eliminate 7,200 calls annually by implementing central user management and single sign-on.

In certain cases, an *identity management system* (or IMS, see Section 6.3) may have to be implemented to meet additional identity management requirements, for example, if a central identity management system is to be implemented that comprises other, non-SAP systems that cannot be mapped with the interfaces described next.

Identity management systems

6.2 Centralized Identity Management with SAP NetWeaver and Microsoft Active Directory

The key element of an identity management implementation is the use of a central repository, which can be accessed by various applications using open standards, such as *Lightweight Directory Access Protocol* (LDAP). Many companies already use a Microsoft Active Directory infrastructure as the basis for their Windows Server 2000 or Windows Server 2003 domains.

The SAP NetWeaver platform provides the technical basis for central identity management in an SAP system landscape. The SAP NetWeaver Application Server can access information from a central directory service, such as Microsoft Active Directory, using LDAP protocol. This enables centralized identity management of an SAP system landscape, integrated into an existing Active Directory landscape. This integration scenario involves the following three interfaces.

User Management Engine

The *User Management Engine* (UME) is the Java-based user management component of the SAP NetWeaver Application Server. The UME can access the internal database of the J2EE Engine and ABAP-based SAP systems, and can use LDAP protocol to access LDAP directory services like Microsoft Active Directory as a data source for user data (see Figure 6.1).

Central User Administration

With *Central User Administration* (CUA) of ABAP systems, all user administration tasks for a system group comprising several SAP systems with several different clients can be executed centrally in a single client. Changes to user masters are replicated from the central CUA system into the connected child systems. CUA continues to store user data in the ABAP system, but periodically is able to synchronize the user data with a directory service.

SAP HR-LDAP interface

The *SAP HR-LDAP interface* creates and updates users in the Active Directory based on information from the employee masters in mySAP ERP Human Capital Management (mySAP ERP HCM).

With this integration scenario, a user can log on to the SAP NetWeaver Portal directly because the Active Directory is used as a data source. The user accounts in the Active Directory can be created manually or with the SAP HR-LDAP interface.[1] The user accounts required to access the mySAP Business Suite systems connected to the portal are automatically created by the LDAP synchronization of CUA.

---

1   Users that are created by the SAP HR-LDAP interface are created as inactive users without a password. These users therefore have to be manually activated and assigned a password.

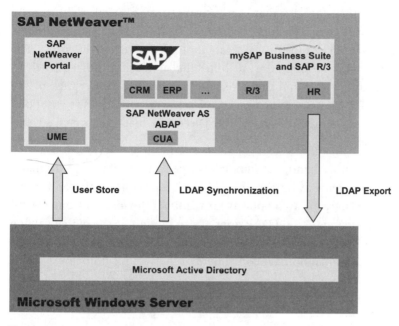

Figure 6.1 Integration of SAP User Management with Microsoft Active Directory

6.2.1 Active Directory

Active Directory is the directory service integrated into Windows Server 2000 and Windows Server 2003. It is used to manage users and resources, such as PCs, printers, and servers, within a company network. Active Directory can be used as a central user repository for an SAP NetWeaver system landscape. LDAP is used for access. Many companies already use Microsoft Active Directory as part of their Windows domain structure. For detailed documentation, refer to Microsoft TechNet.[2]

In most cases, it is sufficient to set up a single *domain* because the delegation of responsibilities allows you to assign users administrative rights in one or more *organizational units* (OU). However, it may be necessary to set up several domains for different areas within the company due to scalability requirements and various security guidelines and settings (for example, user rights and password guidelines).

---

2 *http://technet2.microsoft.com/WindowsServer/en/library/6f8a7c80-45fc-4916-80d9-16e6d46241f91033.mspx?mfr=true.*

Global
catalog server

One or more domains that use the same *schema*[3] and a *global catalog* are referred to as a *forest* (see Figure 6.2). The global catalog contains a partial replica of the domain data for each domain in the forest. The partial replicas contain the attributes that are used most frequently in search operations and those required to locate a full replica of the object. The global catalog thus enables central read access to user and group data stored in an Active Directory that comprises several domains.

If, on the other hand, a system landscape consists of a single domain, LDAP queries can be sent directly to a domain controller for the domain. There are two options for reading information from several domains using LDAP. LDAP queries can be sent to the global catalog on port 3268, or port 389 can be used to send several LDAP queries to the individual domain controllers of the various domains.

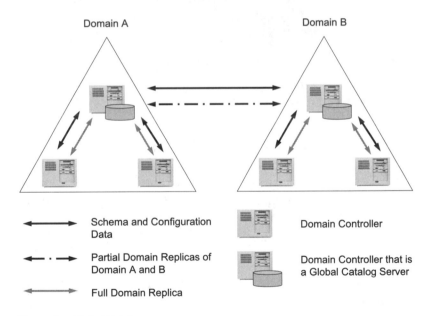

←——→ Schema and Configuration Data	Domain Controller
←—·—→ Partial Domain Replicas of Domain A and B	Domain Controller that is a Global Catalog Server
←——→ Full Domain Replica	

Figure 6.2 Global Catalog

If access is required to attributes of a user object that is not contained in the global catalog, these should be added to the global catalog

---

3 The definitions of the object classes and attributes are stored in the schema. If additional attributes are to be stored for an object, the schema may have to be extended.

because the global catalog only contains the most frequently used object attributes as standard.

As an alternative to using the global catalog for consolidated access to a forest, you can use Microsoft Active Directory Application Mode (ADAM). In contrast to Active Directory, ADAM is an LDAP-specific directory service. Microsoft developed ADAM to support directory service-enabled applications that require the merging of data from several forests. ADAM is therefore ideal for consolidating user data in Active Directory environments consisting of several domains. With *bind redirection*, ADAM as the global catalog provides a proxy function for authentication against a forest that consists of several domains. In contrast to the global catalog, ADAM also enables write access. Any user attributes can replicated from the connected Active Directories.[4]

Microsoft Active Directory Application Mode (ADAM)

However, using ADAM is associated with additional installation and configuration costs. An ADAM instance must be generated, configured, and operated. In addition, mechanisms must be implemented to enable the automatic synchronization of the ADAM user accounts with the user accounts in the Active Directory. An identity management system is essential for this purpose. You can use *Microsoft Identity Integration Server 2003* (MIIS) or the *Identity Integration Feature Pack* (IIFP) from Microsoft. The Identity Integration Feature Pack for Microsoft Windows Server Active Directory is a pared-down version of MIIS 2003 that is available to download free of charge.

Microsoft provides a collection of programs, referred to as *support tools*, for managing the Active Directory. You will find these in the *\Support\Tools* folder on the Windows Server installation CD. The *ADSI Edit* tool is ideal for administrative access to the Active Directory. To use this, you require the *adsiedit.msc* snap-in for the Microsoft Management Console (MMC). Among other things, this allows you to display and maintain all attributes of Active Directory objects required to set up the interfaces in SAP (see Figure 6.8).

Support tools

---

4 *http://www.microsoft.com/downloads/details.aspx?familyID=d9143610-c04d-41c4-b7ea-6f56819769d5.*

6.2.2 User Management Engine (UME)

The User Management Engine (UME) of the SAP NetWeaver Portal supports several data sources for the storage of user data (see Figure 6.3).

This and most of the other functions described in this section are available with SAP Enterprise Portal 6.0 Support Package 9. However, for the sake of readability, the term SAP NetWeaver Portal is used in the following discussion.

User Management Core Layer

Access to the SAP NetWeaver Portal and other J2EE applications is encapsulated using an abstraction layer, referred to as the *User Management Core Layer*. In addition to a Java API, the UME offers access via a Service Provisioning Markup Language (SPML) interface, which can also be used by external applications, such as identity management systems. The UME accesses the individual data sources (also referred to as user persistence stores) using persistence adapters.

In addition to the internal database of the J2EE Engine, the ABAP user database of an SAP NetWeaver Application Server is supported as a data source. The UME can be integrated with Active Directory as an LDAP directory.

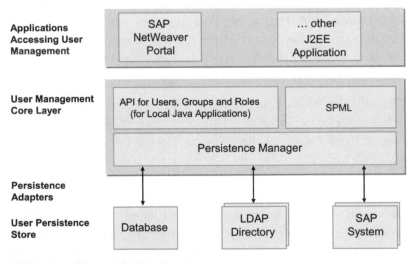

SPML = Service Provisioning Markup Language

Figure 6.3 User Management Engine (UME)

If Active Directory is used as a data source for the UME, no users have to be created in the UME. When a user logs on with a user name and password, the LDAP simple bind mechanism of Active Directory is used for authentication. This means that users do not have to remember any additional passwords for logging on to the SAP NetWeaver Portal. If single sign-on is also configured, the initial user authentication on the Windows PC can be re-used for logging on to the SAP NetWeaver Portal (see Section 6.5.3).

For security reasons, Secure Sockets Layer (SSL) protocol should be used to ensure secure LDAP communication between the UME and Active Directory or ADAM. Otherwise, the users' Windows passwords will be transferred by the network as plain text. LDAP access to the Active Directory uses either standard port 389 for the LDAP protocol to the individual domain controllers or port 3268 for global catalog servers. If the communication is encrypted with SSL, the LDAP communication runs over SSL (LDAPS) to a domain controller via port 636, and to a global catalog server via port 3269. The configuration of SSL is essential if you want to generate users in the Active Directory with the UME. In this case, the individual domain controllers must be accessed via LDAPS because write access to the global catalog is not possible.

SSL

UME Configuration

The UME can only be configured for using an LDAP directory after installation. To do this, start the *User Management Configuration Tool* in the SAP NetWeaver Portal under **System Administration · System Configuration**, and then select the **UM Configuration** menu option on the detailed navigation screen (see Figure 6.4).

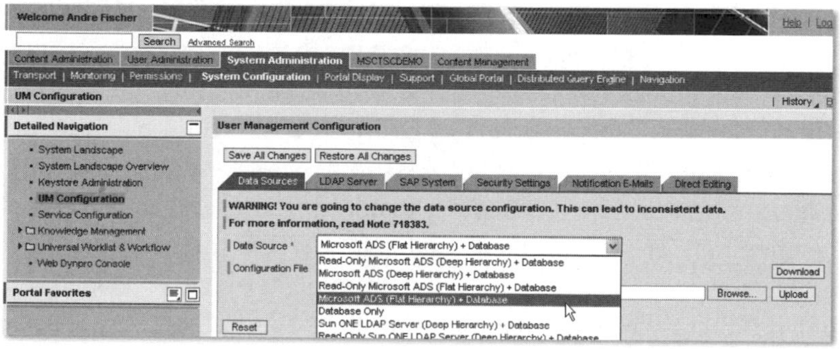

Data sources

Figure 6.4 SAP NetWeaver Portal—Maintaining UME Data: Data sources

With the UME, SAP provides configuration files for various standard scenarios. The following templates can be selected for the Active Directory:

- Write-protected Microsoft ADS (deep hierarchy) + database
- Microsoft ADS (deep hierarchy) + database
- Write-protected Microsoft ADS (flat hierarchy) + database
- Microsoft ADS (flat hierarchy) + database

Deep hierarchy   With a *deep hierarchy*, organizational units are used as UME groups. In a deep hierarchy, group membership is determined by the position of the user object in the DIT (Directory Information Tree). This variant can be used by customers who have mapped their organizational structure in the Active Directory. A user then inherits all roles that have been assigned to organizational units that are located above the organizational unit containing the user object in the container hierarchy.

Flat hierarchy   With a *flat hierarchy*, Active Directory groups are used as UME groups. Group membership of an Active Directory user does not change if the user object is moved within the directory tree.

An existing group structure or organizational structure in the active directory can be used for role management because the UME permits the assignment of portal roles to groups as well as the direct assignment to users. This means that, depending on the selected hierarchy, portal roles can be assigned to Active Directory groups or to organizational units in the Active Directory.

If a portal role is assigned to a UME group, this role is also automatically assigned to all group members. In addition, the UME allows you to use *nested groups*. These are groups that contain other groups as group members. For example, if Group B is a member of Group A, a role assignment for members of Group A is inherited by all members of Group B. The `ume.allow_nested_groups` parameter is set by default as TRUE in the UME. As a result, portal users' actual group memberships are determined recursively when they log on. This means that portal roles can be assigned to higher-level groups in the Active Directory if a flat hierarchy is used. If a deep hierarchy is used instead, portal roles assigned to higher-level organizational units can be inherited by subordinate organizational units.

The connection data for the LDAP server is maintained on the **LDAP Server** tab in the User Management Configuration Tool. To access this tool, select **System Administration · System Configuration** and select the **UM Configuration** menu option on the detailed navigation screen.

Figure 6.5 shows the connection of a multidomain environment using a global catalog server. The domains in this case are MSCTSC.SAP.CORP and WDF.MSCTSC.SAP.CORP. The domain controller, on which the global catalog is also located, has the host name msctscdc1.msctsc.sap.corp and is accessed via port 3268. In this example, the userprincipalname attribute is used for the unique ID and the user ID of the portal user because the individual domains in the forest contain identical Windows user names (sAMAccountName).

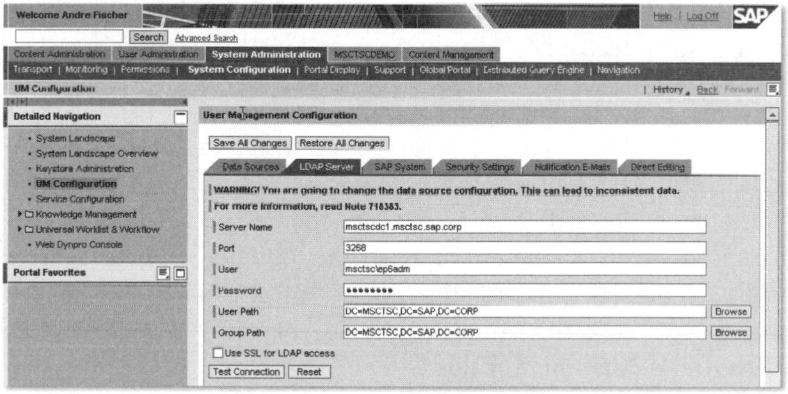

Figure 6.5 SAP NetWeaver Portal—Maintaining UME Data: LDAP Server

In an Active Directory environment consisting of a single domain, you can use port 389 rather than the global catalog to access the domain controller. You can use the ADSI Edit tool, which Microsoft provides in its Support Tools, to determine the user's distinguished name for LDAP access to the UME and the path to the user and group container.

Negative user filter

With the *negative user filter*, you can define that certain users from the LDAP directory used as a data source are not to be displayed or taken into account in the UME. The ume.ldap.negative_user_filter parameter is used for this purpose, which allows you to define the template for names that are to be excluded. This is a useful function because problems may occur in the UME if the connected data sources contain users with names identical to those used by internal portal users that only exist in the portal database.

These users must be created in the Active Directory (for example, for the internal portal user *index_service*) if TREX is to access a Microsoft-based WebDAV repository (see Section 4.2) via the SSO22KerbMap module with single sign-on.

Active Directory Forests with Several Domains

The following options are available if you create a user management configuration that uses an Active Directory with several domains as a data source. These are the connections of:

▸ Individual domains as separate LDAP directories

▸ The global catalog

▸ An ADAM directory service

Individual domains

The UME supports the use of several data sources in parallel. This means that individual domains can be connected to the UME as separate LDAP data sources. Note, however, that SAP can support a maximum of five different LDAP data sources because the performance of the UME deteriorates as the number of data sources increases. However, in this scenario, in contrast to using the global catalog, you have the option of configuring both read and write access to the different domains.

Global catalog

If you want to connect more than five domains to the UME, or if you have fewer than five domains and want to use a single LDAP directory to connect to the UME as a data source, you can access the global catalog. The global catalog permits access to the most frequently used attributes of the Active Directory users and groups. However, access is read-only. If access to attributes is required that are not contained in the global catalog, the global catalog can be adjusted so that additional attributes can be added. Since attributes stored in the global catalog are replicated in each global catalog in the forest, the effect on replication must be checked in this case. A restriction may arise if you use groups in role management because the global catalog can only be used to evaluate the group membership of Active Directory users in *universal groups*. Group membership of *global groups* or *local domain groups* cannot be evaluated.

As an alternative to the global catalog, you can use Microsoft ADAM for consolidated access to data in a forest. You may consider using ADAM if it is not possible to use universal groups or if write access is required. With *bind redirection*, ADAM as the global catalog provides a proxy function for authenticating LDAP queries in Active Directory forests with several domains. If ADAM is used as a data source for the UME, users can authenticate themselves with their Windows password because the LDAP query is forwarded from the ADAM instance to the relevant domain controller.

ADAM

However, as mentioned above, using ADAM is associated with additional installation and configuration costs. The global catalog, in contrast, is available out of the box as part of an Active Directory infrastructure. Therefore, when connecting forests with several domains to the UME, you must consider whether the global catalog can be used for access or whether additional requirements, such as write access, necessitate the installation of an ADAM instance.

Global catalog or ADAM?

Two attributes, the *logon ID* and the *unique ID*, are essential for the LDAP configuration of the UME. This is because the UME assigns a unique ID to LDAP users. All data for these users is stored in the portal database under this unique ID. This includes data such as role assignments or user assignments for these users. A freely configurable attribute of the LDAP user object forms part of the unique ID. If, for example, the attribute userPrincipalName is used as the unique ID, the unique ID of a user in the MSCTSC domain with the DNS name MSCTSC.SAP.CORP is as follows:

Unique ID and logon ID

USER.CORP_LDAP.Jon.Doe@MSCTSC.SAP.CORP

The logon ID is the name of the user account of the portal user, which is mapped to the j_user UME attribute. The logon ID is an attribute of the LDAP user object and can be freely defined with the UME. Since both the unique ID and the logon ID must be unique, they must be mapped to unique attributes of the LDAP user object. The sAMAccountName attribute is used by default for both the logon ID and the unique ID in the current SAP NetWeaver version. The sAMAccountName is the Windows user name used to log on to the Windows domain.

In Active Directory environments consisting of several domains, a problem may occur with users in different domains who have an identical sAMAccountName. This occurs because the sAMAccountname must only be unique within a domain but does not have to be unique within the forest. In cases where company-wide guidelines cannot ensure that the sAMAccountName is unique within a forest, SAP recommends using the userprincipalname attribute because this attribute is unique and indexed in each forest in an Active Directory.

In earlier versions of the SAP NetWeaver Portal, the UME used the distinguished name (DN) of a user as part of the unique ID. This caused a problem because the Active Directory users could not be moved within the Active Directory hierarchy without portal-specific information being lost. This occurred because moving a user from one organizational unit (OU) into another OU changes the distinguished name and thus also the unique ID (see above). In this case, the UME configuration can be changed, as described in SAP Note 777640, *Using an LDAP Directory as a UME Data Source*. Note, however, that subsequent changes to these UME settings result in an irreversible loss of portal-specific user information because the unique ID changes.

6.2.3   Directory Service Integration of ABAP Applications

LDAP Connector   The LDAP Connector enables direct access from ABAP applications via LDAP. The LDAP Connector can be accessed from ABAP using an API, whose function calls allow you to log on to the directory services and to find, generate, delete and change directory service entries, for example. This API is delivered with SAP Basis Release 4.6. However, this release does not contain any functions for synchronizing SAP user management with LDAP-enabled directory services. These functions and the SAP HR-LDAP interface are available as of SAP Web AS ABAP 6.10.

For the sake of readability, the term SAP NetWeaver Application Server is used consistently in the following discussion, even though the LDAP Connector functions are available with SAP Web Application Server 6.10.

Technically speaking, the LDAP Connector consists of the *ldap_rfc* program, which is executed as a registered server program, and is accessed from SAP NetWeaver AS ABAP via RFC (see Figure 6.6). Communication between the Microsoft Active Directory and the executable file *ldap_rfc* uses the standard Internet protocol LDAP, and, at operating system level, requires an LDAP library that is available for most platforms.[5] The LDAP Connector then runs as part of the SAP NetWeaver AS in the *usr\sap\<SID>\SYS\exe\run* (Windows) or */usr/sap/<SID>/sys/exe/run* directory (Unix) and is monitored by CCMS.

The *wldap32.dll* LDAP library is installed as standard on the Windows platform. This allows the LDAP Connector to be installed as a Windows service if an LDAP library is not available or cannot be installed on the SAP NetWeaver AS operating system.

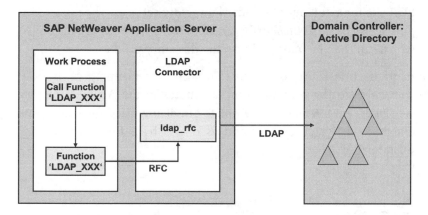

Figure 6.6 LDAP Connector

6.2.4 Central User Administration (CUA)

While the UME of the SAP NetWeaver Portal can use Microsoft Active Directory as a native data source for users, ABAP-based SAP systems use their own user databases. Central User Administration (CUA) can be used to manage the user masters of the ABAP-based SAP systems in a central system and to distribute this data into the connected child systems via ALE. All SAP systems with Basis Release 4.6 and higher can be used as child systems.

With the SAP NetWeaver AS ABAP, the BC-SAP-USR interface, which uses the LDAP Connector, allows you to synchronize user data with an LDAP directory service. Both Active Directory and ADAM are certified by SAP for the BC-SAP-USR interface. In this scenario,

BC-SAP-USR interface

---

5 See also SAP Note 188371, *Configuring the LDAP Connector.*

Microsoft Active Directory or ADAM can be used as the main system for storing user data. If LDAP synchronization is used in the central CUA system, all systems connected to CUA can be synchronized with Active Directory. This is particularly useful for older systems (4.6), which do not offer the option of LDAP integration.

Configuration of the interface is described in detail in the How-To Guides in Section 6.4.

Schema extension and mapping

With schema extension, attributes can be created in the Active Directory for SAP-specific fields, such as the **sap-username** field. The RSLDAPSCHMEAEXT report allows you to generate a corresponding LDIF file for a number of standard directory services. The report outputs a list of attributes to be created for SAP-specific data fields, which can then be imported into the directory product.

In transaction LDAPMAP, you can define the mapping of the SAP data fields to the corresponding attributes in the Active Directory (see Figure 6.7). A mapping template can be imported for the schema extension delivered by SAP and used as a basis for more detailed Customizing.

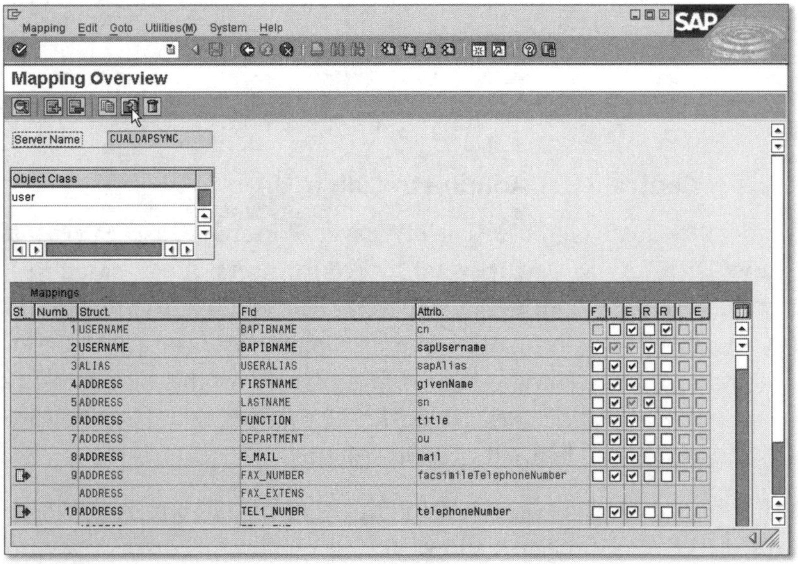

Figure 6.7 Mapping SAP Data Fields to the Attributes in the Microsoft Active Directory

Search accesses can be accelerated if the attribute set as a **filter** in the **mapping overview** (see Figure 6.7) is indexed. Figure 6.8 shows access to the SAP-specific attributes with Microsoft's ADSI Edit support tool.

If no schema extension can be imported into the Microsoft Active Directory, it may be possible in certain cases to access existing schema extensions, such as those provided for Microsoft Exchange (*extensionAttribute1, …, extensionAttribute15*). In this case, however, the imported mapping template must be adjusted accordingly and the attribute used as a filter attribute should be indexed in the Active Directory.

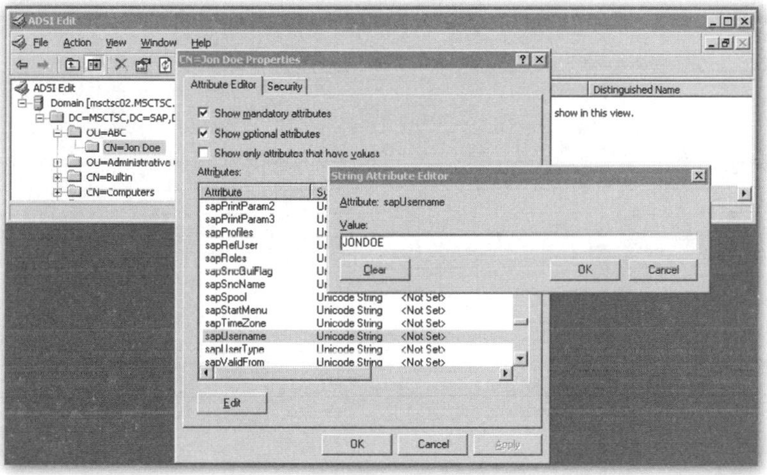

Figure 6.8 ADSI Edit—Maintaining SAP-Specific User Attributes

If new users are created in the Active Directory, new user accounts are created in the Central User Administration system during the next synchronization run, and the changes are distributed to the connected child systems. The RSLDAPSYNC_USER report selects all user accounts to be synchronized with Active Directory. The report must either be scheduled regularly or started as an event-controlled job with the SAP program *sapevt.exe*. Figure 6.9 shows the selection screen of the RSLDAPSYNC_USER report.

Synchronization

In a synchronization run, new users are created in the SAP user database without a password, and existing users are changed (see Figure 6.10).

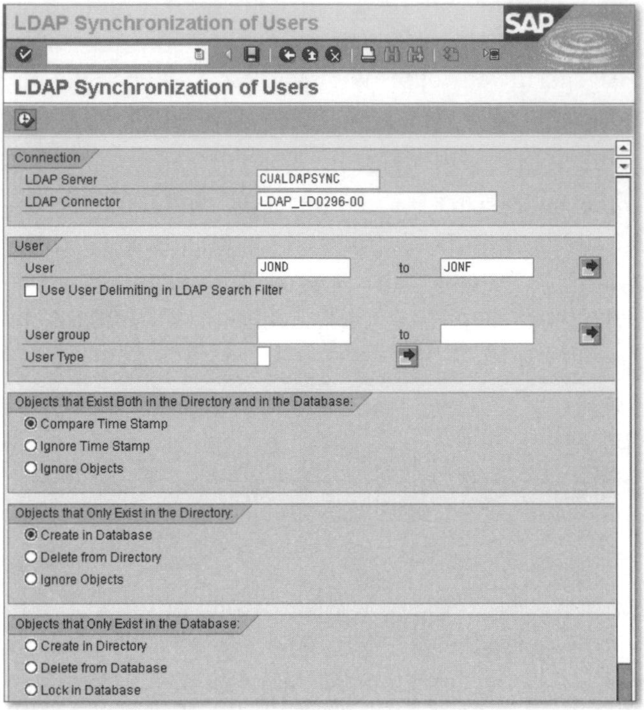

Figure 6.9 The RSLDAPSYNC_USER Report

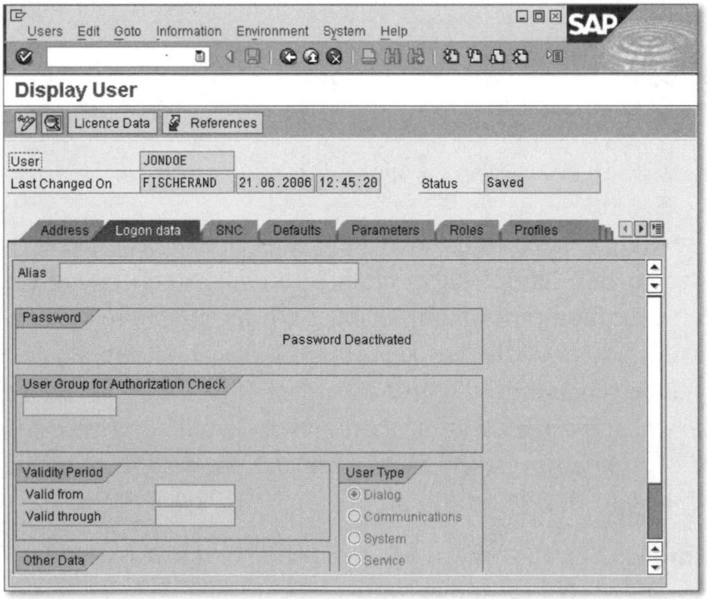

Figure 6.10 Users Created by LDAP Synchronization

A password is not required for user accounts created in this way if a single sign-on mechanism with SAP logon tickets is implemented with the SAP NetWeaver Portal. This approach also ensures that users can only log on to the SAP systems using single sign-on. A password should be assigned to administrators (for example, SAP* or DDIC) to allow them to log on if the SAP NetWeaver Portal, which issues the logon tickets, is not available.

6.2.5 SAP HR-LDAP Interface

Employee master data can be used to control Active Directory users. If a new employee joins a company, the HR department enters this information in the HR master data. The SAP HR system is the system the company uses to manage central user data, such as an employee's first name, last name, employee ID, address, and so on.

SAP NetWeaver provides an interface for generating and changing users in an LDAP directory service such as Microsoft Active Directory. Using a query or ABAP report, data can be extracted from HR via the *HR Data Retrieval in a LDAP Enabled Directory Service* interface (function module SPLDAP_RECEIVE_ATTRIBUTES), and written to the directory service using the LDAP Connector. Data extraction using an ABAP report is the preferred method for extracting complex data and formatting it before export (see Figure 6.11).

Configuration of the interface is described in detail in the How-To Guides in Section 6.4.

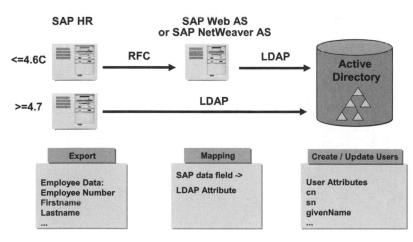

Figure 6.11 SAP HR-LDAP Interface—Architecture

The ABAP code of the SPLDAP_RECEIVE_ATTRIBUTES interface function module is delivered with SAP Basis Release 6.10. If employee data is to be extracted from an SAP HR 4.6 system, the SPLDAP_RECEIVE_ATTRIBUTES function module can be called remotely in a separate SAP Web Application Server or SAP NetWeaver Application Server, which then functions as an LDAP gateway. If the HR system is part of SAP R/3 Enterprise or a higher release, the function module can be called locally.

Since the user data does not have to be entered manually in this case, errors that normally occur during the transfer of application forms or with the exchange of information over the phone can be excluded. As a result, the entire process is greatly accelerated.

Employee Self-Service (ESS) If you use Employee Self-Service (ESS), employees have the option of maintaining some of their HR data themselves. In this case, the task of entering HR data is divided between the HR department and the employees themselves. If, for example, an employee's room number changes, this data can be entered by the employee, and the data is automatically updated in the Active Directory via the SAP HR-LDAP interface.

Result While new users are created in the Active Directory as inactive user accounts without a password, existing user accounts are updated with the information extracted from the SAP HR system. Figure 6.12 shows two inactive user accounts, which were created by the SAP HR-LDAP interface.

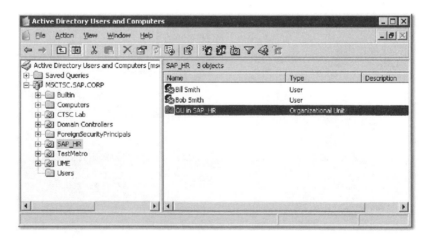

Figure 6.12 Active Directory Users Created by the SAP HR-LDAP Interface

Since these user accounts are inactive and no password can be transferred via the LDAP Connector, manual postprocessing by Active Directory administrators is required.

The SAP HR-LDAP interface provided by SAP only executes a data export. It cannot be used to import data from the directory service. However, a data import can be implemented in a customer-specific report with the LDAP API provided in ABAP. You could, for example, use this to import a user's e-mail address into SAP HR, for which a company's groupware system is the primary system. Another restriction is the lack of delta management for the `SPLDAP_RECEIVE_ATTRIBUTES` function module. This means that the export changes the user object if the same data is exported a second time. However, delta management can be implemented in the ABAP code of a customer-specific extraction report.

Restrictions

6.3 Identity Management Systems

In certain cases, an IMS may have to be implemented to fulfill additional identity management requirements that cannot be covered by the SAP standard integration scenarios described above. In this case, UME user management and ABAP user management provide open interfaces that allow external identity management systems to manage SAP user master records.

SAP provides BAPIs such as `BAPI_USER_CHANGE` for ABAP user management. The API is described in detail in the following document on the SAP Service Marketplace:

BAPI_USER_
CHANGE

http://service.sap.com/security · *Security in Detail* · *Secure User Access* · *Identity Management* · *SAP Identity Management APIs*

The UME provides an interface based on Service Provisioning Markup Language (SPML), which allows you to connect to external systems. SPML is an open standard, which is used, for example, to provision user accounts and access privileges for certain systems and applications. SPML Version 1.0 was released as a standard by the *Organization for the Advancement of Structured Information Standards* (OASIS) in October 2003.

SPML

HiPath SIcurity DirX Based on these open interfaces provided by SAP NetWeaver and the HiPath SIcurity DirX product from Siemens, SAP and Siemens have jointly developed a flexible, standard-based solution for managing users and authorizations.

Other manufacturers can also connect to the SAP NetWeaver platform's open interfaces and certify their solutions. In addition to Siemens, a whole range of other companies offer SAP NetWeaver-certified solutions in the area of identity management. You will find an overview of all certified solutions available on the SAP Service Marketplace under:

http://service.sap.com/security · Certified Security Partners · Partners for user management

6.3.1 How Does an Identity Management System Work?

An identity management system creates user accounts in the connected systems and assigns roles and group memberships to these user accounts. The interfaces are configured centrally in the identity management system. Centralized configuration offers benefits in terms of monitoring, and helps companies meet legal requirements (such as the Sarbanes-Oxley Act).

Data source HR systems such as mySAP ERP HCM are generally used as a data source. However, CRM systems may also function as a data source if, for example, user accounts are to be created for customers and their employees to allow them to access company information.

In this kind of scenario, systems in which user accounts are created include Microsoft Active Directory and CUA, which can be used to distribute the user masters within the SAP system landscape. Alternatively, the SAP systems can be connected to the IMS as individual systems. If the SAP NetWeaver Portal uses Microsoft Active Directory as a data source, these user accounts can be used.

6.3.2 HiPath SIcurity DirX

The HiPath SIcurity DirX identity management solution from Siemens enables the automation of processes for the controlled assignment of authorizations for SAP and non-SAP solutions in an SAP NetWeaver Portal environment.

With HiPath SIcurity DirX, you can integrate SAP NetWeaver user management, components of the mySAP Business Suite, and SAP R/3. HiPath SIcurity DirX also enables the provisioning of Microsoft Active Directory. SAP has certified HiPath SIcurity DirX as a central identity management product for SAP products. A demo and test license for downloading the product is available to SAP customers on the SAP Service Marketplace at *http://service.sap.com/siemensdirx* (see Figure 6.13).

Central identity management product for SAP

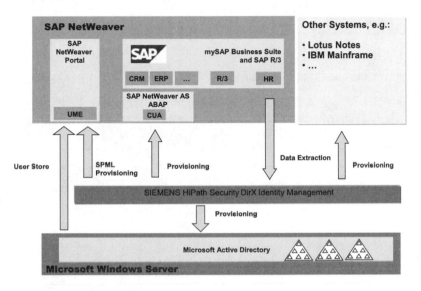

Figure 6.13 HiPath SIcurity DirX

6.3.3 Microsoft Identity Integration Server

Microsoft Identity Integration Server 2003 (MIIS) is a Microsoft product for identity management in heterogeneous environments. Microsoft provides an *SAP Management Agent*[6] for connecting to SAP systems (see Figure 6.14). MIIS thus supports read and write access to SAP HR systems and allows you to connect to SAP NetWeaver AS ABAP user management. However, unlike the Siemens solution, MIIS does not support the SPML interface of the UME, which means that portal roles cannot be assigned directly.

---

6 At the time of writing, the SAP Management Agent as part of MIIS 2003 SP2 was available to Early-Adopter Program Participants.

Mapping between Active Directory groups and portal roles must therefore be executed manually in the UME of the SAP NetWeaver Portal.

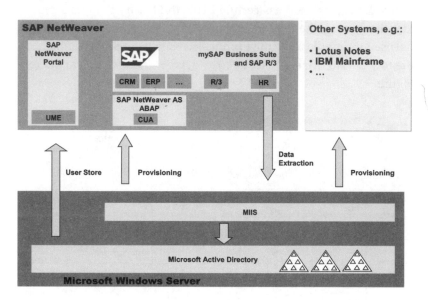

Figure 6.14 Microsoft Identity Integration Server

6.4   How-To Guides

This section describes the steps that must be completed in the Active Directory to configure the SAP HR-LDAP interface and LDAP synchronization for Central User Administration. This discussion is intended to supplement rather than replace the SAP online help. However, the naming convention for various attributes in the Active Directory differs from the other LDAP-enabled directory services.

The configuration is described in three parts:

▸ How to configure the LDAP Connector

▸ How to configure LDAP synchronization for Central User Administration

▸ How to configure the SAP HR-LDAP interface

The configuration of the LDAP Connector for LDAP synchronization for Central User Administration is almost identical to the configuration of the SAP HR-LDAP interface. Therefore, the steps involved are explained only once and any differences are pointed out.

6.4.1 Configuring the LDAP Connector

The LDAP Connector is configured centrally in transaction LDAP (see Figure 6.15).

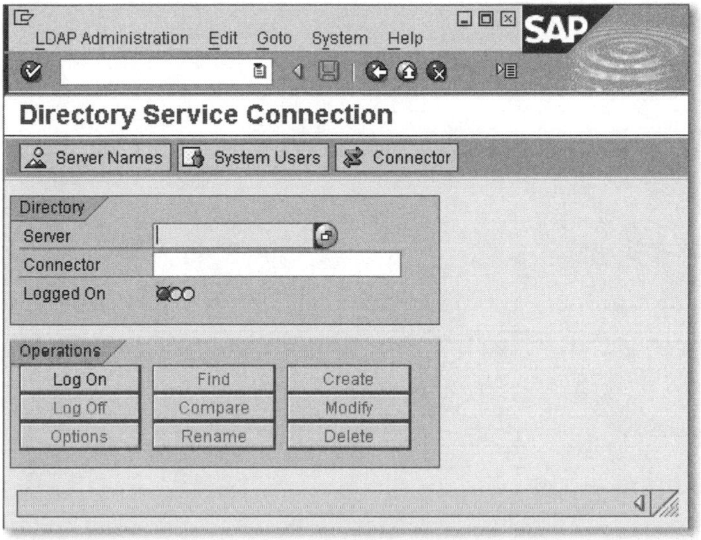

Figure 6.15 Transaction LDAP

First, you must create an RFC destination for the LDAP Connector in Transaction SM59 (see Figure 6.16). This destination must have the type T and its activation type must be **registered server program**. The following naming convention applies to the name of the RFC destination and the name of the program ID:

Creating an RFC destination

LDAP_<name of application server>-<consecutive number>

Next, press the **LDAP Connectors** button in transaction LDAP (see Figure 6.15) to access the maintenance dialog for the LDAP Connector (see Figure 6.17)

Creating an LDAP Connector

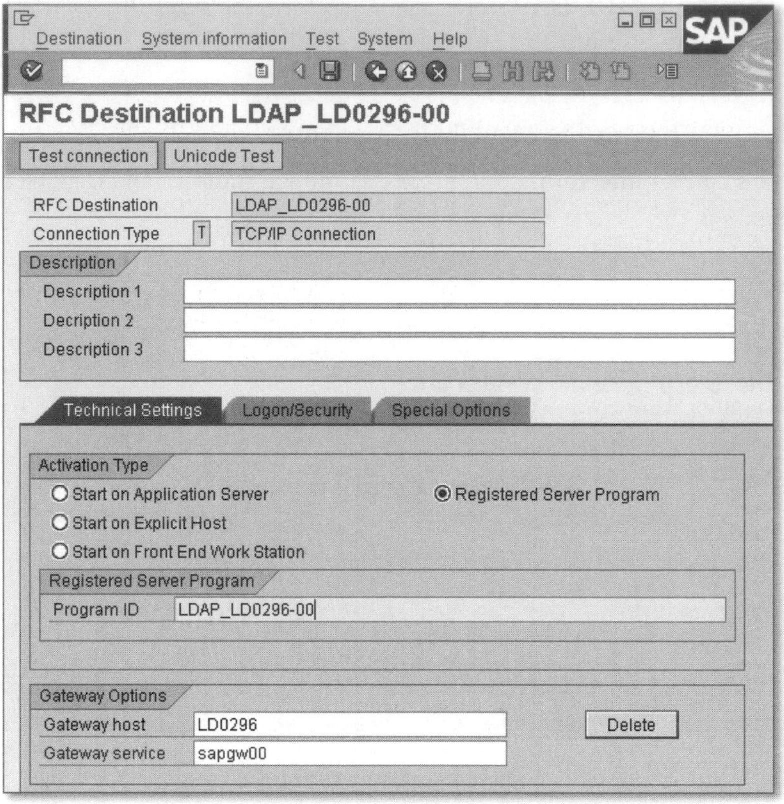

Figure 6.16 RFC Destination of the LDAP Connector

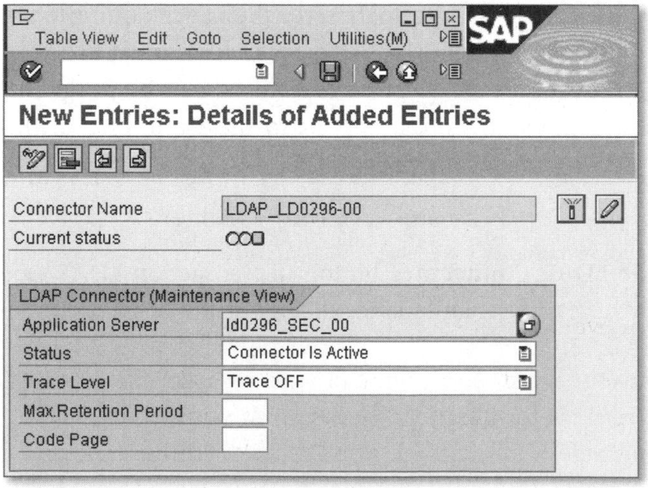

Figure 6.17 Creating an LDAP Connector

The name of the LDAP Connector must be identical to the name of the RFC destination.

The **system user** (see Figure 6.18) is the logical name of the LDAP user, which is used to log on to the directory. The *distinguished name* DN and the password of the Active Directory user for which the connection is to be set up are stored under this logical user. This user's password is encrypted in the *secure store*.

Defining the system user of the directory service

To do this, start transaction LDAP. Press the **System Users** button to access system user maintenance. Select **Simple Bind** (user ID and password) as the authentication mechanism.

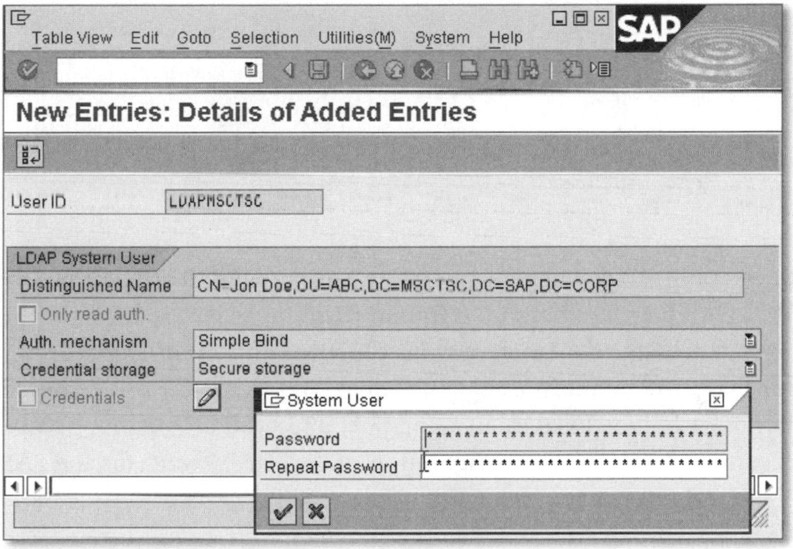

Figure 6.18 LDAP System User

Tip: The distinguished name of an object in the Active Directory can be determined using the *ADSI Edit* MMC snap-in. The snap-in can be started from the command line by calling *adsiedit.msc*. As shown in Figure 6.19, you can use ADSI Edit to access all attributes of the user object in the Active Directory.

You can then use the system user you created to make the required configuration settings for the LDAP server. To do this, start Transaction LDAP and select the menu option **LDAP Administration · Server Names**. Select **Display · Change** and **New Entries**.

Creating an LDAP server

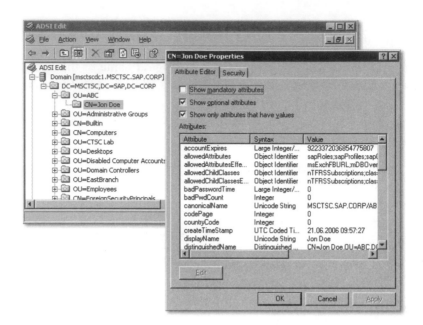

Figure 6.19 Determining the Distinguished Name of the LDAP System User

Separate LDAP servers are created to connect the CUA and the SAP HR-LDAP interface because different mapping rules are used for the interfaces. Figure 6.20 shows the configuration of an LDAP server for the LDAP connection to CUA. Since only read access is required in this case, the global catalog and port 3268 can be used for access. Figure 6.21 shows the configuration of an LDAP server for the SAP HR-LDAP interface.

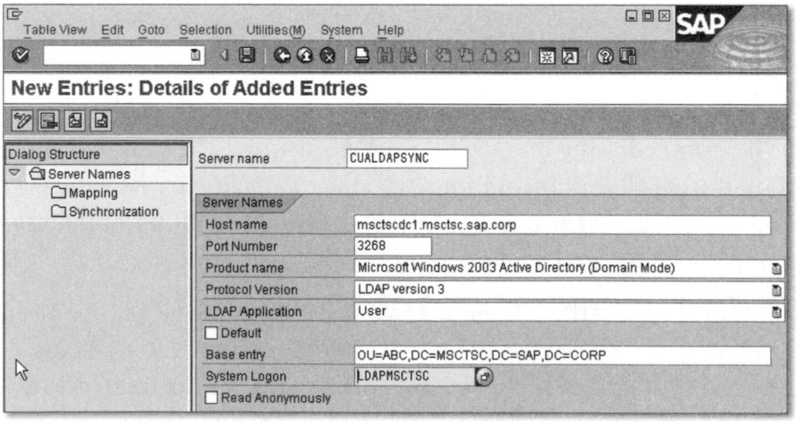

Figure 6.20 LDAP Server Definition for LDAP Synchronization of CUA

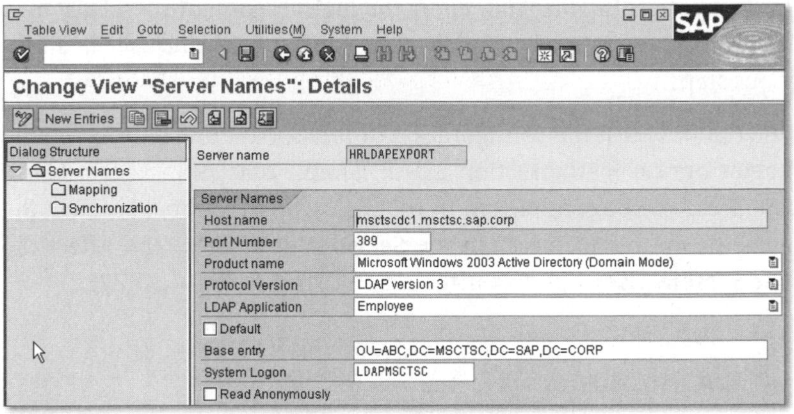

Figure 6.21 LDAP Server Definition for SAP HR-LDAP Interface

The Customizing settings shown in Figures 6.20 and 6.21 are explained below.

LDAP Server Definition

As the port number, select either port **389** for access to a domain controller, or port **3268** for access to the global catalog.

As the **Product name**, select the correct version of the LDAP server from the list. For Microsoft Active Directory, you can choose between the **Microsoft Active Directory (Domain Mode)** and **Microsoft Active Directory (Application Mode)** options.

The option **LDAP v3** must be selected as the **Protocol version** for access to the Microsoft Active Directory because this is accessed using Version 3 of the LDAP protocol.

The value **User** must be selected in the **LDAP Application** field for the synchronization of SAP user administration. If an LDAP server is to be configured for the SAP HR-LDAP interface, the value **Employee** must be entered as the application.

As the **Base entry**, you must enter the DN of the container in the Active Directory that is selected as the root for accessing the Active Directory. All accesses via LDAP take place starting from this container specified as root here. In the example described above, the DN of the OU selected as the root is as follows: **OU=ABC, DC=MSCTSC, DC=SAP, DC=CORP**.

In the **System Logon** field, enter the logical name of the LDAP user that is used to log on to the directory. You created this user in a previous step.

Testing the LDAP connection You can now test the configuration of the LDAP Connector using the **Logon** option in transaction LDAP. Simply start transaction LDAP and press the **Logon** button. In the dialog box that opens, select the name of the LDAP server in the **Server Name** field, and select the **Use System User** option for the logon data (see Figure 6.22).

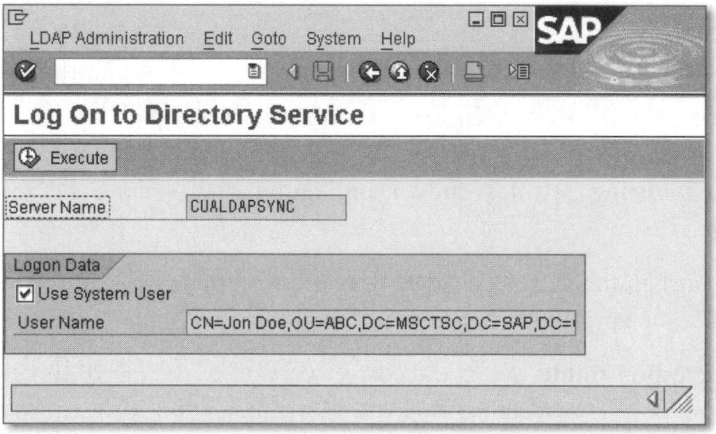

Figure 6.22 Testing the Configuration of the LDAP Connector

After you have successfully configured the LDAP Connector, you can begin configuring the two interfaces for the LDAP connection, that is, the CUA interface and the SAP HR-LDAP interface. Both interfaces use the connection data you have configured to access the Active Directory.

6.4.2 Configuring the SAP HR-LDAP Interface

The ABAP report for data extraction, which is available to download, is based on the standard SAP report RPLDAP_MANAGER, and uses the logical database PNP. The RP_PROVIDE_FROM_LAST macro is used to copy the last entry of a specified period (for example, of a specified subtype) from an internal infotype table into the table header entry. The data is transferred using the remote-enabled function module SPLDAP_RECEIVE_ATTRIBUTES, which is part of the SAP NetWeaver AS ABAP:

```
CALL FUNCTION 'SPLDAP_RECEIVE_ATTRIBUTES'
  DESTINATION
    LDAPDEST
  EXPORTING
    LOGSYS         = LOGSYS
    SERVERID       = LDAPSRV
    ATTRIBUTES_S   = attributes[]
    INITIAL_RUN    = LDAPINITIALRUN
  IMPORTING
    RETURN         = ERRORS[].
```

If the extraction report is run in an SAP HR system with Basis Release 4.6, the function module can be called remotely in a separate SAP NetWeaver AS ABAP, which then functions as an LDAP gateway.

The SPLDAP_RECEIVE_ATTRIBUTES function module receives the data that is to be exported to the directory service in the form of the internal table attributes[]. The value of the **Structure** field is defined by default as EMPLOYEE. The name of the SAP data fields, meanwhile, can be freely defined.

In transaction LDAPMAP, you must then define the mapping of the SAP data fields to the corresponding attributes of the user object in the Active Directory. This setting is shown in Figure 6.23.

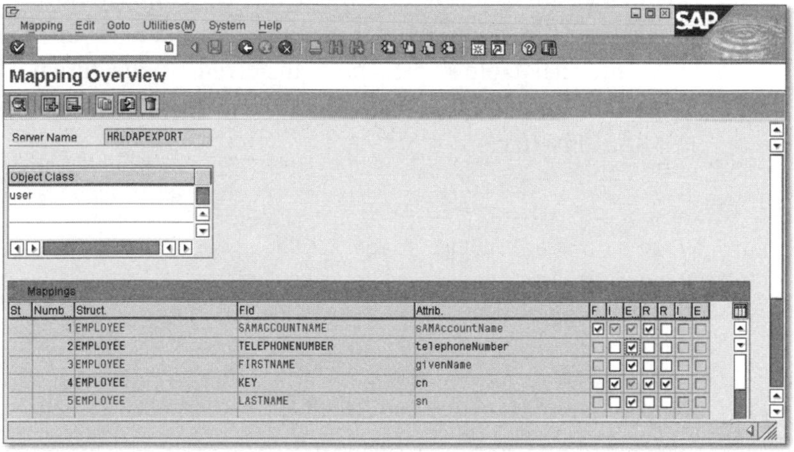

Transaction
LDAPMAP

Figure 6.23 Transaction LDAPMAP—Mapping Overview

> **Remarks**
>
> ▶ The object class `user` of the user object in the Active Directory has two required attributes that must be filled when you create a user object. These are the common name (`CN`) and the Windows log on name, `sAMAccountName`. If these two attributes are not transferred using the data structure, any attempt to create the user in the Active Directory fails. These attributes are therefore referred to as *mandatory*.
>
> ▶ The `sAMAccountName` attribute must be unique and indexed within a domain. The filter indicator is therefore set for this attribute.
>
> ▶ The `SPLDAP_RECEIVE_ATTRIBUTES` function module fills the `KEY` SAP data field internally using the `EMPLOYEE` structure. For this purpose, the function module calls the `GET_RDN` BAdI interface of the `HRLDAP_ATTRIBUTES` BAdI. Mapping is therefore also required for the `KEY` SAP data field. In the `KEY` field, `KEY` is always mapped to the `cn` attribute in the directory service. The default implementation of the `GET_RDN` BAdI interface fills the `KEY` data field with a value comprising the name of the logical system of the SAP HR system and the employee's HR number. If you want to use a value other than the default value for the `cn` attribute, you must implement the BAdI interface with customer-specific source code in the SAP NetWeaver AS.
>
> ▶ Since the `KEY` field is used to form the *relative distinguished name* for the user object, the RDN Mapping indicator must be set for this mapping.

Filling attributes_wa

The `attributes_wa` internal table is filled in the sample report as shown in the source code extract below. No data from the `attributes_s` internal table has to be transferred to the function module for the `KEY` field because the values for this field are filled by the `GET_RDN` BAdI interface.

```
get persno.
  rp-provide-from-last p0001 space keyda keyda.
  rp-provide-from-last p0002 space keyda keyda.
  ATTRIBUTES_WA-PERNR = p0001-persno.
* lastname
  attributes_wa-attr_tab = 'EMPLOYEE'.
  attributes_wa-attr_field = 'LASTNAME'.
  attributes_wa-value = p0002-lastn.
  append attributes_wa to attributes.
* firstname
  attributes_wa-attr_tab = 'EMPLOYEE'.
  attributes_wa-attr_field = 'FIRSTNAME'.
  attributes_wa-value = p0002-firstn.
```

```
  append attributes_wa to attributes.
* sAMAccountName
  attributes_wa-attr_tab = 'EMPLOYEE'.
  attributes_wa-attr_field = 'SAMACCOUNTNAME'.
* --------------------------------
* Using the employee number a unique name is created
* for the sAMAccountName
* --------------------------------
  concatenate 'E' p0001-persno into attributes_wa-value.
  append attributes_wa to attributes.
```

In our example, cn is filled with the first and last name, separated by a blank space:

```
concatenate rdn vals_wa-val into rdn separated by space.
```

This is the default value of cn when a user object is created using the *Users and Computers* MMC snap-in.

To implement the BAdI interface, start transaction SE19, select a new name for the implementation (for example, Z_HRLDAP_ATTRIBUTES), and follow the steps described in the SAP online help *http://help.sap.com · mySAP ERP* under *Implementing a Business Add-in*.

Implementing the BAdI interface

The source code that can be used to implement the BAdI interface is shown below:

```
method IF_EX_HRLDAP_ATTRIBUTES-GET_RDN .
FIELD-SYMBOLS: <fs_data> LIKE LINE OF data.
  DATA vals_wa TYPE valstructc.
  CLEAR rdn.
  CLEAR xrdn.
* create cn that has the following structure
* firstname space lastname
  READ TABLE data
    WITH KEY var = 'EMPLOYEE'
             fld = 'FIRSTNAME'
    ASSIGNING <fs_data>.

  IF sy-subrc EQ 0.
    READ TABLE <fs_data>-vals INDEX 1
                              INTO vals_wa.
    IF sy-subrc EQ 0.
```

```
            rdn = vals_wa-val.
      ENDIF.
    ENDIF.

  READ TABLE data
    WITH KEY var = 'EMPLOYEE'
             fld = 'LASTNAME'
    ASSIGNING <fs_data>.

  IF sy-subrc EQ 0.
    READ TABLE <fs_data>-vals INDEX 1
                              INTO vals_wa.
    IF sy-subrc EQ 0.
       CONCATENATE rdn vals_wa-val INTO rdn
         SEPARATED BY SPACE.
    ENDIF.
  ENDIF.

* CONCATENATE logsys persno INTO rdn
*   SEPARATED BY space.
endmethod.
```

If you then execute the Z_TEST_SPLDAP_RECEIVE sample report, users are created in the Active Directory in the container specified by the LDAP server. You still have to activate the users you have created and assign a password to each before the user accounts can be used.

6.4.3 Setting up the CUA-LDAP Connection

Mapping SAP data fields to directory attributes After you configure the LDAP Connector, you must define the mapping of the SAP data fields to the corresponding attributes of the directory service for the CUA-LDAP connection. You do this in transaction LDAPMAP. SAP provides mapping proposals for the various directory services (including Microsoft Active Directory) for the synchronization of SAP user administration. To accept these proposals, select **Import proposal** (see Figure 6.24). After you import the proposal, you can adjust it to meet your specific requirements.

Filter attribute Active Directory users that are to be selected for synchronization with SAP user administration are identified by a filter attribute. If this attribute is set for an Active Directory user object, the RSLDAPSYNC_USER synchronization report is used to create a new SAP user, or an existing SAP user is updated with the information from the Active Directory. Figure 6.24 shows the default value of the mapping proposal delivered by SAP for the Active Directory.

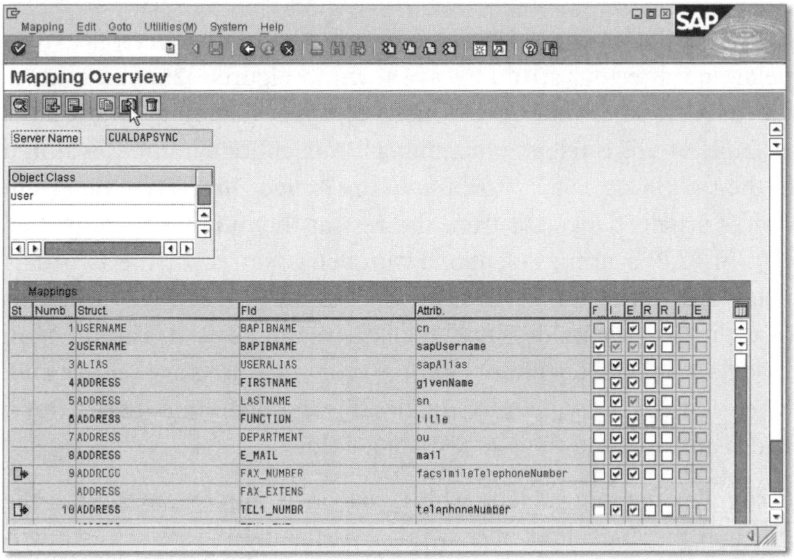

Figure 6.24 CUA-LDAP Synchronization: Mapping SAP Data Fields to the Microsoft Active Directory Attributes

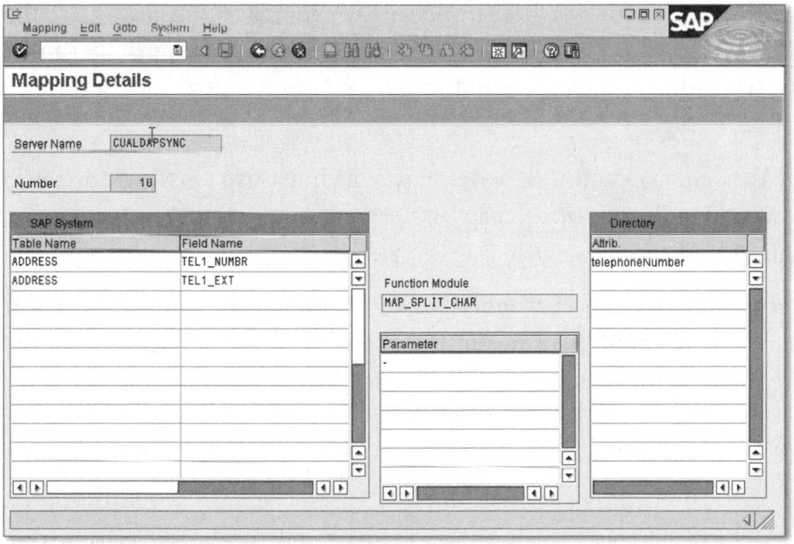

Figure 6.25 Mapping Details—Function Module

For each case in which an SAP data field is mapped to a directory attribute, you can define whether the mapping is to be used for import, export, or for both directions of the synchronization.

Function modules

If there is not a simple 1:1 mapping relationship between SAP data fields and directory attributes as shown in Figure 6.25, you can use function modules that enable more complex mapping. One simple example of this is telephone numbers. A telephone number is stored in the telephoneNumber attribute in the Active Directory. The extension is usually separated from the rest of the number by a hyphen ('-'). In SAP, a user's telephone number is stored in the two data fields ADDRESS-TEL1_NUMBR and ADDRESS-TEL1_EXT. In this case, the function module MAP_SPLIT_CHAR can be used. This function module reads the telephone number from the directory service and, when it finds a hyphen, it divides the number into two strings, which are stored in the two SAP data fields.

If complex mapping relationships cannot be implemented with the function modules delivered in the SAP standard system, customer-specific function modules can also be developed.

Schema extension

The standard SAP mapping proposal is based on a schema extension that includes SAP-specific fields of the directory services supported by SAP. To generate the proposal for schema extension, start the RSLDAPSCHEMAEXT report. This report generates an output that can be downloaded as a text file and imported into the directory service as an LDIF file.

If the schema cannot be extended, you must use existing attributes and adjust the imported mapping proposal (see above) in transaction LDAPMAP.

Synchronization

Synchronization occurs when you start the RSLDAPSYNC_USER report (see Figure 6.26). As a result, the report returns an overview of the replication that has been executed (see Figure 6.27).

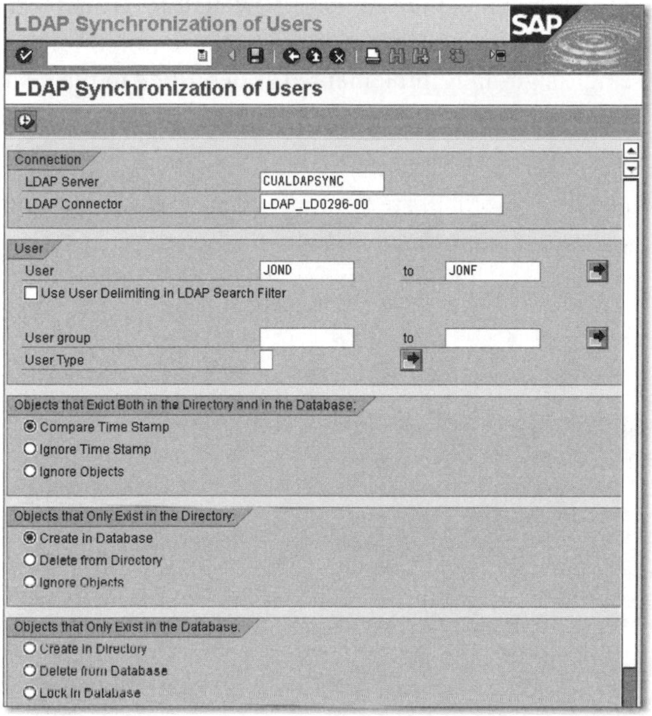

Figure 6.26 CUA—LDAP Synchronization: Synchronization Report RSLDAPSYNC_USER

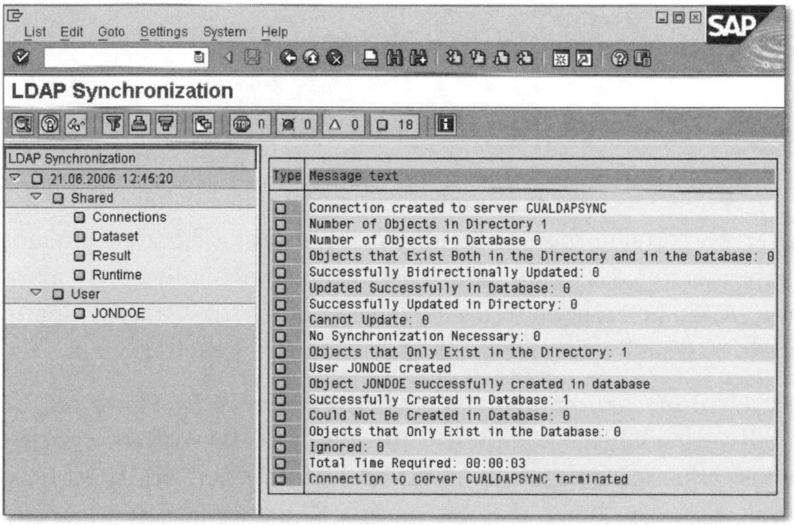

Figure 6.27 CUA—LDAP Synchronization: Log File

As a result of synchronization, an SAP user **JONDOE** is created (see Figure 6.28) without a password. A password is not required for the user created if single sign-on is implemented as described in the next section.

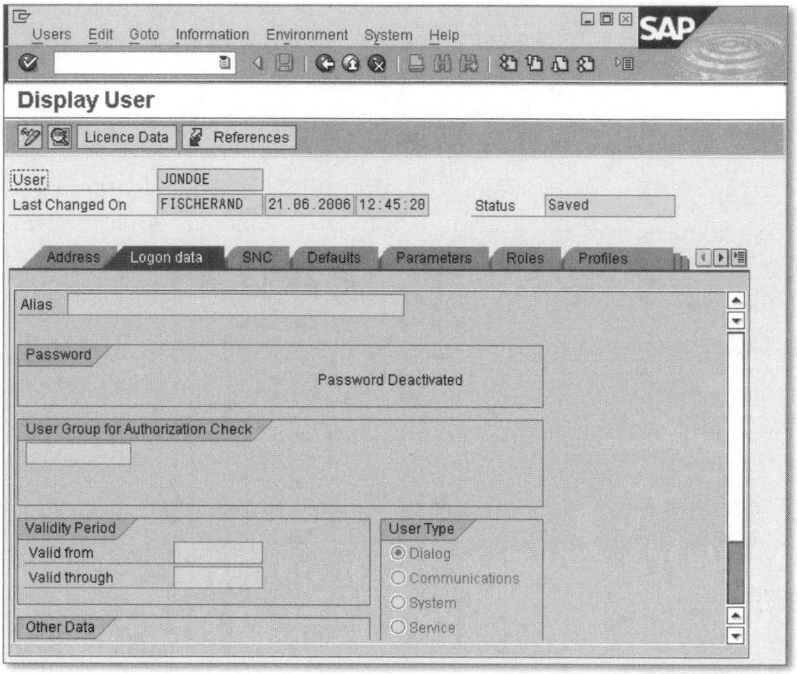

Figure 6.28 CUA—LDAP Synchronization: A Newly Created User Account

6.5 Single Sign-On

SSO greatly improves the usability of an SAP system landscape. However, properly functioning identity management is a prerequisite for implementing SSO. With SSO, users can automatically access all of the SAP and external systems they need to use after a single logon to their workstations or a single authentication in a central system.

In Microsoft environments, the Microsoft Active Directory can be used for the initial authentication because this authentication occurs when users log on to their PC in the company network as the first thing each day. When they log on to a Windows frontend that is a member of a domain, users receive a Kerberos ticket. This initial authentication can be used again for authentication in SAP systems.

For the reasons discussed earlier in this chapter, SAP provides solutions that allow its customers to use Active Directory for single sign-on to SAP systems, thereby cutting operating costs. Some of these solutions have been available from SAP for a long time, while others have only recently been added to the SAP portfolio.

While access was only possible via the SAP GUI for Windows in the conventional SAP R/3 system, web-based access is also possible with SAP NetWeaver. Web-based access to an SAP NetWeaver Application Server, which offers support for both ABAP and Java, is based on the *Internet Communication Manager* (ICM). The ICM processes the incoming web requests and distributes them internally to the ABAP Dispatcher and its work processes, which in turn process the ABAP programs, or to the Java Dispatcher and its server processes.

Internet Communication Manager (ICM)

The ABAP stack of an SAP NetWeaver Application Server can still be accessed with the SAP GUI frontend via the (ABAP) Dispatcher. However, this form of access will gradually become obsolete because the strategic SAP frontend Web Dynpro uses HTTP-based access (see Figure 6.29).

The various access types influence the SSO technologies that can be used.

Secure Network Communications (SNC) can be used for single sign-on for SAP GUI-based access. In this case, SAP provides an implementation for the Kerberos protocol supported by the Active Directory. However, this approach is subject to certain restrictions and is not suitable for Web-based access.

Secure Network Communications (SNC)

SAP logon tickets are the method of choice for SSO to SAP systems. These enable SSO for both web-based access and access via SAP GUI. A two-step approach is therefore recommended.

As shown in Figure 6.30, the first step consists of SSO to the SAP NetWeaver Portal, based on the initial Windows authentication. In this case, the SAP NetWeaver Portal acts as a ticket-issuing instance for SAP logon tickets after a successful authentication.

In the second step, the SSO mechanism provided by the SAP logon tickets allows users to access all systems in the SAP NetWeaver system landscape.

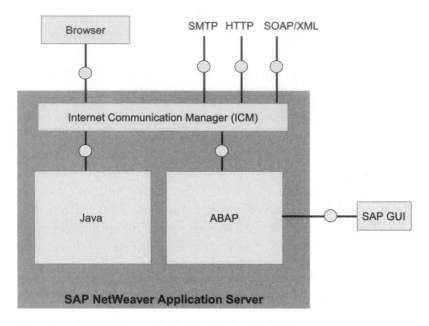

Figure 6.29 SAP NetWeaver Application Server—Architecture

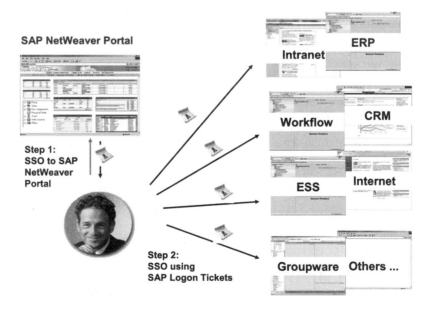

Figure 6.30 SSO in an SAP NetWeaver System Landscape with Kerberos and SAP Logon Tickets

With SSO to the SAP NetWeaver Portal, the single sign-on scenario is fully integrated. A user only has to log on once to his/her PC and can then access all systems in the SAP NetWeaver system landscape.

In other words, users only have to remember a single password, which can therefore be a complex one than would otherwise be the case. Alternatively, the initial PC logon can be protected with additional measures, such as SmartCard.

6.5.1 SAP GUI for Windows

SNC can be used for single sign-on if SAP systems are accessed exclusively with SAP GUI. When you use SNC, users are authenticated by an external security product. Based on this authentication, users are granted access to the SAP system. In addition to the single sign-on function, SNC enables encryption of the data traffic between the SAP GUI and the SAP NetWeaver Application Server.

In environments based purely on Windows 200x, you can use Microsoft Windows 2000/XP/2003-based authentication for single sign-on to SAP backend systems with SAP GUI. With the *gsskrb5.dll* library provided by SAP, you can set up an SNC connection between the SAP system server components and the SAP GUI frontend. In this case, both the client PC and the SAP Application Server must have the *gsskrb5.ll* library provided by SAP. In this implementation of the SNC interface, the Kerberos implementation is used as an external security product.

The single sign-on mechanism described here is subject to the following restrictions:

▶ If the SAP systems run on Unix, the support of UNIX-based Kerberos implementations is limited. As an alternative, SNC-certified third-party products must be purchased and installed on the clients and the servers. Note that SAP provides limited support for this kind of scenario.[7]

▶ In pure Windows environments, the SSO mechanism described here is also limited to scenarios in which access from the frontend uses SAP GUI or RFC because SNC is only available for the SAP protocols RFC and DIAG.

---

7 See the two SAP Notes 352295, *Microsoft Windows Single Sign-On Options*, and 150380, *Is MIT Kerberos 5 Supported for Use with SNC?*

▶ Problems occur with this single sign-on mechanism if you use a combination of different frontends (SAP GUI and a web browser). This is the case, for example, if access to a system is started from the GUI via the web browser.[8]

For cross-system single sign-on scenarios, SAP logon tickets should therefore be used, with an SAP NetWeaver AS or SAP NetWeaver Portal as the instance that issues the tickets. In this scenario, the SAP logon ticket is sent to an SAP GUI shortcut with a Portal iView (see Figure 6.31).

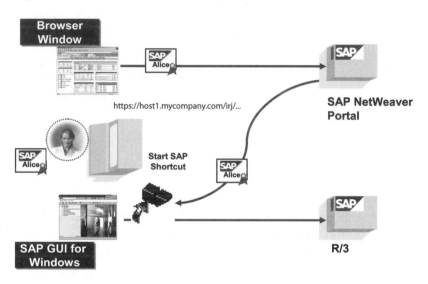

Figure 6.31 SSO with SAP GUI and the SAP NetWeaver Portal

6.5.2 SAP Logon Tickets

SAP logon tickets serve as tokens for authentication. After a successful authentication against the data source specified in the UME, the SAP NetWeaver Portal issues a user with an SAP logon ticket. The SAP logon ticket contains the portal user name and possibly also the SAP backend user name. The ticket is saved in the user's web browser as a session cookie. Digital signatures ensure the authenticity and integrity of the SAP logon ticket, while SSL protocol guarantees confidentiality. In addition, each SAP logon ticket is assigned a certain validity period, which can be configured in the security settings in the SAP NetWeaver Portal.

---

8 See also SAP Note 612670, *SSO for Local BSP Calls Using SAP GUI HTML Control.*

All SAP applications and various non-SAP applications can use SAP logon tickets as a single sign-on mechanism. Web server filters (see the *SAP Web Server Filters* section later in this chapter) and a DLL and Java library (see the *DLL* and *Java library* later in this chapter) allow third-party applications to verify the information in an SAP logon ticket and to use it for authentication. An application that accepts SAP logon tickets must be able to verify the digital signature of the issuing server based on its public key certificate.

If SAP logon tickets are used for authentication with web applications, the user's SAP logon ticket is saved as a temporary cookie in the web browser. This ticket can in turn be transferred to other systems as a token for authentication.

SAP logon tickets contain the SAP user name and, in the case of the SAP NetWeaver Portal, the SAP backend user name and portal user name. Therefore, the SAP backend user name must be unique in all connected SAP systems. You can use SAP Central User Administration (CUA) in this case, which enables central user management of ABAP users with standardized user IDs.

6.5.3 Single Sign-On to the SAP NetWeaver Portal with Integrated Windows Authentication

For authentication in the SAP NetWeaver Portal, a user must go through the login modules configured in the SAP NetWeaver Application Server Java. SAP NetWeaver supports various forms of logon as standard, including authentication with X.509 certificates or authentication of user names and passwords against the data source configured in the UME.

SAP supports *Windows Integrated Authentication* as a mechanism for external authentication. SAP provides the following mechanisms for this purpose:

Windows Integrated Authentication

- IIS proxy module[9]
- SPNegoLoginModule[10]

---

9 See SAP Note 886214, *End of Maintenance of IIsProxy ISAPI Module*.
10 SPNego is short for *Simple and Protected Negotiate*. SPNego is a security standard and is described in an RFC.

Using Windows Integrated Authentication for SSO to SAP NetWeaver or SAP NetWeaver solutions offers customers several benefits. The solutions provided by SAP enable the implementation of this single sign-on mechanism without costly third-party software.

IIS Proxy Module

SAP previously provided the IIS Proxy Module for Integrated Windows Authentication. However, SAP will not continue to support this module in the long term. The IIS Proxy Module requires a separate Microsoft IIS, on which an ISAPI filter developed by SAP (the IIS Proxy module) is installed. The IIS Proxy Module acts as a Reverse Proxy filter in this cases, and forwards all requests to the portal. If the user accesses the SAP NetWeaver Portal via the IIS Proxy Module installed on the IIS server, this extracts the Windows logon name from the Windows desktop session, and forwards the Windows user name to the portal with the HTTP request in a header variable. If the header login module is configured for the J2EE Engine, the SAP NetWeaver Application Server Java uses the information to identify the portal user and then logs the user on to the portal.

JAAS SPNegoLogin-Module

The SPNegoLoginModule is a JAAS login module for the SAP J2EE Engine Version 6.40 and higher, which enables logon to the SAP NetWeaver AS Java using the integrated Windows authentication mechanism. The SPNegoLoginModule is available with Support Package 15 as part of the SAP standard system in the Java stack of the SAP NetWeaver Application Server.

A special feature of this solution is that the J2EE Engine can also be run on a Unix platform. In contrast to authentication with the IIS Proxy Module, a separate IIS is not required.

Authentication and communication

The SPNego protocol is used for authentication and communication between the browser and the J2EE Engine. Kerberos, an integral component of the Active Directory, is used for authentication of the J2EE Engine against the Active Directory. To enable Kerberos communication for a J2EE Engine running on a Unix server, a user account must be created for the Unix server in the Windows domain.

If a user calls the URL of an application in the J2EE Engine and sends a GET request to the J2EE Engine, the J2EE Engine returns HTTP return code 401 with an HTTP header variable WWW Authenticate: Negotiate. The user then knows that the server of the J2EE Engine is a member of a Kerberos realm, and requests a Kerberos session ticket for this server. This Kerberos Ticket is not sent to the server directly. First, it is packed into an SPNego token, which is sent to the server as an authorization header in a second call. The JAAS login module reads the SPNego token from the HTTP request and sends it to the Java-Kerberos implementation. The request may either succeed (authentication is successful) or fail (authentication fails).

At this point, an explanation of why the login module is called *SPNegoLoginModule* and not *KerberosLoginModule* is necessary. The reason is that the login module uses the SPNego protocol. SPNego is used to negotiate the security mechanism between client and server that is to be used for authentication. SPNego thus functions as a protocol wrapper (discussed earlier), whereby the Kerberos tickets exchanged are wrapped in SPNego tokens.

SPNego or Kerberos?

In reality, the SPNegoLoginModule does not execute Kerberos authentication. This is handled by the Kerberos implementation of the Java Virtual Machine (JVM) on which the J2EE is running.

The Kerberos protocol uses UDP port 88 as standard. Since Kerberos is used for communication between the browser and the domain controller, and between the J2EE Engine and the domain controller in the scenario described above, the Kerberos protocol must be activated for these communication channels. For communication between the browser and the J2EE Engine, HTTP or HTTPS is required. If Active Directory also serves as a data source for the J2EE Engine, this requires access to the domain controller via LDAP port 389 or 3268 if the global catalog is used.

Communication channels

If you want to use the SPNegoLoginModule in the SAP NetWeaver Portal, it must be added to the login module stack.

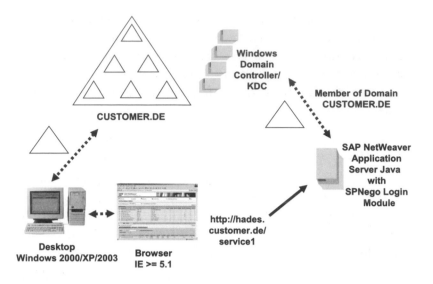

Figure 6.32 SSO with the SPNegoLoginModule

6.5.4   Single Sign-On to SAP Backend Systems

All SAP applications support SAP logon tickets. In addition to browser-based access via iViews, BSP pages, HTML GUI or Web Dynpro, SAP logon tickets can also be sent from the SAP NetWeaver Portal to the SAP GUI.

Since all access types via the various protocols for single sign-on are supported, the SAP NetWeaver Portal offers clear benefits compared to the previously described SSO mechanisms based purely on SNC technology, which can only be used for the SAP GUI.

6.5.5   Single Sign-On to Non-SAP Backend Systems

In many cases, web-based applications are integrated into the SAP NetWeaver Portal by adding the URL to a URL iView or an Application Integrator iView. A number of different options can be used for SSO for these applications when being integrated into the portal.

User Mapping

High
administrative
costs

User mapping enables single sign-on to systems where the only shared authentication mechanism permitted is authentication by user name and password. In the case of the SAP NetWeaver Portal, the portal user name is mapped to the user name and password in the component system. The disadvantage of user mapping is that users must maintain a user name and password for each system connected in this way. Using this SSO mechanism is therefore associated with high administrative costs. However, it sometimes cannot be avoided if the system that must be connected offers no alternative.

SAP Web Server Filters

For the integration of web-based applications that support authentication via HTTP header variables, SAP offers web server filters for IIS and other web servers. These can be downloaded from the SAP Service Marketplace.[11] These web server filters verify the logon ticket using the digital certificate of the portal server. The user name of the portal user is extracted from the logon ticket and written to an HTTP header variable. The name of the HTTP header variable can be defined using the remote_user_alias parameter in the configuration file of the filter.

The following sample source code provides a simple example of an ASP application that uses a web server filter. In this case, the remote_alias_user parameter is set to the value MY_SAP_USER.

```
<%@ LANGUAGE="VBSCRIPT" %>
<%
Dim strUser
strUser = Request.ServerVariables("MY_SAP_USER")
If MY_SAP_USER <> "SecretUserID" Then _
UserNotAuthenticated
If MY_SAP_USER = "SecretUserID" Then UserAuthenticated
Sub UserNotAuthenticated()
Response.Write " User is NOT authenticated. "
End Sub
Sub UserAuthenticated()
Response.Write " User is authenticated. "
End Sub
%>
<HTML>
<HEAD>
```

---

11 For more detailed information about the availability of these filters and how to download them, see SAP Note 723896, *EP 6.0: Web Server Filters for SSO to Third-Party Systems*.

```
Test page check user id
</HEAD>
<BODY>
Welcome to the test page
</BODY>
</HTML>
```

Integrated Windows Authentication and the SSO22KerbMap Module

With the IIS, Microsoft-based web applications usually only support Windows Integrated Authentication (Kerberos) or, as a fallback, Basic Authentication as an authentication mechanism.

Intranet scenarios

Integrating these applications into the SAP NetWeaver Portal using an Application Integration iView enables seamless integration with *intranet scenarios*. If a user accesses the IIS server via a URL retrieved by the iView, he/she is authenticated on the IIS server by means of Windows Integrated Authentication with a Kerberos ticket. A typical example of this scenario is the integration of Outlook Web Access into the SAP NetWeaver Portal.

Extranet scenarios

However, the Kerberos protocol does not work over the internet because the relevant ports are normally blocked by the company firewalls. In *extranet scenarios*, this used to mean that *user mapping* was the only available SSO option for these applications.

A SSO solution based on SAP logon tickets could only be developed by SAP when Microsoft provided the mechanism of *Kerberos Constrained Delegation using Protocol Transition* with Active Directory 2003. *Constrained Delegation*, the delegation model introduced with Active Directory 2003, allows you to delegate client credentials to a service. The term Constrained Delegation indicates that user credentials only enable authentication for certain services. Based on this technology, SAP now provides the *SSO22KerbMap Module*. This new ISAPI filter from SAP requests a *constrained Kerberos ticket* for users who have been successfully authenticated with a valid SAP logon ticket. This Kerberos ticket can then be used to log on to Microsoft-based web applications.

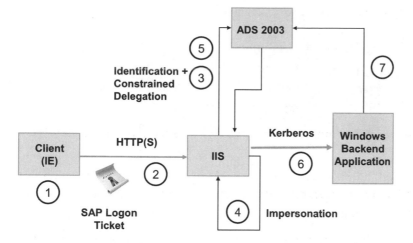

Figure 6.33 SSO22KerbMap Module—Kerberos Constrained Delegation Using Protocol Transition

Figure 6.33 shows the authentication procedure with the **Process flow**
SSO22KerbMap Module. The individual steps are as follows:

1. A client uses a valid SAP logon ticket to access the IIS server.

2. The ISAPI filter DLL checks the validity of the SAP logon ticket and extracts the name of the portal user.

3. Identification: The ISAPI filter searches for a user in the Active Directory. The portal user name, which is saved as a user attribute in the Active Directory, serves as a filter criterion.

4. After successful identification of the user, the filter executes *impersonation* as the user with the LogonAsUser function.

5. The Active Directory issues a constrained Kerberos ticket, which only permits access to certain resources (*Constrained Delegation managed by ADS*).

6. Kerberos authentication of the HTTP request is performed in the backend system with the Kerberos ticket that was issued. The user is thus authenticated as a Windows domain user in the backend system.

7. The Windows backend application accepts the constrained Kerberos ticket.

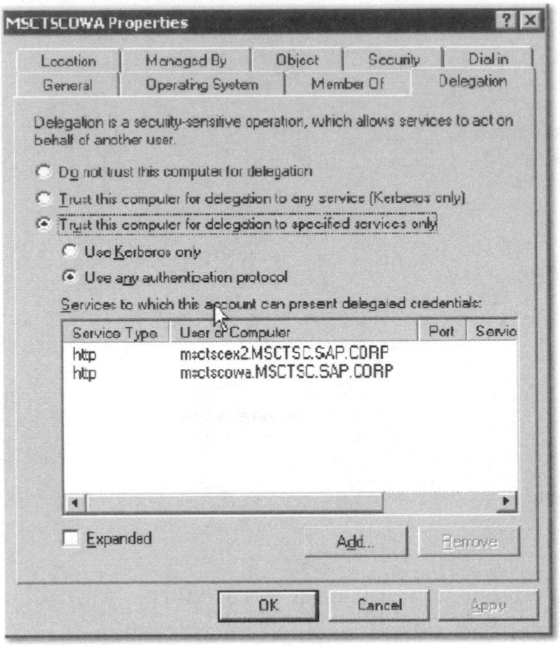

Figure 6.34 Delegation Configuration in the Active Directory

Figure 6.34 shows the configuration of the delegation settings for a computer in the Active Directory. As you can see, the options **Trust this computer for delegation to specified services only** and **Use any authentication protocol** must be selected for the computer because authentication with the SSO22KerbMap Module is based on SAP logon tickets.

DLL and Java library

Native support for SAP logon tickets In addition to the ISAPI filters, you can also implement native support for SAP logon tickets in customer developments. The *sapssoext.dll* library or a Java library from SAP can be used in this case. The C and Java sample programs provided by SAP can be used as an aid by developers.

6.5.6 SAML

Security Assertion Markup Language (SAML) is an XML-based specification for exchanging security-relevant information. SAML is developed and standardized by the *Organization for the Advancement of*

Structured Information (OASIS). An encryption protocol such as SSL or TSL is a prerequisite for using SAML in order to protect the transfer of messages.

The SAP J2EE Engine supports SAML for single sign-on. A user is authenticated by a system (external), which acts as an "SAML authority." Following a successful authentication, the SAML authority issues the user with a confirmation referred to as an *assertion*. Currently (NetWeaver 2004s), the J2EE Engine cannot yet be used as an SAML authority. However, this situation will change with future releases of NetWeaver.

To conclude, we take a look at today's software market. This chapter examines the competition and coexistence between SAP and Microsoft, and discusses how the concept of service-oriented architectures influences collaboration between the two companies.

7 Future Possibilities

It would, of course, be very interesting to know how the partnership between SAP and Microsoft will develop within the highly competitive software industry, and which technologies and solutions will be offered by the two companies. Unfortunately, it is difficult to make forecasts in the software industry, even for the next few months. The reasons for this are as follows:

▸ In practically no other industry are decisions regarding technology subject to so many constantly shifting influences.

▸ New technologies and standards are established and then become obsolete at an extremely fast rate.

Therefore, we will not attempt to predict the specific functionalities that will be available with Duet 3.0, for example. Such predictions are almost inevitably doomed to fail.

Instead, we will examine the position of both SAP and Microsoft in the market (as a continuation of our discussion in the Introduction) in order to gain a better insight into the likely future of this partnership. In addition, we cannot neglect the move toward service-oriented architectures, which is so central to this discussion and is, furthermore, being driven by so many companies that its success is guaranteed. We will therefore also examine its significance for the integration of SAP and Microsoft products.

7.1   SAP and Microsoft in Today's Software Market

Competition   Both companies are undisputed global market leaders in their respective markets. SAP tops the market for business applications, and Microsoft the market for desktop operating systems and office applications. It is striking that there does not appear to be stiff competition between the two companies, as is explicitly the case between many other players in the industry. But why should this be so?

During the last decade, both companies have built up a complete technology stack in the form of NetWeaver and the Windows Server System family of products. Even though issues frequently arise in relation to certain product combinations (NetWeaver Portal and Microsoft SharePoint Portal, NetWeaver Exchange Infrastructure and Microsoft BizTalk Server), SAP and Microsoft technology components nonetheless dovetail very well in customers' system landscapes.

In relation to business application software for medium-sized and large enterprises, SAP applications are very clearly to the fore. Competition is only starting to emerge in the market for small enterprises, where a large number of smaller providers are also active.

In the area of desktop applications, Microsoft Windows and Office are clearly the globally recognized standards.

Reasons for coexistence   In addition to product range, there are a number of other factors that favor coexistence between the two companies:

► With SAP NetWeaver, SAP provides a complete business process platform, while the mySAP Business Suite is the most comprehensive range of turnkey applications that can be configured to suit customer requirements. Microsoft Windows, on the other hand, is the most successful operating system for clients and servers, and Microsoft Office is practically the standard for all productivity tools. In addition, Microsoft focuses on development tools that allow its partners and customers to build their own applications.

► SAP operates an end-to-end sales, consulting and support organization, which works closely with customers to support the rollout and operation of SAP software. In contrast, Microsoft covers the entire customer spectrum, from private consumers to major enterprises, and relies exclusively on its partners for sales, consulting and support.

All in all, this means that a company's IT management will likely be able to meet the needs of end users by choosing products from SAP and Microsoft. It is for precisely this reason that a growing number of companies, including multinational groups, are opting for a dual-vendor strategy.

Dual-vendor strategy

But what would happen if the partnership between SAP and Microsoft turned instead into a heated competition? This possibility can never be completely ruled out. After all, companies naturally strive to improve growth and increase their market share. It is likely that very little would change in terms of interoperability. Despite their size and standing, SAP and Microsoft have both remained very customer-focused and, if their customers want new interoperability scenarios, the companies would only do themselves damage by ignoring these demands.

We can therefore assume that SAP and Microsoft are essentially willing to develop complementary (integration) solutions, and that they will remain so for the foreseeable future.

7.2   The Future of Interoperability

The number of conceivable integration scenarios has grown rapidly as both companies have developed their range of technical components to a very significant degree over the years. From the customer's perspective, this is a desirable situation, as it opens up new realms of possibility for system landscape design.

This new diversity presents a range of challenges for SAP and Microsoft. The integration scenarios required by the market must be designed, developed and maintained over many years. If you also consider the various release strategies and versions of the products involved, it becomes clear that the potential costs involved require serious consideration, even by two software giants like SAP and Microsoft.

Challenges for SAP and Microsoft

So, how can the challenges of interoperability be overcome efficiently and economically? This question has already been answered in a number of different places in this book. The answer boils down to two key concepts: SOA and open standards.

Web services It is beyond dispute that proprietary and release-dependent interfaces in software products constitute obstacles to integration, and should therefore be avoided as far as possible. They are to be replaced by web services, which offer, among other things, the advantage of being based on recognized open standards such as XML, SOAP, WSDL and UDDI. The other main advantages of web services are as follows:

▶ Web services are easily comprehensible to software applications, and they can bridge the problematic gap between .NET and J2EE applications, for example.

▶ Well-defined web services are release-independent. It is therefore relatively easy to replace or update individual components in an SOA.

▶ Web services can be easily implemented over the Internet, and thus also between companies, because they use HTTP, which is firewall-compatible.

Over the past decade, all leading software manufacturers have made clear commitments to SOAs and open standards. In their 2004 joint statement, SAP and Microsoft also emphasized their joint efforts in relation to emerging advanced web service protocols. These will address issues in relation to authentication, encryption and guaranteed provision of web services, for example.

Enterprise SOA SAP is going one step further in this regard with its Enterprise Service-Oriented Architecture (Enterprise SOA). Enterprise SOA introduces the concept of Enterprise Services. These are context-specific services at business level. They use low-level, technically defined web services from one or more applications, conceal their technical complexity, and emphasize their operational benefits instead.

The value of using enterprise services is perfectly illustrated by the example of a sales order comprising a range of web services and application functions. If the order is cancelled half way through processing, the enterprise service ensures clean reverse processing from a business point of view.

In the future, interoperability between SAP and Microsoft will therefore be based increasingly on web services and enterprise services and related open standards, which will allow it to remain manageable. Agreement on jointly recognized standards will replace coordination of implementation details for individual products. This makes interoperability much simpler.

A first step in this direction has already been taken. All scenarios in the Duet, the first joint product from the two companies, are based exclusively on SAP Enterprise SOA.

The Authors

Andreas Rohr holds a diploma in business administration with a focus on information management. Since January 2005, he has been working as a freelance consultant. In this role Andreas focuses on the areas of interoperability and interface architecture. Many of the projects he completed in the past focused on interfaces between SAP R/3 or SAP NetWeaver and Microsoft products. Andreas is also a certified Microsoft Partner.

After finishing his studies and a subsequent scholarship at Siemens Nixdorf Informationssysteme AG (SNI), Andreas worked as a developer, solutions architect, and project manager at a medium-size IT service provider where he successfully supported projects for several large German enterprises. After that he worked as an IT coordinator for a subsidiary of Deutsche Post (German Postal Services).

In addition to his freelance consulting work, since 2004 Andreas has been teaching information management and EAI with a focus on SAP at the Institute of Management in Berlin, Germany.

You can send any suggestion or criticism to Andreas via the following email address: *a.rohr@conaro.de*.

Thomas Meigen is an employee at SAP AG. After finishing his studies in business administration in Ludwigshafen, Germany, he started his professional career as an R/2 technology consultant at a large SAP consulting partner. After several years of consulting for many customers in Germany and other European countries, Thomas decided to join SAP in 1992. Within the team of SAP R/2 Basis consultants (which was still relatively small at that time), he specialized in IBM MVS mainframes and IBM DB/DC.

From 1994 to 1998 he took the opportunity to work for SAP in Melbourne, Australia, where he was responsible for one of the last major

R/2 projects. In 1996, Thomas switched to SAP R/3 on Windows NT, whose potentials he identified right away. After his return to Walldorf in 1998, he assumed the newly created position of a product manager for the Microsoft platforms, Windows NT and SQL Server. During that time, he drove several Microsoft-related topics such as the roll-out of new versions of Windows, SQL Server, and other Microsoft products.

In 2003, Thomas became responsible for building and managing the newly created Collaboration Technology Support Center Microsoft (CTSC-MS) for SAP. The CTSC consists of equal numbers of SAP and Microsoft employees and acts as a trusted advisor for customers who use both companies' products. The team addresses all technical and non-technical aspects of Microsoft interoperability. Among other things, Thomas regularly presents the most up-to-date roadmap of the collaboration between SAP and Microsoft at the annual SAP TechEd conferences.

With the experience of almost 20 years in SAP business and more than 8 years in the partnership with Microsoft, Thomas Meigen knows the details of this partnership extremely well.

You can send your questions and suggestions to Thomas Meigen via the following email address: *thomas.meigen@sap.com*.

André Fischer has worked in the area of Strategic Alliance Microsoft at SAP AG since 2004. After finishing his studies of physics at RWTH Aachen University and Heidelberg University, Germany, he started his professional career in 1995 as a technology consultant for an SAP partner. From the beginning, he specialized on SAP solutions operating on Microsoft platforms as well as the authorization system in SAP R/3. During his work as a consultant, he supported many customers in building up their system landscapes and forming SAP Basis teams.

From 1999 to 2000 he was responsible for setting up a data center for a newly founded joint venture outsourcing company. The successful SAP audit of the data center, which was based on the Windows/SQL Server platform, resulted in the certification of the company as an SAP Hosting Partner in 2000. From 2002 onward, André worked as a senior consultant with a focus on SAP security. In this context, his work focused primarily on identity management and single sign-on of SAP solutions in the interaction with Microsoft Active Directory.

In 2004, he joined the newly created Collaboration Technology Support Center Microsoft (CTSC-MS) at SAP AG. His current work focuses on integrating SAP and Microsoft technologies in the areas of single sign-on, identity management, knowledge management, and process management. He has published numerous articles on those topics on the SAP Developer Network.

You can contact André via the following email address: *andre.fischer@sap.com.*

Index